THE LUCKY FEW
AND THE WORTHY MANY

THE
LUCKY FEW
AND THE
WORTHY MANY

*Scholarship Competitions and
the World's Future Leaders*

Edited by
Alice Stone Ilchman,
Warren F. Ilchman,
and Mary Hale Tolar

Indiana University Press

Bloomington and Indianapolis

Publication of this book was made possible in part with grants from the Rockefeller Foundation, the John D. and Catherine T. MacArthur Foundation, the Thomas J. Watson Foundation, the Paul and Daisy Soros Fellowships for New Americans, and the National Association of Fellowship Advisors.

This book is a publication of

Indiana University Press
601 North Morton Street
Bloomington, IN 47404-3797 USA

http://iupress.indiana.edu

Telephone orders   800-842-6796
Fax orders   812-855-7931
Orders by e-mail   iuporder@indiana.edu

The paper used in this publication meets the minimum requirements of American National Standard for Information Sciences— Permanence of Paper for Printed Library Materials, ANSI Z39.48-1984.

Manufactured in the United States of America

Library of Congress Cataloging-in-Publication Data

The lucky few and the worthy many : scholarship competitions and the world's future leaders / [edited by] Alice Stone Ilchman, Warren F. Ilchman, and Mary Hale Tolar.
      p. cm. — (Philanthropic and nonprofit studies)
Includes index.
   ISBN 0-253-34476-X (cloth : alk. paper)
   1. Scholarships—Social aspects. 2. Educational evaluation.
I. Ilchman, Alice Stone. II. Ilchman, Warren Frederick. III. Tolar, Mary Hale, 1966– IV. Series.
   LB2338.L83 2004
   378.34—dc22
                                                2004013089

1 2 3 4 5   09 08 07 06 05 04

Contents

ACKNOWLEDGMENTS

Many individuals contributed to this volume. We would like to thank them all: First, we are grateful to the Rockefeller Foundation for inviting us and our colleagues to their Study and Conference Center in Bellagio, Italy, to address the issue of "Strengthening Nationally and Internationally Competitive Scholarships." A number of practitioners and scholars helped us to frame the questions: Louis Blair, Allan Goodman, Stanley Katz, Kenneth Prewitt, and Harriet Zuckerman. Gordon Conway, president of the Rockefeller Foundation, and Jonathan Fanton, president of the John D. and Catherine T. MacArthur Foundation, encouraged knowledge-based papers and broader international participation through their grants. We thank Paul and Daisy Soros and their foundation, David McKinney and the Thomas J. Watson Foundation, and the officers of the National Association of Fellowship Advisors for their interest in and support of these questions. Norvell Brasch and Kamilah Briscoe traveled to Bellagio in the service of better fellowship evaluation, with the Thomas J. Watson Fellowship as a case in point. There is always a home team of energetic and steady support: Tonji Wade Barrow, Leah Donahue, Carmel Geraghty, Max Hale, Anna Humphreys, Leigh Hallingby, Wei Chang, and Stephanie Ramos deserve commendation. Not least, the person most responsible for managing the "purposeful and productive paradise" that serves so many at Bellagio is the incomparable Gianna Celli. We thank her and her able assistants. Finally, and above all, we are grateful to the participants and authors of the first-ever conference on this topic.

Alice Stone Ilchman
Warren F. Ilchman
Mary Hale Tolar
Bellagio, October 10, 2003

THE LUCKY FEW
AND THE WORTHY MANY

1 | Strengthening Nationally and Internationally Competitive Scholarships:

An Overview

Alice Stone Ilchman, Warren F. Ilchman, and Mary Hale Tolar

Why This Is Important

In choosing the talented and promising, the stakes are high and the outcomes matter. Moreover, the concerned communities are many: those who award these scholarships, those who seek them, and those advising candidates and universities on "improving their odds." At stake also are the goals of the funders—foundations and governments—and the many individuals associated with enhancing the potential of young people to lead more useful and creative lives, both for themselves and for others. Because many of the scholarship programs are international in character (both in terms of the origins of candidates and of their academic destinations), these programs have a common concern to build a world of constructive internationalism. Finally, nationally and internationally competitive scholarship programs advance the acquisition of skills important to building better societies. What can be done to strengthen these scholarship programs redounds to the advantage of successive generations and the world they will inhabit.

To the end of testing the proposition that these programs have much in common and that an understanding of processes would be mutually instructive, the authors convened in November 2002 at the Rockefeller Foundation Conference Center in Bellagio, Italy, a meeting of the responsible officers of many of the major European, British, and American competitive scholarship programs. To enrich the discussion, we also invited leaders from higher education in Asia and Africa whose students were increasingly beneficiaries of these schemes, and social scientists concerned with leadership and creativity, selection, and evaluation. This essay is an overview of the field in general and an introduction to the following chapters.

We are particularly drawn to the subject of strengthening nationally and internationally competitive scholarships for three reasons. First, as individuals charged with producing results wished by donors—whether philanthropic or government—we want to know what constitutes "good evidence" that we have been successful in our missions, and we want to have these answers in good time to improve our process and outcomes. Second, as people responsible for such scholarships, we are concerned about how to choose the "lucky few" from among the "worthy many." Our task in practice becomes finding grounds for rejecting applicants rather than for their selection because there are so many individuals qualified and capable to fulfill the objectives of our programs. Surely, we think, there must be positive measures to take that would better discern "worthiness." And finally, given the amount of experience in managing existing programs, there must be better ways to organize panels, conduct interviews, and add value to the fellowship for our finalists. From so much collective experience, we should find insights that will assist us all.

We had an additional concern, born of a commitment to equity and productivity. As citizens in societies concerned with merit, we believe that talent is broadly, even randomly distributed, but only selectively developed. Because many able, talented people have not had the privilege of selective development—experiences that make candidates more attractive and available to those who select them—we are concerned that we may be missing many qualified individuals, often from groups underrepresented in many ways in our societies. Missing their potential contributions deprives not only them but all of us as well. It seems worthwhile to broaden the pool, even at the expense of having more disappointed people—those worthy but unchosen many.

One more dimension of fairness concerns us. While no economist has estimated what difference the possession of a Rhodes or similar scholarship means in terms of a lifetime's income, we assume that it can be substantial. More particularly, by anecdote and experience, we have noted in recipients of scholarships what Harriet Zuckerman calls the "accumulation of advantage," where receiving one scholarship leads to other forms of support in critical periods of building a career.[1] In science this has been called the "Matthew Effect."[2] In addition, based on the work of Pierre Bourdieu, we note how scholarship programs tend to reproduce certain characteristics of dominant groups in their recipients, how finalists tend to look like, talk like, and value what we find in the panelists who select them.[3] Within the twin commitments to merit and equity, how have various scholarship programs addressed these concerns?

The Universe of Nationally and Internationally Competitive Scholarships

Nationally and internationally, competitive scholarships have long been a tool used by foundations and governments to advance the acquisition of critical skills and to further valued goals. After a very long history of their use (in one case, a full century), three major new competitive fellowships have been launched. The Ford Foundation inaugurated in 2000 a program of $280 million, the largest grant in its history, to support graduate study anywhere in the world. The goal is to fund, within ten years, 3,500 individuals from Africa, Asia, and Latin America.[4] Another major new undertaking is the Gates Cambridge Scholarship through an endowment of $210 million dollars from the Bill and Melinda Gates Foundation to the University of Cambridge. When this program is in full operation, the Gates-Cambridge Trust expects to support 225 students annually from around the world, studying at the graduate level at Cambridge in fields that relate to such global problems as health equity, technology, and learning. Finally, within the last decade, the Open Society Institute (George Soros' philanthropic organization) has established many competitive graduate scholarship programs for Central and Eastern Europe and Central Asia as well as for Burma and Africa. Approximately one thousand scholarships are awarded annually among thirty countries.

These dramatic new efforts at nationally and internationally competitive scholarships join a field of well-established programs with long experience in managing both domestic and international scholarship programs. Originating from Europe, there are many, including the oldest, the Rhodes Trust (1904). The German Deutscher Akademischer Austauschdienst (DAAD), the ERASMUS/SOCRATES program of the European Union, the Commonwealth Scholars program of the Association of Commonwealth Universities, the British Marshall Fund, and the many programs associated with the Academic Cooperation Association involve significant numbers of students. These scholarly exchanges have as their objectives teaching critical skills, nurturing creativity, furthering goals of citizenship and mobility among university students, and developing leadership.

Apart from the ERASMUS/SOCRATES program of the European Union, the DAAD may be the largest scholarship-awarding program in the world. In 2002, DAAD made grants for its undergraduate and graduate scholarship and related programs to 14,687 Germans to study outside of Germany and for 21,334 non-Germans to study in Germany.[5]

For the United States such longstanding programs as the Fulbright, the Woodrow Wilson National Fellowship Foundation, the Luce Scholars, the Hertz Fellowships, the Mellon Humanities Fellowships, the Howard Hughes Fellowships, the Truman Scholars, and the Thomas J. Watson Fellowships come to mind. In addition, there are competitive graduate fellowships sponsored by the U.S. government through the National Science Foundation and the National Institutes of Health.

In U.S.-related programs alone, there are an estimated six thousand nationally competitive scholarships annually (not including those offered by the universities themselves), with an annual direct cost of one hundred million dollars. Many of these are multiple-year scholarships (e.g., Howard Hughes, Hertz, National Science Foundation, etc.) and, conservatively estimated, probably bring the direct expenditure annually for U.S. residents to over four hundred million dollars.

To show the variety and size of the principal programs, we offer the taxonomy in Table 1.1 (the programs with asterisks were represented at Bellagio).

The Challenges of Strengthening Competitive Scholarships

Those who gathered in Bellagio were asked to list in advance what they saw as the external and internal challenges to their programs in the next decade. Managers of those scholarships supported by endowments saw substantial decreases in their income due to the decline in stock markets, while those dependent on governments for annual appropriations found a growing skepticism about the value of their programs to attain their country's foreign policy objectives. In Europe, the rise of the massive ERASMUS program provided the need for renewed justifications for other programs. World turmoil has caused some programs to question the safety of certain geographic destinations. Other scholarship programs expressed concern over the decline of interest in certain subjects, such as the humanities or German or Russian language.

Internally, the challenges involved issues of program performance and how to gauge and compare it. The pressure for evaluations that went beyond outputs and assessed outcomes (e.g., is there more world understanding because of a particular program?) became stronger. These queries were accompanied by the absence of benchmarks that made questions of cost effectiveness more difficult to answer. Nor was there clear evidence on whether scholarships were more effective than institutional grants to achieve a program's goals. In addition, there were questions of how to maintain the reputation of fairness in the selection process and how to strike the balance between time and resources spent on selection, and those spent on improving the experience during and after the scholarship. Finally, all participants felt the universal challenge to improve the diversity among candidates and finalists—diversity both in the sending and receiving institutions and in socioeconomic, racial, ethnic, gender, and regional backgrounds.

What did the participants expect of such a gathering? First, no participant, including the conveners, was acquainted with more than a quarter of the other participants. To meet colleagues in the field, long known by name or by personal or program reputation, face-to-face was a singular attraction. Second, the prospect of comparing performance and expectations as well as defining the larger field of competitive national scholarships began

Table 1.1.
Taxonomy of Selected Nationally Competitive Scholarships

Name (Year Founded, Source of Funds)	# Applicants (approx.)	# Awards	Duration	Award Value (max.)[1]	Selection Process[2]	Institutional Endorsement[3]	Origin	Destination
Beinecke Fellowship (1971, Private Foundation)	100	20	5 years	$32,000	Delegated	Yes; 100 invited institutions only	US	US or international
Churchill Scholarship (1959, Private)	150	11	1 year	$27,000	Delegated	Yes; 75 invited institutions only	US	UK
Commonwealth Scholarship and Fellowship Plan — General Scholarships * (1959, Government)	25,000-30,000	600	up to 3 years	T, F, M, B, E, Tr, Fa	Delegated	Varies by country	Commonwealth countries	UK; 12-13 Commonwealth countries
Jack Kent Cooke Graduate Fellowship (1997, Private)	675	50	2 years	$60,000	Delegated	Yes	US	Not stated
DAAD – Deutschlandjahr Scholarship for Graduating Seniors * (1971, Government)	200-250	150-200	1 academic year	$6,650; B, Tr, I	Delegated	Yes	US, Canada	Germany
European Commission — Socrates/Erasmus Program * (1987, Government)	N/A	N/A	1 semester; 1 year	Varies by country	Delegated	Yes	EU	EU

Continued on the next page

Table 1.1. *Continued*

Name (Year Founded, Source of Funds)	# Applicants (approx.)	# Awards	Duration	Award Value (max.)[1]	Selection Process[2]	Institutional Endorsement[3]	Origin	Destination
Ford Foundation International Fellowships Program (IFP) * (2000, Private)	N/A	Varies; 95 in 2000; 557 by end of 2002	3 years	T, M, Tr, F	Delegated	No	21 IFP countries [Africa, Asia, L. America, Middle East, E. Europe]	Europe, Russia, US, L. America, Canada, Africa, Asia, Australia
Fulbright Program — Incoming Student Program * (1946, Government)	N/A	2,200+	1 academic year (plus renewals)	Full award: T, M, B, Tr, I. Varies by country	Direct	Yes; US university admission required	140 countries	US
Fulbright Program — US Scholar Program * (1946, Government)	4,000–5,000	1,000+	1 year (plus extensions, renewals)	T, M, B, Tr, I, L. Varies by country	Delegated and direct	Yes, but may also apply at-large	US	140 participating countries
Gates Cambridge Scholarships * (2001, Private)	500	100–120	1 to 3 years	T, M, Tr	Direct and delegated	No	All countries except UK	UK
German Chancellor Scholarship/Humboldt Foundation (1990, Private)	N/A	10	1 year	M, B, L	Delegated	No	North America	Germany
Hertz Fellowship (1963, Private)	500–700	25	5 years	$125,000; T	Direct	No; 36 invited institutions only	US	US
HHMI/EMBO Young Investigators and Scientists * (2002, Private)	35	5	3 years	$30,000/ year	Direct	No	Czech Republic, Hungary, Poland	Czech Republic, Hungary, Poland

Program								
HHMI – Research Training Fellowships for Medical Students * (1989, Private)	180	77	1 or 2 years	$37,000	Direct	No	US	US; abroad in some cases
HHMI/NIH Research Scholars * (1985, Private)	170	42	1 or 2 years	$37,000	Direct	No	US	US
Kennedy Memorial Scholarships (1966, Private)	N/A	12	1 or 2 years	T, M, Tr, I	Direct	Yes	UK	US
Luce Foundation Scholars Program (1974, Private)	130	18	1 year	M, H	Direct and delegated	Yes; 65 invited institutions only	US	Asia
MacArthur Fellows Program * (1981, Private)	N/A	20-30	5 years	$500,000	Delegated	No; anonymous "Nominators"	US	Not stated
British Marshall Scholarship * (1953, Government)	800-900	Up to 40	2 or 3 years	T, F, M, B, Tr	Delegated	Yes	US	UK
Mellon Fellowships in Humanistic Studies (1982, Private)	775	85	1 year	$17,500; T, F	Delegated	No	US	US or Canada
Mitchell Scholarships * (1998, Government / Private partnership)	250	12	1 year	$11,000; T, H, Tr	Delegated	Yes	US	Ireland and N. Ireland
National Science Foundation (NSF) Graduate Research Fellowship (1952, Government)	5,000-6,000	900	3 years, over 5-year period	$21,000; $10,000 to institution; $1,000 (Tr)	Delegated	No	US	US

Continued on the next page

Table 1.1. *Continued*

Name (Year Founded, Source of Funds)	# Applicants (approx.)	# Awards	Duration	Award Value (max.)[1]	Selection Process[2]	Institutional Endorsement[3]	Origin	Destination
Open Society Institute * (1993, Private, Government, University cost-share)	8,000	1,000	1 year, some multi-year	$1,500 to $70,000. Varies by country	Direct and delegated	Yes	E. & C. Europe, Mongolia, former Soviet Union, Burma	US, UK, France, Germany, SE Asia & countries of origin
Rhodes Scholarship * (1904, Private)	N/A	94	2 or 3 years	T, M, Tr, F	Delegated	Yes	Commonwealth, US, Germany, & Hong Kong	UK
Rotary Scholarship (Ambassadorial) (1947, Private)	1,300	1,000	1 year	$25,000	Direct	No; by local Rotary club	100 Rotary countries	100 Rotary countries
Paul & Daisy Soros Fellowships * (1997, Private)	1,000	30	up to 2 years	$20,000/yr; ½T	Delegated	No	US	US
Truman Scholarship * (1975, Government)	600	75 to 80	4 years	$30,000	Delegated	Yes	US	US or international
Thomas J. Watson Fellows * (1968, Private)	180-190 interviewed	Up to 60	1 year	$22,000; F	Direct	Yes; 50 invited institutions only	US	Varies; international

*Program presented at Bellagio.

[1] Value stated in US Dollars. For those programs that do not provide award value in currency, the following key is used. Key: T = Tuition, F = University fees, M = Maintenance/living expenses, H = Housing, B = Books/research expenses, E = Equipment, Tr = Travel, Fa = Family allowance, I = Health/accident insurance, L = Language course/tuition.

[2] "Direct" indicates selection of awardees by program trustees or staff. "Delegated" indicates selection of awardees by a committee of volunteers invited by program staff/trustees. A multi-tiered selection process may include both.

[3] Institutional Endorsement signals if the candidate's application must be endorsed by his or her sponsor institution, e.g. undergraduate university (Yes), or if direct application by candidate is acceptable (No).

tangibly to fill a need many felt important to their professional performance. Finally, there was a widely shared feeling that there was a community of interest, with academic underpinnings, between and among these large scholarship programs.

Commonalities and Differences in Scholarship Programs

Scholarship Objectives

An important point of departure is what these several scholarships wish to achieve and which candidates they believe can best achieve it. A classic statement is the one contained in the 1901 will of Cecil Rhodes establishing the Rhodes Scholarships. To foster and encourage an appreciation of the advantages of the union of English-speaking peoples throughout the world, his will identified four criteria for selection:

> My desire being that the students who shall be elected to the Scholarships shall not be merely bookworms I direct that in the election of a student to a Scholarship regard shall be had to (i) his literary and scholastic attainments (ii) his fondness of and success in manly outdoor sports such as cricket football and the like (iii) his qualities of manhood truth courage devotion to duty sympathy for and protection of the weak kindliness unselfishness and fellowship and (iv) his exhibition during school days of moral force of character and instincts to lead and to take an interest in his schoolmates for those latter attributes will be likely in afterlife to guide him to esteem the performance of public duties as his highest aim.[6]

Several fellowship programs followed this model. The Commonwealth Fund in New York, for instance, created in 1924 a "reverse Rhodes" called Harkness Fellows with similar qualifications for students from Great Britain and the Commonwealth.[7] When the Fulbright program was founded in 1946, Senator Fulbright claimed lineage from his Rhodes experience.[8] In many subsequent scholarship programs, the language of the Rhodes will was adopted to describe the objectives and criteria for appointment. It is significant that the privilege of further study did not depend on academic qualifications alone, but on traits and experiences that Rhodes believed were important in the kind of leaders he hoped to encourage. Many programs have endorsed these broad criteria for selection.

A more contemporary description of objectives can be seen in the case of the Deutscher Akademischer Austauschdienst. While the DAAD has had more than a million grantees since 1950 in its two hundred programs, the overarching purpose is summed up in a recent report as

> encouraging members of the international, young, up-and-coming academic elite to come to Germany for a study or research stay and, as far as possible, of maintaining these contacts as life-long partners, as well as the

goal of qualifying young German research scientists at the very best locations around the world in a spirit of tolerance and liberal-minded, cosmopolitan attitudes, of assisting the developing countries of the South as well as the reforming states of the East [to] establish efficient higher education structures and, finally, the goal of maintaining or establishing German studies and the German language, literature and area studies at important universities and colleges around the world at a level worthy of and appropriate to a great cultural nation.[9]

A hundred years apart in terms of their public description, the Rhodes and DAAD are very similar in spirit and mission. Both sought an appreciation of a cultural tradition by individuals who were considered exceptionally able, even superior. Both saw that, as a result of exposing superior young people to other systems of education, their own systems of education might be strengthened.

Having identified these common themes, it should be noted that there are also different, though sometimes overlapping, missions for the many nationally and internationally competitive scholarships, whether these are offered in Europe, Japan, the British Commonwealth, the United States, or elsewhere. Among the outcomes many scholarship programs seek are:

- Imparting specific substantive skills and knowledge
- Redirecting or raising career objectives
- Strengthening leadership skills
- Encouraging public service
- Increasing international understanding
- Sustaining creativity
- Increasing participation of the underrepresented
- Furthering international mobility
- Developing a global or national perspective or affinity
- Creating new knowledge

For each outcome there are indicators, signs at the point of award that the recipient is likely to achieve what is wanted. Any evaluation of these programs must begin with the extent to which the recipients achieved the mission of the program (e.g., entered the public service, became a biomedical scientist, continued to keep in touch with the culture of the exchange site, etc.). The more lofty and abstract the mission (e.g., increasing international understanding), the more difficult it is to evaluate what was accomplished by the recipients or the program in general.[10]

Common to all of them, however, is the need to choose from among the many worthy applicants. For this, in addition to the specific characteristics sought (e.g., interest in German culture, biomedical science), those who pre-

Chart 1.1
Selection Markers

Talent	Leadership	Creativity
Public recognition through official results, winning of prizes and other confirmations of quality	*Speaks authoritatively for others, as head of publicly recognized group or organization*	*Expresses self in a complex medium normally associated with older persons*
Performance in a medium at a standard normally associated with older individuals	*Sustains group to address issue of imputed public importance*	*Contributes new or different approach to existing formulation*
Other?	*Other?*	*Other?*

vail in these competitions show more "leadership," "talent," and/or "creativity" than those candidates who do not prevail. Even those programs addressing opportunity for underrepresented groups seek the most "promising" from those considered underrepresented.

Knowing that the majority of our candidates are relatively young, it is important to speculate on what they could have accomplished by their early or mid-twenties that would convince selection panelists of their superior promise. How does one detect "promise" in individuals so relatively inexperienced? Is it easier to do so in the case of field-specific programs such as the Howard Hughes Fellowships in biological science or the Mellon Fellowships in Humanities, as opposed to general fellowships such as the Rhodes and Marshall? In contrast, to use a U.S. example, the judges of the Guggenheim Fellowship, which is normally given to a scholar or artist in mid-career, have one or two decades of work to appraise.

What do talent, leadership, and creativity look like when they appear in the credentials of candidates? How are they elicited by instructions to applicants, application forms, essays, and interviews? Chart 1.1 suggests "manifestations" of these three most commonly used criteria. The presumption is that if these manifestations are evident in young individuals, they will likely continue to be present in later life, and that the more they are present in youth, the more likely they will be to characterize adult performance. "Risks" are recipients who do not evince the criteria and are chosen by "gut feelings" of panelists. Neither method is "scientific," but those who rely on selection markers are at least able to compare candidates.

LEADERSHIP LITERATURE

Is it possible to improve on these markers? Does the vast literature on leadership and creativity suggest what are the indicators in the young that promise a life "marked" by either leadership or creativity or both? Is there a developmental psychology that could assist the selection process? To that end, a paper coauthored by Robert Sternberg and Elena Grigorenko (Chapter 2 in this volume) reviewed the literature and proposed a way that staff and selection panelists might think about these terms.

Using the model of WICS (i.e., wisdom, intelligence, creativity, synthesized), they propose ways of looking at existing markers and how their model would improve on the selection process. In every case, they argue against single-dimension markers of intelligence, especially where the student has been trained to perform but not to think independently or creatively. Indeed, adaptability and demonstration of practical application of intelligence are more valuable in assessing differences among candidates. Going beyond intelligence, Sternberg and Grigorenko call for the recognition in finalists of creativity, which includes such behaviors as the redefining of problems, the questioning and analyzing of assumptions, the selling of an idea, the willingness to take sensible risks, and the ability to delay gratification. The third and most appropriate attribute for scholarship holders, according to the authors, is wisdom—the balancing of goals, interests, time horizons, and values. Synthesizing wisdom, creativity, and intelligence is the stuff of future leaders.

Sternberg and Grigorenko demonstrate in their research how all of these attributes can be measured. While competitive scholarship programs might not be able to adopt their very inventive approaches as they now stand, some new measures might be adapted for our needs. Moreover, assuming our present and past recipients might possess the characteristics they describe, no matter how they are apprehended by selection panelists, a sample of scholarship holders might provide a further test of the authors' views.

EVIDENCE FROM THE STUDENT DEVELOPMENT LITERATURE

In addition to the literature reviewed by Sternberg and Grigorenko, it is helpful to look at the literature on student development with a focus on the conditions that nurture the traits we seek in our finalists. The point of award for many of the scholarship programs represented at Bellagio is at the conclusion of the first university degree. The undergraduate experience, thus, is common to all and allows us to ask about the nature of undergraduate education and its impact on the most able students. What experiences or environments most encourage those traits we seek? Are there settings in which they are already visible?

The literature on how college affects students and how students can make the most of their college years is vast. Regrettably, only examples from the United States are presented here, though we assume that these characteristics and their relationship to success are found in many systems of higher education.

The student development literature presents its findings across a broad spectrum, from highly quantitative longitudinal studies to the anecdotal and qualitative. On the one hand, some two hundred U.S. colleges and universities and more than 20,000 students and faculty have participated annually over several decades in a longitudinal study of student attitudes, values, and ambitions.[11] At the other end of the spectrum is a highly qualitative study, drawn from just twenty colleges, of how students can most benefit from college and how faculty can help them.[12] There are literally hundreds of studies that seek to measure how students develop in college.[13]

Social scientists are cautious about establishing cause and effect. A brief summary of the literature, plus a generous sprinkling of common sense derived from nearly half a century in the university, give the authors the temerity to suggest here some settings, interventions, and events that seem to give students the greatest sense of values, ambition, and confidence.[14]

For those who choose to invest in human capital (and all scholarship programs are such investments) the reassuring answer seems to be that "people make the difference." It is particular people and the settings for interaction—not the size or selectivity of the college, not the major or focus of a curriculum, not visibility or resources of the university, or even how well its faculty is paid—that create the most powerful influence on the choices and performance of undergraduates.

From all the evidence, it is clear that there are three sometimes overlapping undergraduate environments or experiences that have the greatest effect on ambition, confidence, and achievement. They are (1) the stimulation and influence of peers; (2) small group interaction, both in and out of class; and (3) the sustained attention of teachers. In support of the strong influence of peers, one large study finds that the most significant variable for outcomes in ambition, self-reported learning, and career choice is the peer group of "high intellectual self-esteem."[15] Students generally tend to change their values, behavior, and academic plans in the direction of the dominant orientation of their peer group. From this data, the author, Alexander Astin, asserts that "the values, attitudes, self-concept, and socioeconomic status of the peer group are much more important determinants of how the individual student will develop than are the peer group's abilities, religious orientation, or racial composition."[16] Perhaps selection committees should be asking a candidate, "Who are your friends and what do they want to do?"

Small group interaction is also cited as a powerful teacher. Many faculty and deans assume students respond best when they are respectfully treated as adults, entrusted to do the work, and directed to write a long, thoughtful paper at the course's conclusion. But data supporting learning, intellectual engagement, and passion correlate strongly with courses that are more "interactive." Such courses offer frequent discussion with the professor, require numerous writing assignments often shared with other students, and may demand cooperative homework assignments. The amount of writing is a key indicator. The connection between the amount of writing in a course and a student's engagement in it is dramatic, whether measured by time spent on that course, by the intellectual challenge it presented, or just how much the student liked doing the work.[17]

What might be the implication of this finding for selection panels? It is not easy to make a direct connection. Perhaps a key to assessing the quality of the candidate's intellectual experience through the file or an interview could be the amount of writing done in class and how much interaction was possible with the professor. Letters of recommendation may attest to both.

The importance of the intervention of a wise advisor follows closely after the overall effectiveness of the peer group and engaged learning. Such a person may, but need not be, associated with an academic class. Some thirty students who had been selected as Rhodes and Marshall Scholars believed that *the* significant factor in their success was that at "key points in their college years, an academic advisor asked questions, or posed a challenge, that forced them to think about the relationship of their academic work to their personal lives."[18] The point here is the importance of a respectful adult who engages the student in questions of both making a life and making a living. Such individuals may be especially astute referees. Candidates might be asked to send a recommendation letter from a person he or she considers to be a "mentor" or major professor.

Although certain kinds of institutions, for example, liberal arts colleges and prestigious universities, might be more likely to enable settings for small group interaction or attract students who would form peer groups of "high intellectual self-esteem," the findings suggest that such settings and peer group formations occur across many kinds of institutions and seem to provide the same positive direction for their students. Elite institutions or not, this learning is positively correlated with residential campuses and living away from home.

What specifically does the student development literature say about developing and identifying leadership, the goal that most scholarships say their programs seek? Little research appears useful beyond that fact that election to student office is correlated with strong participation in volunteer, social, literary, and artistic enterprises and with intramural sports. Racial and cultural awareness is also correlated with leadership.[19] Selection panels looking for "demonstrated leadership" need to look beyond the resume and identified campus offices to ad hoc settings to find examples of the initiative, imagination, and judgment so often found in successful leaders.

Broadening and Deepening the Pool

All scholarship programs represented at our conference indicated that they want to draw from broader applicant pools. They aspire to find more grantees outside elite institutions and away from metropolitan cities; they actively seek more racial and national diversity and a greater socioeconomic range. Some scholarships look for greater gender balance. The officers of most programs contend that the tension between excellence and diversity is a false one. There was also agreement that the effort to add diversity to the candidate pool requires a steady commitment.

Programs have used a number approaches to broadening the pool. Some have advertised in student and regional newspapers and in publications of nonprofit organizations. Others have used already appointed scholarship-holders from the desired populations to serve as role models and advocates among their peer groups. The new Ford International Fellows Program (IFP) is the most focused on this objective, restricting participation to those groups underrepresented at the graduate levels in their own societies in Asia, Latin America, and Africa and utilizing the assistance of those groups growing out of and serving the underrepresented communities. In addition, the IFP tailors the graduate destination to the particular needs of the candidate and the institution the candidate will later serve.

There was also the recognition at the conference that other modifications need to accompany the commitment to broadening and deepening the pool, such as providing candidates with computer access and, on occasion, with prepaid postage for applications. Selection panel make-up and the interview process may need to be adjusted. Using the American embassy as the site of Fulbright interviews or even as the application distribution point, for example, can intimidate candidates in some countries.

Once appointed, attention should be given to the particular needs of recipients in this new pool, such as providing support for child care or interest on student loans. Several programs have provided basic equipment, including laptop computers. The Commonwealth Scholarship program includes a split-site scheme where individuals doing a degree in developing countries spend a year of research in the United Kingdom with joint supervision from the two institutions. Again, because of the explicit targeting of underrepresented communities, the Ford IFP recognizes the need for up to two years in which finalists can work on language, computer, or methodological skills before beginning their graduate programs.

Evidence regarding the performance of those who were appointed as a conscious effort to broaden and deepen the pool in scholarship programs is not yet substantial. A study of ten years of Ford Foundation and Danforth Foundation competitive scholarships for minorities found almost 100 percent degree completion and concluded that "many of these successful minority students now holding Ph.D. degrees would never have gotten the chance to prove themselves if they had been considered for admission to graduate school only on the basis of test scores or undergraduate grades."[20]

There is some evidence from American undergraduate education. Over the past three decades, what has changed most on U.S. college campuses is the "the new student diversity"—students bringing their different backgrounds to campus. Many universities have allocated significantly more financial aid to assure this end. Some of the most selective institutions have pushed the hardest to offer access to traditionally barred groups and to assure that all students have the experience of learning from a more diverse faculty and student body.

Briefly, what has been the U.S. university experience in pressing for excellence *and* diversity? How, for example, do race-aware admissions policies work in practice? In their landmark study, *The Shape of the River,* Bowen and Bok measure the success of black students admitted to academically selective colleges under race-aware admissions policies to see how well these students have met the expectations placed on them.[21] The study shows that in relation to their white classmates, black students have functioned well in competitive universities. More particularly, in measures of graduate degrees and entry into the professions, income, life satisfaction, and success in achieving leadership positions in their working and volunteer lives, black students have performed very well indeed. Those in the most demanding institutions performed the best of all.

Two other recent studies stress the advantages for all students who attend colleges with such diversity. These studies also emphasize how positively many students regard learning from others with different points of view. Greater self-reported gains in cognitive and affective development and in increased satisfaction in their college experience are positively associated with increased institutional commitment to promoting racial understanding.[22]

What do the data suggest for our efforts to include candidates from new groups in our scholarship awardees? Bowen and Bok suggest that students from diverse backgrounds will use these opportunities no less well than those from the traditional pool and that the environments for learning will be richer. To conclude from Astin: "Clearly, the dire claims about the detrimental effects of emphasizing diversity are not supported by the data. On the contrary, findings suggest that there are many developmental benefits that accrue to students when institutions encourage and support the emphasis on multiculturalism and diversity."[23]

Selection

Among the scholarship programs included in Table 1.1, there are literally dozens of combinations of processes in selection. Some programs allow candidates to nominate themselves; other programs require institutions to pre-select candidates. Some programs are more universalistic in their requirements for candidates; others require distributive, often particularistic requirements (e.g., geography, field) to be met. Some programs have staff members make final decisions; others delegate the decisions to selection panels. Some programs use interviews; others do not. Some programs prepare their interviewers for the responsibility; others assume that formal credentials suffice as preparation. Some programs use their former recipients as selection panelists; other programs choose panelists because of their public eminence.

To our knowledge, there is little discussion as to which combinations constitute "best practices" in terms of achieving one's mission. If you take the brochures of programs at face value, you would believe that all these arrangements were determined in light of such discussions. Issues of convenience and eminence, however, affect many arrangements. The amount of attention each application gets depends on its length and on the time available before the interview or final decision schedule; the length of interviews is likely to be determined by the number of candidates, the number of days that interviews can be scheduled, and the length of time panelists can be made available. Who serves as a selection panelist is affected by availability or desire for a particular balance. Often "best practice" is what prevailed when the officer in charge took responsibility for a program.

Whether or not to have an interview is a major question. How many? With whom? For how long? In what format? In a personal communication, Allan Goodman, president of the Institute of International Education in the United States, maintained that "there can be a wide variety of nomination, application, and selection processes . . . with no appreciable effect on quality," though he favors "hands-down" nominators plus oral interviews.[24] On the other hand, a reviewer for the U.S. National Science Foundation, a program in which interviews are anathema, argued that actuarial approaches (i.e., giving numerical status to applicant's department and chief professor, grade point average, and scores on the Graduate Record Examination) should be used to check on evaluators and that the only reason for not using actuarial standards exclusively was that the numbers don't always keep up with changing fields fast enough.[25]

While a compelling personal interview can salvage a less meritorious case on paper, interviews are surely a means by which individuals well polished in the "presentation of self" can secure advantages in competition. Students from privileged circumstances may be more at ease in an interview setting and the attendant social functions such as dinners and cocktail receptions than students of more modest means or experience. Students in selective institutions in the United States are often groomed for their interviews by faculty and staff responsible for advancing the competitiveness of their students. Indeed, the website for a very selective U.S. institution has a PowerPoint presentation on how to interview for Rhodes and Marshall scholarships, giving suggestions about clothes and posture and how to respond to questions.[26] Non-elite institutions are also eager to present their candidates as strongly as possible in national fellowship competitions. The National Association of Fellowships Advisors (NAFA), founded in 2001 in the United States, is a resource for the growing cohort of fellowship professionals in higher education.[27]

The issue of what difference our selection practices make is the subject of Chapter 3 in this volume by Stanley Heginbotham. Dividing his remarks between "science" and "art," he demonstrates how the application of statistical insights could improve outcomes. For example, significant improvements could be achieved by rating panelists and the frequency of their agreements, by requiring all panelists to read applications and interview the same candidates on the same day (rather than dividing candidates between different panelists for simultaneous interviews), and above all, by requiring rank-ordering by panelists as opposed to having them grade by abstract categories.

Suggesting that selection is really an art form, Heginbotham shows how the characteristics identified in the Sternberg and Grigorenko chapter could be translated into application materials and could be used by those who write letters of recommendation and those who serve as selection panelists to elicit and confirm the characteristics associated with leadership, intelligence, creativity, and wisdom. In written materials from the candidates, panelists should give more weight to the essays providing evidence of past achievement than to candidates' future aspirations. In the latter, there should be a clear relationship between aspiration and the proposed educational plan.

Heginbotham demonstrates how various filters—regional quotas and institutional pre-selection—to handle the "big numbers problem" can have unintended consequences. Regarding efforts at quotas for special groups, his experience has shown the concept of "trajectory" or "distance traveled" to be more useful than other measures. By this measure, the applicants can be judged on the starting point and its effects—family, culture, income, gender, and such life adversities as war, asylum, and refugee status—and the level of achievement at the point of evaluation. A U.S. Hmong, born in a refugee camp and coming from a preliterate group in Laos, completing a D.Phil. at Oxford would have among the steepest trajectories imaginable.

Need for Partnerships

Selection is never an isolated or even a final event. Often other collaborators —partner foundations, governments, and higher educational institutions— need to be enlisted. Not only must the administrators of the Rhodes and Marshall scholarships depend on the recommending colleges and universities to do their work in initial nominations, but they must also secure the agreement of the host colleges and institutions for admissions of their finalists. Fulbright, DAAD, the Commonwealth Scholarships, and the Open Society Institute typically depend on cost-sharing with host institutions, other government programs, or other foundations. Because of its size and the aegis of the European Union, the ERASMUS/SOCRATES program requires complex departmental agreements to accept work done by students at cooperating institutions as well as financial calculations on comparative national costs. The new Ford International Fellows Program is even more complex. The IFP relies on nontypical organizations to recommend candidates in the first place, and then often chooses as destinations for study, institutions without long traditions of educating international students.

In contrast, few nationally and internationally competitive scholarship programs have the management autonomy enjoyed by the Thomas J. Watson Foundation or the Paul and Daisy Soros Fellowships for New Americans. While the Watson program depends on selected institutions to make nominations, once a Fellow is appointed, the responsibility for the "wanderjahr of one's own devising" rests entirely on the recipient. There is no sharing with other funders or institutions. The thirty Paul and Daisy Soros Fellows each year are self-nominated, and if they fail to gain admission themselves to graduate programs, they forfeit the award. The formal cooperation of no other institution, funder, or government is necessary.

Programs pursue partnerships for a variety of reasons particular to the needs and organization of the scholarship. Some scholarship programs partner to generate funding, to gain access to the knowledge or expertise of others, to reduce administrative costs, or to maintain quality and relevance. For some, partnering simply makes political sense. While partnerships are often essential to the goal, the relationships can be complex, even volatile, and may require careful and time-consuming stewardship. From the outset, partners must appreciate and be faithful to the scholarship's mission. While partnering can extend the reach and scope of a scholarship program, it also runs counter to the culture of philanthropy. Prestige is conferred upon founders of programs, not brokers.

Little has been written on partnerships.[28] What are the conditions for their effective formation, sustaining, and termination? How do new programs earn the "currency of respect" to enlist partners? Are there benefits for lead partners? Are partners best enlisted at the outset of programs? What in the Rhodes or Marshall history might help the administrator of the new Gates Cambridge Scholarships to manage the complex relationships with Cambridge colleges and graduate programs? What can the administrators of the Commonwealth Fellowships share with the new Ford International Fellows Program that would ease recruitment in Africa and Asia and in forming alternatives to expensive advanced degrees in Europe or North America? How might the Ford IFP partner with the Mandela Rhodes Foundation for work in Africa?

Value Added

Selection is only the beginning. What happens during the course of the scholarship (and after) is a key to whether or not a program's objective will be reached.

In the personal communication cited earlier, Allan Goodman argues that what makes the difference is the "enrichment process." He continues: "It is the experience they have while on the scholarship that matters. I suspect the programs which make sure that the winners have a chance to network and support strong alumni programs, promote interaction across generations with established leaders, and convey the impression that a young person should not hesitate to get seized with a set of global issues (beyond their discipline) . . . produce the kinds of persons which we all wish would inherit the earth."[29]

Several of the older scholarships have developed highly articulated programs to enrich the scholarship period and to provide continuing growth for scholars and enduring connection to the mission of the program. The Fulbright and the Rhodes programs specifically seek to foster mutual understanding and respect between the scholar and the people of the host country. Both hold that a diffusion of talented leaders with global views will make the world a better place. (While Senator Fulbright had a vision of what such an impact might mean in the relations between nation states, the Rhodes scholars were to be a deeply personal cohort motivated to serve their societies. The alumni programs reflect these differences.) Both programs invest time and attention to the adjustment of the scholar (and sometimes the scholar's family) to the new country. Both programs aspire to long-term professional and personal association between scholars and people in the host countries.

Specifically, the American Fulbright program typically begins with an orientation for recipients and follows up with in-country conferences for assessment and evaluation. Forty-two countries have Fulbright alumni associations—including Uzbekistan and Burkina Faso. Presumably, these associations do what good alumni do everywhere: sustain relationships and loyalty to the institution, encourage "networking" for opportunities and effectiveness, and build support—financial, political, and intellectual—for the Fulbright program. Out of roughly 100,000 U.S. Fulbrighters, 6,000 belong to a U.S. Fulbright Alumni Association, which publishes a newsletter and features an annual awards dinner. The association, with alumni in every congressional district, is an important advocate for sustained public funding. Finally, the U.S. Fulbright program has developed a grant-in-aid program for sustaining research relations in the country where the scholarship was earlier held.

The Rhodes scholarship provides an example of what careful nurture at Oxford and established connections throughout life might look like. Cecil Rhodes did not specify in his will more care than admission to an Oxford college. His successor trustees, however, decided to increase the likelihood of positive outcomes by having a resident counselor, later called the Warden of Rhodes House, to be present during the academic term. In its centenary year, the Rhodes Trust held international celebrations in both the United Kingdom and in South Africa.

Although Rhodes scholarships are received each year (94 in number) by nationals from twenty-four countries, the American Rhodes organization provides an example of how imaginative "aftercare" might be instituted. Since 1919, there has been an American secretary paid by the Rhodes Trust. The American secretary organizes the selection process and oversees the publication of a journal, *The American Oxonian,* and a newsletter. Rhodes alumni are active in regional and state selection panels. Alumni regularly organize class reunions in the United States. There have been two national reunions, and the Rhodes women have recently met as group.

Some programs, however, have not shown interest in adding value to their award. They leave this task to the recipients themselves and to the institutions they attend. There is no orientation to the program; there are no meetings with other holders of the scholarship, no newsletter, and no association to keep the recipients in touch. The philosophy here, commonly found in corporate assumptions about human capital development, is that true talent, like cream, rises to the top. Able people will create their own opportunities and use them well. Indeed, "making your own way" and learning by mistakes is intrinsic to the philosophy of the Thomas J. Watson Fellowship.

Program directors at Bellagio agreed that as with the Rhodes and Fulbright, a greater percentage of funds and time should be set aside to make it more likely that the original investment in the scholarship will bear fruit. It is also important to persuade both funders and staff of the usefulness of these programs. With the growth of websites and e-mail, the problems with maintaining contact are significantly reduced. Moreover, there is scope in a number of countries to share their alumni activities. Fulbright and Commonwealth scholarships provide a case in point.

Most scholarship programs have pre-departure orientations for the country or university and to the scholarship requirements. Several programs undertake remedial work to ensure the scholar is minimally prepared. Once embarked on the scholarship, however, the responsibility for the welfare and progress of the scholar is often delegated to the institution attended. This scholarship-university partnership is of key importance, but the program has to maintain a capacity to monitor academic problems and intervene in crisis situations. Because many scholarships provide inadequate stipends, this capacity to intervene on behalf of the student is especially important.

Beyond the universities themselves, many communities have private organizations to support international students, such as the English Speaking Union; the Goethe Institute; and, in New York as an example, a non-profit hospitality organization called MetroInternational, serving international scholars at all the universities in the area. This support might include home stays, conferences, and other ways to make connections in an alien environment.

Many programs gather their recipients at various points during the scholarship in order to build a "cohort effect," a harnessing of the prestige of the program and the network it implies to further its aims. Both the new Ford IFP and the Commonwealth Scholarship programs have "sandwich" courses during the period of the scholarship to increase negotiating skills (e.g., workshops on leadership, conflict resolution, advocacy, etc.) and to prepare the recipient to return to his or her home country. With a similar objective, the Rockefeller African Dissertation program brings the supervisors from the home universities and the European and American counterparts together at critical times in the student's dissertation process.

The ultimate in "aftercare," or longer term attention, however, is what the scholarship program does to ensure that the objectives of the program are more likely to be met in the careers of their recipients. How might a program empower the new alumna or alumnus to pursue the achievements, alone and together, for which the scholarship was created in the first place? Here the program directors were divided about how active their programs should be. Some argued that it should be demand-driven; unless alumni wish to network and give this allegiance priority among competing allegiances, the program may have little effect. Others felt the effort should be very active, including mentoring, career advising, networking, and intellectual stimulus. Alumni might be the source of new gifts for the program and political support if the fellowship is supported by the government. One scholarship director argued that funds to sustain a professional career (e.g., for research equipment, books, and participation in international networks) should be made available, lest the recipient languish or be tempted to emigrate.

Staffing to Meet the Program's Mission

Exactly half of the scholarship directors had spent their careers administering selective scholarships; the other half came to this work after careers in university teaching or administration. For the former, the route was often through the student services side of higher education. Once engaged in the managing of scholarships, new opportunities opened up, creating a claim for more responsibility. They learned their work "on the job." For the latter, there had been cognate experiences: being selection panelists, chairing graduate admissions as a faculty member, or serving as trustees or officers of philanthropic organizations and colleges. Regardless of route, there was agreement that strengthening nationally and internationally competitive scholarship programs required systematic and comparative knowledge. It was agreed that building and diversifying a pool of candidates, creating an effective selection process, enhancing the experience during and after the scholarship, and improving evaluation were subjects worthy of research. The outcome—more knowledge and more skill—was important to us and to the next generation of staff and leaders in this work. Several scholarship managers offered their programs as training sites for each other's new staff.

Maintaining Reputation and Relevance

All the scholarship programs at Bellagio value their reputation for quality, fairness, and thoroughness. However, few international programs can exercise their full mission alone. The partnerships they need to recruit in many countries in the world, to secure cooperation from admitting institutions, and to finance joint awards may affect the quality of their operations. The vast European Union ERASMUS/SOCRATES program must depend on the highly decentralized agreements between sending and receiving departments to ensure what is otherwise very difficult to monitor centrally. New programs such as the Gates Cambridge Scholarship and the Ford International Fellows Program have to build a reputation, though they can draw on Cambridge and Ford Foundation reputations to protect their processes. Either by public mandate or by donor commitment, all the programs see the broadening and deepening of their applicant pools and distribution of their eventual finalists to be a factor in their long-term reputation. To be seen as fair and impartial is a mutually shared goal.

Maintaining relevance affects selective scholarships differently. Funding sources encourage and limit what scholarships can do, and scholarship missions may need to be modified to meet a changing environment. The Thomas J. Watson Fellowship assumed that their award would, for most undergraduates, enable the first overseas trip. After thirty-five years, most applicants have had at least one trip abroad before their fellowship year. The Fellowship has modified its expectation to say that a Watson Fellow may not return to a country where he or she has already enjoyed a sustained period of residence. The Rhodes Scholarship also provides an example of successful adaptation. Because the program specified in general terms who was to be appointed (countries of origin and personal characteristics) and then left it to Oxford University to provide the program, the scholarship could accommodate changes in academic aspirations. Once a program for a "second BA," it is now largely a graduate program. As it has become more graduate (post-graduate) in character, the colleges play a lesser role and Rhodes House plays a greater one.[30]

While the will of Cecil Rhodes became an act of Parliament and thus major changes require Parliamentary action, the original commitment to a selection without regard to race and creed meant that many of the restrictions later found in other scholarship programs were in the Rhodes case obviated. The first African American was appointed in 1907, though the next ones were not appointed until 1963. Although the will laid out specific allocations by nation (United States and Germany) and colonies (South Africa, Australia, Canada, and New Zealand), these have changed over time. As they became independent, colonies were added and allocations changed. In the 1970s, U.S. scholars constituted half of all Rhodes Scholars; today they are a third. Within the United States, the commitment to decentralization in the selection scheme—and hence standards more sympathetic to local conditions—has led to a more representative group of finalists (see Chapter 3 in this volume). Finally, in response to public pressure from the United States and elsewhere, the trustees got Parliament to amend the act in 1974 to permit the appointment of women.

While the process of working through Parliament, a board of trustees, a decentralized nation-based selection and alumni process, and an ancient university strikes one as a bit glacial, the Rhodes has demonstrated over the last century a capacity to stay relevant to changing times. It has become more worldwide in its recipients, more encouraging to developing countries, more inclusive in terms of race and gender, and more plural in the subjects pursued and the qualifications achieved. The Rhodes's history reflects the major changes in universities and national relationships in the last half-century.

A chief factor in the capacity to retain reputation and relevance in the Rhodes Trust is an endowment whose income exceeds the costs of the scholarship program. Over the years this has meant that, beyond the scholarships and through grants, the Rhodes Trust could build a potentially unifying structure in Rhodes House, assist the expansion of residence halls of various colleges, encourage research on colonialism and American studies, and host international leaders able to bring a cosmopolitan view to the university community. In preparing for its centenary, however, the trustees turned outward from Oxford and authorized a grant to establish the Mandela Rhodes Foundation in Southern Africa, where the Rhodes fortune was originally made. The foundation will undertake projects that strengthen universities and schools, courts and legal processes, and health and the environment. This capacity to seek collateral actions beyond the scholarships themselves is a way to remain relevant to a changing world. Such choices might be possible for other nationally and internationally competitive scholarships as well.

Evaluation

Whether a scholarship is achieving its mission is a continuing concern. Sustaining reputation and remaining relevant to a changing environment are subjects for any evaluation. Another question is: How do other programs get such strong results?

That use of the word *evaluation,* however, is only part of the larger industry of "evaluation," the formal examination of the practices and results, with a view often of whether to continue to fund such activities. While Cecil Rhodes may not be waiting in eternity to see if the objectives of his will have been achieved in practice, other more contemporary programs have such interests. As a generalization, the more a nationally selective scholarship program depends on government money, the more frequently it is evaluated.[31] A recent evaluation of the mammoth ERASMUS/SOCRATES program of the European Union found that participants liked their mobility experience at another European country's campus, that the experience had not significantly delayed the receiving of a degree, and that it had not made an appreciable difference in employment or income except for those who were engaged in language translation.[32]

A recent evaluation of the U.S. Fulbright program stressed the importance of "the multiplier effects" in achieving the program's goal of increasing mutual understanding, those activities during and after the Fulbright year that communicated U.S. and host country interests to audiences larger than the immediate institution. The evaluation concluded in language perfect for advocating the program to its funders: "Without exception, the Scholars reported that they found their Fulbright experiences to be valuable and that they are proud to have been Fulbright Scholars. Ninety-seven percent agreed that they would like to obtain another Fulbright grant. This level of approbation is extremely rare in program evaluation research."[33]

There is no comprehensive history of efforts to evaluate privately supported competitive scholarship programs. Though it has been the subject of much analysis, the Rhodes program has not—to our knowledge—been subject to an evaluation of its methods and outcomes. A large uncompleted study is focusing on trying to demonstrate the "accumulation of advantage" among American Rhodes Scholars, but not to assess how well the Rhodes Trust has chosen, educated, and sustained a community of American Rhodes Scholars (see Chapter 5 in this volume). After thirty years of supporting graduate education in the basic sciences for medical school faculty, the Markle Foundation could announce that it had assisted education of faculty at every medical school in the United States and was therefore able to conclude its program.[34] Quite favorable evaluations for the Danforth-Kent Fellows program and the Woodrow Wilson Fellows program were completed shortly before they lost their funding from private foundations. The needs that spawned the programs appeared to have been met.[35] The Thomas J. Watson Foundation has evaluated its program every decade or so and has made some programmatic changes based on the recommendations.

An optimistic sign regarding evaluation is that the new Ford Foundation International Fellows Program has built this process in at the beginning. In addition to several independent studies about the program to be completed by research organizations around the world, the Center for Higher Education Policy Studies (CHEPS) at the University of Twente in the Netherlands will design an evaluation framework for IFP to incorporate the results while the program is still in progress.

In Chapter 4 in this volume, Michele Lamont brings her own experience in evaluating scholarship programs to dissect the various stages in the decision process—from building the applicant pool to completion of the grant—to show where processes may affect outcomes. Appropriately, she begins with the purposes of the program, since many scholarship programs have objectives that defy evaluation. She proceeds through the process of selection, noting the importance of selection panel dynamics and the "gamed" aspects of interviewing. On the larger question of how well the various programs have chosen recipients relative to their goals, she rightly points out that "success" is situational and affected by factors outside the control of the program. Both structural factors, such as gender, and social determinants, such as socially distributed cultural capital, affect how well recipients do in life.

From existing evaluations, we learn little about the life trajectories of those not selected. In a perhaps apocryphal story, we were informed that a distinguished undergraduate competitive scholarship mixed the list of alternates and finalists, and invited the alternates by mistake. Rather than undo the mistake, the trustees treated it as an experiment and found, not surprisingly, that the performances of the two groups were substantially the same. To be an alternate in that very competitive process required the same characteristics as the finalists—literally, the "lucky few" among the worthy many.

There are two other questions pertinent to proper evaluation. The first is the double-blind question of evaluation: How did others not associated with the program appear to achieve those same goals as those who received the scholarship? And second, the ultimate question of evaluation: What is the opportunity cost of the nationally competitive scholarship programs? The latter has seldom been considered. Andrew Carnegie built libraries; he did not give fellowships. Are the roads to the donors' or governments' ends better served by competitive scholarships than by other possibilities? We believe so, but it is surely worth the discussion.

Issues for Future Discussion

Scholarship directors identified several issues for future discussion. The issues fell under two large categories: making the case for financial and institutional support, and improving selection and management.

MAKING THE CASE FOR FINANCIAL AND INSTITUTIONAL SUPPORT

- Making the case for individual fellowships as tools for institutional change;
- Comparing the effectiveness of individual scholarships and institutional grants;
- Addressing the tension between numbers of scholarship-holders and the value of each scholarship as well as the competitive size of stipends;
- Estimating the effect of scholarship programs on both institutions and higher education in general;
- Developing a rationale for scholarships that would attract new and future donors;
- Articulating a comprehensive message that is stronger and clearer than those of individual programs about the importance of investment in human resources.

STRENGTHENING SELECTION AND MANAGEMENT

- Exploring and evaluating selection criteria—how we define and articulate those qualities, and what confidence we have that they predict lifetime performances;
- Identifying opportunities for cross-program sharing in such common

responsibilities as staff training, marketing, orientation, and alumni events;

- Developing a methodology for benchmarking that allows comparison of costs (e.g., cost per applicant or cost per scholarship-holder);
- Conceptualizing the quality question in higher education to guide our scholarship-holders to the best and most appropriate resources.

A strong consensus confirmed that the work of managing nationally and internationally competitive scholarships was substantial, important, and critical—in the very best sense, professional in nature.

There is a community of individuals that believes that awarding scholarships to young people is a profoundly moral activity. To advance promising youth on their careers and at the same time advance the missions of our several scholarships—whether providing leadership or fostering international understanding—is a rare opportunity. We know that the group affirming these views is substantial. Second, we believe that the pool of applicants should be coterminous with all the aspiring and able young people capable of undertaking the work and pursuing the ends to which a scholarship is dedicated. Third, we agree that it is important to specify concretely the values determining selection and to make the process by which finalists are determined as robust, uniform, and insightful as possible. Fourth, we contend that what happens during and after the scholarship tenure should receive the same kind of attention and imagination as is invested in the selection process. Finally, we look to forms of evaluation that are timely and useful, that focus on ways to improve performance, and that relate performance to achieving the ends of the scholarship program.

As a community of individuals committed to competitive scholarships, we seek to demonstrate the leadership, talent, and creativity we celebrate in our scholars. Scholarship programs must continue the conversation started here so that we may better serve our scholars, our funders, and ultimately, our world. In all of this, we go forward in modesty, bearing in mind the words of a contemporary, borrowing from the ancient Greeks: "Whom the gods wish to destroy, they first call promising."[36]

Notes

1. See Harriet Zuckerman, *Scientific Elite: Nobel Laureates in the United States* (New Brunswick, N.J.: Transaction Books, 1996), 248–54.

2. Robert K. Merton, "The Matthew Effect in Science," *Science* 159 (1968): 56–63. From the gospel of Matthew: "For unto every one that hath shall be given and he

shall have abundance; but from him that hath not shall be taken away even that which he hath."

3. See, for example, Pierre Bourdieu and Jean-Claude Passeron, *Reproduction in Education, Society and Culture* (London: Sage, 1977); Pierre Bourdieu and Jean-Claude Passeron, *The Inheritors: French Students and their Relation to Culture* (Chicago: University of Chicago Press, 1979); Pierre Bourdieu, *Homo Academicus* (Stanford, Calif.: Stanford University Press, 1988).

4. For a full description, Ford Foundation Fellowship Program, *Learning/Leadership/Commitment* (Report 2003-04); also see www.fordifp.net/.

5. See Deutscher Akademischer Austauschdienst (DAAD), *Annual Report 2000/2001 Summary* (Bonn, 2001), 9. The numbers associated with the European Union's ERASMUS/SOCRATES program are, literally, too large to comprehend and, because of the fundamental commitment to "European academic mobility," might be considered as a special case. In 2000, 140,000 European students attended a campus in a country other than their own. See Ulrich Teichler, "Student Mobility in the Framework of ERASMUS: Findings of an Evaluation Study," *European Journal of Education* 2 (1996): 153–79.

6. Punctuation—or lack of it!—in the original will. See Anthony Kenny, ed., *The History of the Rhodes Trust 1902-1999* (Oxford: Oxford University Press, 2001), chap. 1. Rhodes's will is reprinted pp. 568–78. Instructing those panelists how to weigh these criteria in their choice, he initially gave 40 percent to literary and scholarly attainments and 20 percent each to the other three. In a later codicil he modified the allocation, reducing academic qualifications to 30 percent and raising to 30 percent the qualities of courage and concern for the weak. In other words, young men from the United States, Germany, and the then–British Empire, educated at Oxford and selected competitively on the basis of a record of leadership, concern for justice, strength and resilience, and ability to do the academic work at Oxford would more than likely provide the public leadership Rhodes sought. These male scholars were to be selected without regard to creed or race and to be limited only by the basis of number for each area, such as two for each state and territory in the United States. See also Jeffrey Stewart, "A Black Aesthete at Oxford," *Massachusetts Review* 34 (Autumn 1993): 411–28; Robert Bruce Slater, "Black Rhodes Scholars in Academia," *Journal of Blacks in Higher Education* (Winter 1993–94): 102–107; Frank Aydelotte, *The Oxford Stamp and Other Essays* (New York: Oxford University Press, 1917); Laurence A. Crosby and Frank Aydelotte, eds., *Oxford of Today: A Manual for Prospective Rhodes Scholars* (New York: Oxford University Press, 1922); Lord Elton, ed., *The First Fifty Years of the Rhodes Trust and Rhodes Scholarships, 1903-1953* (Oxford: Blackwell 1956); Thomas J. Schaeper and Kathleen Schaeper, *Cowboys into Gentlemen: Rhodes Scholars, Oxford, and the Creation of an American Elite* (New York: Berghahn Books, 1998); Don K. Price, "A Yank at Oxford: Specializing for Breadth," *American Scholar* 55 (1986): 195–207; and unpublished reports of Theodore Youn and Karen Arnold. See also Chapter 5 in this volume.

7. Commonwealth Fund, *Annual Report 1974* (New York, 1974). In that year 38 Fellows were appointed to the two-year terms: 17 from the United Kingdom; 16 from Europe (Germany, France, Belgium, Italy and the Netherlands); and 5 from Australia and New Zealand. The program became policy-focused in the 1980s and terminated in 1998. The qualities sought were "all-around 'ambassadorial qualities' and leadership qualities as well as outstanding professional or academic achievement" (p. 96).

8. Leonard R. Sussman, *The Culture of Freedom: The Small World of Fulbright Scholars* (Lanham, Md.: Rowman and Littlefield, 1992).

9. See DAAD, *Annual Report 2001, 9-10.*

10. An evaluation of the Fulbright Scholar Program asserted that their assessment "found strong quantitative and qualitative evidence that the program is achieving its legislative mandate of promoting mutual understanding and cooperation between the U.S. and other nations" (Executive Report, *Outcome Assessment of the US Fulbright Scholar Program* [Stanford, Calif.: Stanford Research Institute International, May 2002]).

11. Alexander Astin, *What Matters in College: Four Critical Years Revisited* (San Francisco: Jossey-Bass, 1993).

12. Richard J. Light, *Making the Most of College* (Cambridge, Mass.: Harvard University Press, 2001).

13. For example, Ernest T. Pascarella and Patrick T. Terenzini, *How College Affects Students* (San Francisco: Jossey-Bass, 1991).

14. Two of the authors have eighty years of higher education experience between them.

15. Astin, *What Matters in College.* The "Intellectual Self Esteem" peer group is made up of self-reported academic achievement and abilities in leadership, public speaking, writing, aspiration, confidence, and so forth.

16. Ibid., 363.

17. Light, *Making the Most of College,* 44.

18. Ibid., 88.

19. Astin, *What Matters in College,* 233.

20. Rodney Hartnett and Benjamin F. Payton, "Minority Admissions and Performance in Graduate Study: A Preliminary Study of Fellowship Programs of the Ford Foundation and the Danforth Foundation" (Washington, D.C.: Aspen Institute, 1977), 8.

21. William Bowen and Derek Bok, *The Shape of the River* (Princeton, N.J.: Princeton University Press, 1998).

22. Astin, *What Matters in College;* Light, *Making the Most of College.*

23. Astin, *What Matters in College,* 431.

24. Personal communication to Alice Ilchman from Allan Goodman, October 8, 2002.

25. Allen Neuringer, "National Science Foundation Graduate Fellowship Evaluations," *American Psychologist* 48 (August 1993): 913–15.

26. See websites for Stanford University: www.stanford.edu/dept/icenter/orc/scholarships/rhodesmarshall.html and www.stanford.edu/dept/CDC/students/jobhunt/Rhodes/sldoo1.htm.

27. See website for National Association of Fellowship Advisors: www.nafadvisors.org.

28. An exception is Friedhelm Maiworm and Ulrich Teichler, *Study Abroad and Early Career: Experiences of Former ERASMUS Students,* Higher Education Policy Series 35, ERASMUS Monograph 21 (London: Jessica Kingsley Publishers, 1996).

29. Personal communication to Alice Ilchman from Allan Goodman, October 8, 2002.

30. While much of this and the next two paragraphs were gleaned from the works listed in note 7, the personal conversations and public contributions of John Rowett, Warden of Rhodes House, are the major source.

31. See, for example, John Berry, *An Evaluation Framework for the Commonwealth Scholarship and Fellowship Plan,* Commonwealth Secretariat (August 1994).

32. Maiworm and Teichler, *Study Abroad and Early Career.*

33. Catherine P. Ailes and Susan H. Russell, *Outcome Assessment of the U.S. Fulbright Scholar Program,* Stanford Research Institute International, Washington (May 2002).

34. See Markle Foundation website: www.markle.org/about/_about_history.stm.

35. Hans Rosenhaupt, "Report on Woodrow Wilson Fellows, 1945–77," report to the Ford Foundation, January 1978; Susan Uchitelle and Robert Kirkwood, *The Danforth and Kent Fellowships: A Quinquennial Review* (St. Louis: Danforth Foundation, April 1976).

36. Quotation by Cyril Connolly in *Simpson's Contemporary Quotations,* compiled by James B. Simpson (Boston: Houghton Mifflin, 1988).

2 | WICS

A Model for Selecting Students for Nationally Competitive Scholarships

Robert J. Sternberg and Elena L. Grigorenko

Two students apply for an internationally known, highly prestigious graduate fellowship. One student has demonstrated exceptional academic achievement and has devised a new piece of software that already is being used in industry, but she has shown no leadership skills of distinction. The other student is a good but not great student academically who has not yet demonstrated exceptional creativity, but he has shown outstanding leadership skills, having held top leadership roles in both high school and college. Which student does one choose, if either?

Scholarship and fellowship programs have created various criteria for selecting students for their particular programs. We examined these criteria based on those listed on websites of major scholarship and fellowship programs. On the surface, these criteria, as shown in Table 2.1, seem to make good sense in terms of selecting future world leaders in a variety of fields. The question we address in this chapter is whether it is possible to generate a unified model of selection that would work across a wide variety of scholarship programs. This would enable various programs to present a common face to students in terms of what they believe is important for their scholarships and fellowships.

Our goal is to create a model that would comprise most of the general attributes that scholarship-awarding programs seek. We do not attempt to cover all possible attributes. For example, the attribute of "good health" is listed by one program but not by most others. Rather, we suggest a model that: (1) encompasses the attributes scholarship programs generally seek; (2) does not encompass attributes that scholarship programs do not generally seek; (3) is conceptually coherent; (4) is psychologically defensible; and (5) can be operationalized—that is, the stated attributes can be assessed in one or more ways.

In a sense, our essay is about how to avoid selecting the "Dennys" of the world.[1] Roger "Denny" Hansen, a Rhodes Scholar who had all the markings of early success, was a classmate of author Calvin Trillin. But life

Table 2.1

Sample List of Attributes Sought in Nationally Competitive Scholarships

Attribute Sought by Scholarship Program	Mapping onto WICS Framework
Ability to contribute to field of study	ICW
Ability to contribute to society	ICW
Activity in support of human rights and the rule of law	W
Adaptability	I
Advancing the responsibilities of citizenship in a free society	W
Appreciation of participation in arts and humanities	W
Capacity for future influence	ICW
Character	W
Clearly defined career interest	I
Commitment to improving the commonweal	w
Commitment to integrating research and education	IC
Commitment to values in the U.S. Constitution and the Bill of Rights	W
Communication skills	I
Community service	IW
Concern for problems of society	W
Creative ability	C
Creativity	C
Critical-thinking ability	I
Ethical character	W
Experience in community service or development	W
Health	none
Imagination	C
Initiative	IC
Integrity of character	W
Intellectual ability	I
Intellectual distinction	I
Intellectual merit	I
Intelligence	I
Intention to serve communities or countries of origin	IW
Interest in fellow human beings	W

Continued on the next page

Table 2.1 *Continued*

Leadership	ICW
Originality	C
Personal promise	W
Potential for decision making	I
Potential for innovative research	IC
Potential for future achievement	ICW
Potential for human and effective participation in the world community	W
Potential to influence opinions	ICW
Promise of creative achievement	C
Promise of effective service to the world	W
Public service	W
Respect for fellow human beings	W
Scholarship	IC
Scholastic achievement	IC
Significant accomplishment	IC
Understanding of physical principles	I
Vision	CW
Volunteerism	W
Wide attainments	ICW
Wide interests	IC

I = Intelligence
C = Creativity
W = Wisdom

Sources for attributes: Websites for Beinecke Fellowships, Churchill Scholarships, Commonwealth Scholarship and Fellowship Plan, Jack Kent Cooke Graduate Fellowships, DAAD (German "Fulbright"), European Commission—Socrates/Erasmus Program, The Ford Foundation International Fellowship Program, Fulbright Program, German Humboldt Fellowships, Hertz Fellowships, Bill and Melinda Gates Cambridge Scholarships, Howard Hughes Medical Institute, Kennedy Memorial Scholarships, Luce Foundation Scholars Program, MacArthur Fellows Program, Marshall Scholarships, Andrew W. Mellon Fellowships in Humanistic Studies, George Mitchell Scholarships, National Science Foundation Graduate Research Fellowship, Rhodes Scholarships, Paul and Daisy Soros Fellowships, Truman Scholarships, Thomas Watson Fellows.

did not prove kind to him, and after a series of failures, Denny committed suicide at the age of 55. Of course, there are other examples of spectacular failures, such as William James Sidis, who never lived up to the potential he had shown as an intellectual child prodigy.[2] The question then becomes how selection committees can identify the people who are not only talented but are most likely to translate this talent into actions that have a meaningful impact on the world.

The WICS Model

We propose the WICS model as a possible common basis for awarding scholarships and fellowships. This model is an expansion of a mode' of abilities for leadership proposed elsewhere.[3] WICS is an acronym standing for: Wisdom, Intelligence, Creativity, Synthesized.

It is our belief that wisdom, intelligence, and creativity are *sine qua non* for the leaders of the future. Without a synthesis of these three attributes, someone can be a decent leader and perhaps even a good one, but never a great one.

In the remainder of this chapter, we discuss each of these attributes, although for didactic purposes we do not discuss them in the order they are stated above. We start with intelligence, which is a basis for creativity and wisdom and so should be discussed first. Then we discuss creativity, which is essential as well in wisdom. Next we discuss wisdom, which builds on, but goes beyond, intelligence and creativity. Then we briefly describe some of our research findings. Finally, we draw some general conclusions.

Intelligence

Two scholarship applicants are hiking in the woods. One of them "aced" her college courses, getting almost straight A's. Her standardized test scores were phenomenal, and her professors found her to be brilliant. The other student barely made it through college. Her standardized entrance test scores were marginal, and she just squeaked by even getting into college. Nonetheless, people say of her that she is shrewd and clever—her teachers and friends call her "street-smart." As the friends are hiking, they encounter a huge, ferocious, and obviously hungry grizzly bear. Its next meal has just come into sight, and they are it. The first student calculates that the grizzly bear will overtake them in 27.3 seconds. At that point, she panics, realizing there is no escape. She faces her friend, the fear of death in her eyes. To her amazement, she observes that her friend is not scared at all. To the contrary, her friend is quickly but calmly taking off her hiking boots and putting on jogging shoes. "What do you think you're doing?" the first hiker says to her companion, "You'll never be able to outrun that grizzly bear." "That's true," says the companion, "but all I have to do is outrun you."

This obviously apocryphal story points out something many of us feel intuitively. There is more to intelligence than just grades and test scores. But what is intelligence?

Although there are many definitions, intelligence is typically defined in terms of a person's ability to adapt to the environment and to learn from experience. Our own definition of intelligence is somewhat more elaborate and is based on Sternberg's theory of successful intelligence.[4] According to this definition, successful intelligence is

1. the ability to achieve one's goals in life, given one's sociocultural context;
2. by capitalizing on strengths and correcting or compensating for weaknesses;
3. in order to adapt to, shape, and select environments;
4. through a combination of analytical, creative, and practical abilities.

Consider item 1 first. Most programs that award scholarships do not attempt to specify precisely what candidates should do with their lives. Rather, they seek people who have formulated a meaningful and coherent set of goals and have shown the ability to reach those goals. One student may wish to be a statesperson, another a scientist, and another an artist. The question typically is not what goals students have chosen, but rather, what the students have done to show that they can realize those goals in a distinguished way. Thus, this item actually includes three sub-items: (a) identifying meaningful goals; (b) coordinating those goals in a meaningful way so that they form a coherent story of what one is seeking in life; and (c) moving a substantial distance along the path toward reaching those goals.

This first item recognizes that intelligence means a somewhat different thing to each individual. The student who wishes to become a Supreme Court judge will be taking a different path from the student who wishes to become a distinguished novelist—but both will have formulated a set of coherent goals toward which to work. A program granting scholarships often will care less what goal is chosen than that the individual has chosen a worthwhile set of goals and shown the ability to achieve them.

Item 2 recognizes that although psychologists sometimes talk of a "general" factor of intelligence, virtually no one is good at everything or bad at everything.[5] People who are the future leaders of society are people who have identified their strengths and weaknesses and have found ways to work within that pattern of abilities.

There is no single way to succeed in a job that works for everyone. For example, some lawyers are successful by virtue of their very strong analytical skills. They may never argue in a courtroom, but they can put together an airtight legal argument. Another lawyer may have a commanding presence in the courtroom but be less powerful analytically. The legal profession in the United Kingdom recognizes this distinction by having separate roles for the solicitor and the barrister. In the United States, successful lawyers find different specializations that allow them to make the best use of their talents. Unsuccessful lawyers may actually attempt to capitalize on weaknesses, for example, litigating cases when their legal talent lies elsewhere.

This same general principle applies in any profession. Consider teaching, for example. Educators often try to distinguish characteristics of expert teachers, and they have indeed distinguished some such characteristics.[6] But the truth is that teachers can excel in many different ways. Some teachers are better in giving large lectures, others in small seminars, and others in one-on-one mentoring. There is no one formula that works for every teacher. Good teachers figure out their strengths and try to arrange their teaching so that they can capitalize on their strengths and either compensate for or correct their weaknesses. Team teaching is one way of doing so, in that one teacher can compensate for what the other does not do well.

In general, teams can be a highly effective means for capitalizing on strengths and correcting or compensating for weaknesses. At Yale University, we direct the Center for the Psychology of Abilities, Competencies, and Expertise. Knowing that each member of the center has a unique pattern of strengths and weaknesses, we strongly encourage teamwork so that each person can find a role that best enables him or her to contribute to the collective enterprise.

Some years ago one of the coauthors was listening to a lecture by a famous educator and was greatly impressed with his highly effective manner of presentation. He commented to the individual sitting next to him that he wished he could teach like the lecturer. The individual turned to the coauthor, and told him he was wishing for the wrong thing. He ought to wish that he could become an effective teacher in his own way of teaching. At a practical level, this individual grasped the basic idea of the definition of successful intelligence better than did the coauthor! We all have to find our own way of capitalizing on strengths and compensating for or correcting weaknesses.

Scholarship applicants might have very different patterns of abilities. Sometimes selection committees will have feelings of discomfort, recognizing that they are having to choose between "oranges and apples"—that is, to evaluate people whose strengths are very different on a single scale that does not seem to apply across all applicants. When the committee looks at their task from the standpoint of the theory of successful intelligence, their job becomes easier. The question is not how well people do on some common scale, but rather, how well they do on whatever scales are relevant to their making the most of their own aspirations—in other words, how well they capitalize on their strengths without letting their weaknesses get in their way.

Item 3 recognizes that intelligence broadly defined refers to more than just "adapting to the environment," which is the mainstay of conventional definitions of intelligence. The theory of successful intelligence distinguishes among adapting, shaping, and selecting.

In adaptation to the environment, one modifies oneself to fit an environment. The ability to adapt to the environment is important in life and is especially important to scholarship holders. Most of them will be entering a new environment that is quite different from the one in which they previously have spent time. They may be entering a new university and perhaps even a new country or a new culture. If they are not adaptable, they may not be able to transfer the skills they showed in the previous environment to the new one. Over the course of a lifetime, environmental conditions change greatly. A kind of work that at one point may be greatly valued (e.g., forming a start-up company) may at another time be valued little if at all. In research, the problems change, and sometimes people who were effective in solving the problems of one decade are relatively ineffective in solving the problems of another decade. In governmental leadership, some elected leaders prove to be dinosaurs—people who were able to lead the country effectively under one set of conditions but not under another set of conditions (such as when the national or world economy declines). Clearly, adaptability is a key skill in any definition of intelligence. A scholarship applicant ought to be able to show the ability to adapt to a variety of environments.

In life, adaptation is not enough, however. Adaptation needs to be balanced with shaping. In shaping, one modifies the environment to fit what one seeks of it, rather than modifying oneself to fit the environment. Truly great people in any field are not just adapters; they are also shapers. They recognize that they cannot change everything, but if they want to have an impact on the world, they have to change some things. Part of successful intelligence is deciding what to change and then how to change it.

For example, one of the coauthors (Robert J. Sternberg, henceforth referred to as RJS) is currently president-elect of the American Psychological Association. The association is an extremely complex organization comprising 155,000 individuals who represent many constituencies and interest groups. It is difficult to effect change because no matter what one does, some special-interest group will be offended by the change. Yet an effective president must not just adapt to all the special-interest groups, but try to shape the environment in which he or she works. This means effecting change even though some groups will not want it. Effectiveness, however, also requires recognizing what changes plausibly can be made and what changes cannot be.

When a scholarship-holder goes to an institution of higher learning, one hopes that the scholar will not only adapt to the environment but will shape it in a way that makes it a better place than it was before. Selection committees will wish to look for evidence not just of a scholar's having engaged in a variety of activities, but of the scholar's having made a difference in his or her involvement in those activities. We often tell our own students that a career is about having an impact—about making a field or a place better, more interesting, or more enriched for one's having been there. *Shaping* is how one has this kind of impact.

Sometimes one attempts unsuccessfully to adapt to an environment and then also fails in shaping that environment. No matter what one does to try to make the environment work out, nothing, in fact, seems to work. In such cases the appropriate action may be to select another environment.

Many of the greatest people in any one field started off in another field and found that the first field was not really the one in which they had the most to contribute. Rather than spend their lives doing something that turned out not to match their pattern of strengths and weaknesses, they had the sense to find something else to do where they really had a contribution to make. In our own graduate program at Yale, we have a somewhat different philosophy from some of our faculty colleagues. Many colleagues are determined to have students succeed in the program, regardless of what must be done to help the students achieve success. Our own view is that one should help students greatly, but only up to a certain point. Some students may simply be in the wrong field or in the wrong institution. If the students were admitted, they obviously have great strengths. They should not graduate by the skin of their teeth. They should find an environment that enables them to make a distinguished, not a mediocre, contribution.

Item 4 points out that successful intelligence involves a broader range of abilities than is typically measured by tests of intellectual and academic skills such as the SAT, ACT, GRE, LSAT, MCAT, GMAT, and so forth. Most of these tests primarily or exclusively measure memory and analytical abilities. With regard to memory, they assess the abilities to recall and recognize information. With regard to analytical abilities, they measure the skills involved when one analyzes, compares and contrasts, evaluates, critiques, and judges. These are important skills during the school years and in later life. But they are not the only skills that matter for school and life success. One needs not only to remember and analyze concepts but also to be able to generate and apply them. Consider three students (who are genuine examples, but whose names have been changed).

When we admitted "Alice" to our graduate program, she was the teacher's dream. She scored high on tests, performed well in class, and in general did everything a teacher would expect a bright student to do. As a result, Alice was initially considered to be at or near the top of the class. Her stellar test scores were accepted as a valid indicator of her ability to do outstanding work throughout her academic career. Yet by the time she had finished graduate school in psychology, she was performing at a very modest level. About 80 percent of her classmates were doing better than she was. What went wrong? The answer, quite simply, is that whereas Alice was excellent at remembering and analyzing other people's ideas, she was not very good at coming up with ideas of her own. Consequently, she faltered in advanced studies, where (as in life) it is necessary to have original ideas and not just to remember or analyze what one has learned from one's teachers.

Consider, in contrast, "Barbara." Her grades were good, although by no means spectacular, and her undergraduate teachers thought she was just terrific, despite the fact that her standardized test scores were very weak. When Barbara applied to our graduate program in psychology, she included a portfolio of her work that was tremendously impressive. Her chances of getting a job at Yale as an assistant professor (for which one needs a Ph.D.) seemed actually higher than her chances of being admitted to graduate school, because getting a job does not require a standardized ability test, whereas getting into graduate school does.

Nevertheless, despite Barbara's mediocre scores on standardized tests, one of us (RJS) anticipated that she would be admitted. For one thing, the psychology department claimed to care about creativity, and Barbara had amply demonstrated creativity in her work. What better predictor of future creative work could one find than past creative work? Certainly, a test like the Graduate Record Examination, which does not measure creativity, will not be as good a predictor of creative work as the creative work itself. In general, the best predictor of any kind of behavior in the future is the same kind of behavior in the past. This principle applies universally.

At the time of Barbara's application, RJS was the director of graduate studies in the psychology department, so he assumed that the other members of the admissions committee would more or less have to listen to him. Besides, he was the expert on the committee with regard to abilities and how to test them. The committee did not, in fact, just ignore Barbara's application. They spent close to a half-hour discussing it in great detail, but there was a distressing aspect to the discussion. It became apparent that the test scores were coloring everything else about the application. In other words, having seen the weak test scores, the committee members were looking to interpret other aspects of Barbara's admissions file as supporting the scores.

By the end of the discussion, the members of the committee felt very satisfied with the decision they made, which was to reject her. RJS was the only person who voted to admit her. Even though Barbara had included a portfolio of her work that demonstrated a high degree of competence, the other committee members had made their decision largely on the basis of her test scores. In other words, they had more confidence in fallible and often weak predictors of creative work than in the creative work itself. The predictor was seen as more important than what it was supposed to predict!

The situation was actually quite a bit worse than it sounds. If Barbara had been rejected at the range of graduate schools to which she applied because of her GRE scores, she probably would not have had much better luck if she decided to pursue some other calling. Law schools require the LSAT, medical schools the MCAT, business schools the GMAT. These tests are all highly similar. Someone who does well on one of them is likely to do fairly well on the others; someone who does not do well on one of them is likely not to do well on the others.

After Barbara was rejected by our graduate program, RJS decided to hire her as a research associate because he believed that she showed much greater potential than her test scores indicated. He was not disappointed. Her work as a research associate was highly creative and innovative. Two years later she was admitted as the top pick into our graduate program.

When "Celia" applied to our graduate program in psychology, she had grades that were good but not great, test scores that were good but not great, and letters of recommendation that were good but not great. In fact, just about everything in her application seemed to be good but not great. So we admitted Celia, because every program needs people who are good but not great. Indeed, her work proved to be exactly what we predicted—good but not great—so we thought we hit it on that one!

But Celia gave us quite a surprise when it came to getting a job. Everyone wanted to hire her. And that raised an intriguing question. Why would someone who lacked Alice's analytical ability and Barbara's creative ability do spectacularly well in the job market? The answer was actually very simple. Celia had an abundance of practical intelligence and social competence—or, put simply, common sense. She could go into an environment, figure out what she needed to do to adapt successfully in that environment, and then do it. For example, Celia knew how to interview effectively, how to interact well with other students, how to get her work done. She was also aware of the kinds of things that do and do not work in an academic environment. She knew something that is seldom acknowledged—that in school, as in other aspects of life, one needs a certain amount of practical savvy in order to succeed.

It is interesting to compare Alice, Barbara, and Celia with "Paul." Paul was a student who combined Alice's analytical skills with Barbara's creative ones. As a result, many faculty members thought he would be extremely successful. RJS did not. The reason was that although Paul was very bright in some ways, he was notably challenged with regard to practical intelligence. He was the kind of student who was bright and who knew it. His knowledge made him very arrogant. But even arrogant people can get where they want to go if they know how to control their arrogance. Paul did not know. Although he received many job interviews, he was offered only one job, the worst one for which he applied. The reason was that he was unable or unwilling to hide his arrogance on the one day that it is essential to do so—the day of the job interview. Almost no one wanted to hire him. And he did not last long even at the place that was willing to hire him.

We have described these four students at some length in order to make what we believe to be an important point. Intelligence is not, as Edwin Boring once suggested, merely what intelligence tests test.[7] Intelligence tests and other tests of cognitive and academic skills measure part of the range of intellectual skills. They do not measure the whole range. One should not conclude that a person who does not test well is not smart. Rather, one should merely look at test scores as one indicator among many of a person's intellectual skills.

Other Views of Intelligence

We need to state that not everyone shares our views on intelligence.[8] Over the course of the years, investigators have had somewhat different ideas of what constitutes intelligence. Spearman believed in the primacy of a single general factor of intelligence.[9] Thurstone suggested that there are seven primary mental abilities: verbal comprehension, verbal fluency, number, inductive reasoning, memory, perceptual speed, and spatial visualization.[10] Cattell suggested two major aspects of intellectual abilities: fluid abilities, which are used to think flexibly and in novel ways; and crystallized abilities, which represent the accumulated information one has attained over the course of a lifetime.[11] Many theorists believe in hierarchical models, where intelligence is at the top, and more specific abilities further down, in the hierarchy.[12] And Gardner has proposed a theory of multiple intelligences, according to which there are eight and possibly nine relatively distinct intelligences: linguistic, logical-mathematical, spatial, bodily-kinesthetic, musical, naturalist, interpersonal, intrapersonal, and possibly existential. Gardner's theory differs somewhat from the theory presented here, but he is in agreement that there is more to intelligence than conventional tests test.[13]

Intelligence is important for making a meaningful contribution to the world. But some people are intelligent but offer up little. Like Alice, they are good critics but not good creators. Creative skills matter at least as much as do analytical intellectual ones.

Creativity

A politician and his wife decide to eat dinner in a fancy French restaurant in Washington, D.C. The waiter approaches their table and asks the wife what she would like as an appetizer. "The pâté de foie gras," she tells the waiter. "And the main course?" the waiter asks. "The filet mignon," responds the politician's wife. "And the vegetable?" asks the waiter. "He'll have the same," responds the politician's wife.

This story demonstrates that creativity is not an attribute limited to the historic "greats"—the Darwins, the Picassos, the Hemingways. Rather, it is something anyone can use. It also shows that creativity is a decision. The politician's wife decided, through her cutting remark, for creativity. So when we think about "creative ability," we think of it largely in terms of a person's decision to be creative—or not to be.

According to the investment theory of creativity, creative thinkers are like good investors: they buy low and sell high.[14] Whereas investors do this in the world of finance, creative people do it in the world of ideas. Creative ideas are like undervalued stocks (stocks with a low price-to-earnings ratio), and both the stocks and the ideas are generally rejected by the public. When creative ideas are proposed, they often are viewed as bizarre, useless, and even foolish, and are summarily rejected. The person proposing them often is regarded with suspicion and perhaps even with disdain and derision.

Creative ideas are both novel and valuable. But they are often rejected because the innovator stands up to vested interests and defies the crowd. The crowd does not maliciously or willfully reject creative notions. Rather, it does not realize, or does not want to realize, that the proposed idea represents a valid and advanced way of thinking. Society generally perceives opposition to the status quo as annoying, offensive, and reason enough to ignore innovative ideas.

Evidence abounds that creative ideas are often rejected.[15] Initial reviews of major works of literature and art are often negative. Toni Morrison's *Tar Baby* received negative reviews when it was first published, as did Sylvia Plath's *The Bell Jar*. The first exhibition in Munich of the work of Norwegian painter Edvard Munch opened and closed the same day because of the strong negative response from the critics. Some of the greatest scientific papers have been rejected, not just by one journal, but even by several journals before being published. For example, John Garcia, a distinguished biopsychologist, was immediately denounced when he first proposed that a form of learning called classical conditioning could be produced in a single trial of learning.[16]

From the investment view, then, the creative person buys low by presenting a unique idea and then attempting to convince other people of its value. After convincing others that the idea is valuable, which increases the perceived value of the investment, the creative person sells high by leaving the idea to others and moving on to another idea. People typically want others to love their ideas, but immediate universal applause for an idea usually indicates that it is not particularly creative.

Creativity is as much a decision about and an attitude toward life as it is a matter of ability. Creativity is often obvious in young children, but it is harder to find in older children and adults because their creative potential has been suppressed by a society that encourages intellectual conformity.

Creative work requires applying and balancing the three intellectual abilities—creative, analytic, and practical—all of which can be developed.[17] *Creative ability* is used to generate ideas. Everyone, even the most creative person, has better and worse ideas. Without well-developed *analytic ability,* the creative thinker is as likely to pursue bad ideas as to pursue good ones. The creative individual uses analytic ability to work out the implications of a creative idea and to test it. *Practical ability* is the ability to translate theory into practice and abstract ideas into practical accomplishments. An implication of the investment theory of creativity is that good ideas do not sell themselves. The creative person uses practical ability to convince other people that an idea is valuable. For example, every organization has a set of ideas that dictate how things, or at least some things, should be done. When an individual proposes a new procedure, he or she must sell it by convincing others that it is better than the old one. Practical ability is also used to recognize ideas that have a potential audience.

Creativity requires these three types of ability. The person who is only creative may come up with innovative ideas, but cannot recognize or sell them. The person who is only analytic may be an excellent critic of other people's ideas, but is not likely to generate creative ideas. The person who is only practical may be an excellent salesperson, but is as likely to promote ideas or products of little or no value as to promote genuinely creative ideas.

What kinds of attributes should one look for in scholarship applicants in order to assess their creativity?

1. *Redefining problems.* Redefining a problem means taking a problem and turning it on its head. Many times in life individuals have a problem, and they just don't see how to solve it. They are stuck in a box. Redefining a problem essentially means extricating oneself from the box.

A good example of redefining a problem is summed up in the story of an executive at one of the biggest automobile companies in the Detroit area.

The executive held a high-level position, and he loved his job and the money he made on the job. However, he despised the person he worked for, and because of this, he decided to find a new job. He went to a headhunter, who assured him that a new job could be easily arranged. After this meeting the executive went home and talked to his wife, who was teaching a unit on redefining problems as part of a course she was teaching on Intelligence Applied.[18] The executive realized that he could apply what his wife was teaching to his own problem. He returned to the headhunter and gave the headhunter his boss's name. The headhunter found a new job for the boss that he—having no idea of what was going on—accepted. The executive then got his boss's job. The executive decided for creativity by redefining a problem.

The scholarship winner will encounter many kinds of novel situations that resist easy definition in terms of past experience. The more flexible the individual is in redefining these situations so that they make sense to him or her, the more likely he or she is to succeed.

2. *Questioning and analyzing assumptions.* Everyone has assumptions. Often one does not realize that one has them because they are so widely shared. Creative people question assumptions and eventually lead others to do the same. Questioning assumptions is part of the analytical thinking involved in creativity. When Copernicus suggested that the earth revolves around the sun, the suggestion was viewed as preposterous because everyone assumed on the basis of what they could see that the sun revolves around the earth. Galileo's ideas, including the relative rates of falling objects, caused him to be banned as a heretic.

Sometimes it is not until many years later that society realizes the limitations or errors of their assumptions and the value of the creative person's thoughts. The impetus of those who question assumptions allows for cultural, technological, and other forms of advancement.

Schools in particular tend to make a pedagogical mistake by emphasizing the answering and not the asking of questions. The good student is perceived as the one who rapidly furnishes the right answers. The expert in a field thus becomes the extension of the expert student—the one who knows and can recite a lot of information. As John Dewey recognized, *how* one thinks is often more important than *what* one thinks.[19] Schools need to teach students how to ask the right questions (questions that are good, thought-provoking, and interesting) and lessen the emphasis on rote learning. Programs perhaps should not choose as scholarship winners those who merely are experts in spitting back what others have previously said.

3. *Realizing that creative ideas do not sell themselves.* Everyone would like to assume that their wonderful, creative ideas will sell themselves. But as Galileo, Edvard Munch, Toni Morrison, Sylvia Plath, and millions of

others have discovered, they do not. On the contrary, creative ideas and those who propose them are usually viewed with suspicion and distrust. Because people are comfortable with the ways they already think, and because they probably have a vested interest in their existing way of thinking, it can be extremely difficult to dislodge them from their current viewpoints. Scholarship winners need to be people who are not only highly creatively competent but who also have convinced others of their creative competence.

4. *Recognizing that knowledge is a double-edged sword.* Some years ago, RJS was visiting a very famous psychologist who lives abroad. As part of the tour he had planned, the psychologist invited RJS to visit the local zoo. They went past the cages of the primates who were engaged in what euphemistically could be called "strange and unnatural sexual behavior." RJS, of course, averted his eyes. However, his host did not do the same. After observing the primates for a short amount of time, he was able to analyze the sexual behavior of the primates in terms of his theory of intelligence. Whatever is responsible for sexual behavior, it is not intelligence, as Bill Clinton and so many others have compellingly demonstrated. This experience reminded RJS of how knowledge and expertise can be a double-edged sword.

On the one hand, one cannot be creative without knowledge. Quite simply, one cannot go beyond the existing state of knowledge if one does not know what that state is. Many students have ideas that are creative with respect to themselves, but not with respect to the field, because others have had the same ideas before. Those with a greater knowledge base can be creative in ways that those who are still learning about the basics of the field cannot be.

At the same time, those who have an expert level of knowledge can experience tunnel vision, narrow thinking, and entrenchment. Experts can become so stuck in a way of thinking that they become unable to extricate themselves from it. Such narrowing happens to everyone, ourselves included. For example, at one point in RJS's career, every theory he proposed seemed to have three parts. At that point, he was "stuck on threes." Learning must be a lifelong process, not one that terminates when a person achieves some measure of recognition. When a person believes that he or she knows everything there is to know in a field, he or she is unlikely to ever show truly meaningful creativity again.

We tell our students that the teaching-learning process is a two-way process. We have as much to learn from our students as they have to learn from us. We have knowledge they do not have, but they have flexibility that we do not have—precisely because they do not know as much as we do. By learning from, as well as teaching to, one's students, one opens up channels for creativity that otherwise would remain closed. Scholarship winners need to be individuals who use knowledge to move beyond where things are, rather than to replicate what others have already done or to get stuck in old ways of thinking that no longer are serving a constructive purpose.

5. *Willingness to surmount obstacles.* Buying low and selling high means defying the crowd. And people who defy the crowd—people who think creatively—almost inevitably encounter resistance. The question is not whether one will encounter obstacles but whether the creative thinker has the fortitude to persevere. We have often wondered why so many people start off their careers doing creative work and then vanish from the radar screen. We think we know at least one reason: sooner or later, they decide that being creative is not worth the resistance and punishment. The truly creative thinkers pay the short-term price because they recognize that they can make a difference in the long term. But often it is a long while before the value of creative ideas is recognized and appreciated.

One example of having to wait for ideas to be recognized occurred in RJS's own experience. When he was very young, he became interested in intelligence and intelligence testing as a result of poor scores on intelligence tests. As a seventh grader of age thirteen, he decided it would be interesting to do a science project on intelligence testing. He found the Stanford-Binet Intelligence Scales in the adult section of the local library and started giving the test to friends. Unfortunately, one of his friends tattled to his mother, who reported RJS to the school authorities. The head school psychologist threatened to burn the book that contained the test if RJS ever brought it into school again. He suggested that RJS find another interest. Had he done so, however, he never would have done all the work he has done on intelligence, which has meant a great deal to his life and, he hopes, something to the world. The school psychologist's opinion presented a major obstacle to RJS as an early adolescent. However, because he surmounted that obstacle, he has been able to do research on intelligence, which has been very fulfilling for him.

Scholarship winners will encounter many obstacles in their lives. Some of them have led "charmed" lives, as did Trillin's Denny. But sooner or later the obstacles start to present themselves. The ones who go on to greatness will be those who are prepared to surmount rather than succumb to these obstacles.

6. *Willingness to take sensible risks.* When creative people defy the crowd by buying low and selling high, they take risks in much the same way as do people who invest. Some such investments simply may not pan out. Moreover, defying the crowd means risking the crowd's wrath. But there are levels of sensibility to keep in mind when defying the crowd. Creative

people take sensible risks and produce ideas that others ultimately admire and respect as trend-setting. In taking these risks, creative people sometimes make mistakes, fail, and fall flat on their faces.

Nearly every major discovery or invention entailed some risk. When a movie theater was the only place to see a movie, someone created the idea of the home video machine. Skeptics questioned if anyone would want to see videos on a small screen. Another initially risky idea was the home computer. Many wondered if anyone would have enough use for a home computer to justify the cost. These ideas, once risks, are now ingrained in our society.

RJS took a risk as an assistant professor when he decided to study intelligence because the field of intelligence has low prestige within academic psychology. When he was being considered for tenure, it came to his attention that the university was receiving letters that questioned why it would want to give tenure to someone in such a marginal and unprestigious field. He sought advice from a senior professor, Wendell Garner, asking whether perhaps he had made a mistake in labeling his work as being about intelligence. Indeed, he could have done essentially the same work but labeled it as being in the field of "thinking" or of "problem solving"—fields with more prestige. Garner's advice was that RJS had come to Yale wanting to make a difference in the field of intelligence. He had made a difference, but now he was afraid it might cost him his job. He was right: RJS had taken a risk. But Garner maintained that there was only one thing RJS could do— exactly what he was doing. If this field meant so much to him, then he needed to pursue it, just as he was doing, even if it meant losing his job. RJS is still at the university, but other risks he has taken have not turned out as well. One must realize that some risks just will not work, and that is the cost of doing creative work.

Willingness to take risks is especially important for scholarship winners. Many of them got to where they are by *not* taking risks. They played the academic game with consummate skill, doing what needed to be done and playing it safe so that they would not get "burned." But there is a transition in the life of every great contributor. He or she needs to start taking risks. It is important, therefore, to select people who are willing to risk.

7. *Tolerance of ambiguity.* People like things to be in black and white. They like to think that a country is good or bad (ally or enemy) or that a given idea in education works or does not work. The problem is that there are a lot of grays in creative work. Artists working on new paintings and writers working on new books often report feeling scattered and unsure in their thoughts. They often need to figure out whether they are even on the right track. Scientists often are not sure whether the theory they have devel-

oped is exactly correct. Creative thinkers need to tolerate ambiguity and uncertainty until they get the idea just right.

A creative idea often comes in bits and pieces and develops over time. However, the period in which the idea is developing tends to be uncomfortable. Without time or the ability to tolerate ambiguity, many people may jump to a less than optimal solution. Scholarship winners will often be undertaking major projects in their graduate years. They should be individuals who are willing to tolerate ambiguity long enough to make these projects not just good, but great.

8. *Self-efficacy.* People often reach a point where they feel that no one believes in them. We reach this point frequently, feeling that no one values or even appreciates what we are doing. Because creative work often does not get a warm reception, it is extremely important that the creative people believe in the value of what they are doing. This is not to say that individuals should believe that every idea they have is a good one. Rather, individuals need to believe that, ultimately, they have the ability to make a difference. In the course of their studies, there will come times when scholarship winners will doubt themselves. That is what happened to Trillin's Denny. He seemingly lost confidence in himself at Oxford, and he never was able to gain it back. To succeed in life, one has to believe, not in each and everything one does, but in one's ability to get done what needs to be done and to recover from the inevitable setbacks that life throws at one.

9. *Finding what one loves to do.* To unleash their students' best creative performances, teachers must help students find what excites them. This may not be what really excites the teacher. People who truly excel creatively in a pursuit, whether vocational or avocational, almost always genuinely love what they do. Certainly, the most creative people are intrinsically motivated in their work.[20] Less creative people often pick careers for the money or prestige and are bored with or loathe their careers. Most often, these people do not do work that makes a difference in their field.

We often meet students who are pursuing a certain field, not because it is what they want to do, but because it is what their parents or other authority figures expect them to do. We always feel sorry for such students because we know that although they may do good work in that field, they almost certainly will not do great work. It is hard for people to do great work in a field that simply does not interest them.

Of course, taking this attitude is easier said than done. RJS was heartened to learn that his young son wanted to play the piano. RJS plays the piano, and he was glad that his son also wanted to play. But then his son stopped practicing and ultimately quit, and RJS felt bad. A short time thereafter, when his son informed him that he had decided that he wanted to play the trumpet, RJS reacted very negatively, pointing out to him that he had already quit the piano and probably would quit the trumpet too.

RJS later found himself wondering why he had been so harsh. How could he have said such a thing? But then he quickly understood it. If someone else's child wanted to play the trumpet, that was fine. But he couldn't imagine any Sternberg child playing the trumpet. It did not fit his ideal image of a Sternberg child. He realized he was being narrow-minded and doing exactly the opposite of what he had told everyone else to do. It's one thing to talk the talk, another to walk the walk. He backpedaled, and his son started playing the trumpet.

Selection committees should select those students who genuinely love what they do and wish to keep doing it, not because it brings them extrinsic rewards (such as scholarships), but because they feel a calling to do it. The people who feel such a calling are the ones who later can make a true difference.

10. *Willingness to delay gratification.* Part of being creative means being able to work on a project or task for a long time without immediate or interim rewards. Students must learn that there are benefits to delaying gratification. In the short term, people are often ignored when they do creative work or even punished for doing it.

Hard work often does not bring immediate rewards. People do not immediately become expert baseball players, dancers, musicians, or sculptors. And the reward of becoming an expert can seem very far away. The people who make the most of their abilities are those who are willing to wait for a reward.

Because students have not learned delayed gratification, they often succumb to the temptations of the moment, such as watching television or playing video games. The short-term focus of most school assignments does little to teach students the value of making incremental efforts for long-term gains. Projects are clearly superior in meeting this goal, but it is difficult for teachers to assign home projects if they are not confident of parental involvement and support.

Because much of learning at all levels—and especially university levels— is about short-term rewards, many of the applicants who are seeking scholarships will not truly have learned the importance of delaying gratification. Yet it is a lesson they need to learn, because the great contributions to the world are rarely made quickly. RJS's undergraduate mentor, Endel Tulving, once commented to him that "young people end up being surprised by the amount of time it takes for work to make a difference." Tulving was right, of course. And because of the time lapse, students need to learn that good things can come to those who actively seek them—and then wait.

11. *Courage.* Defying the crowd takes, above all, courage. Those who

do not have courage may be many things—they will not be creative. A scholarship winner can be many things. If he or she is not courageous, the other things may not matter.

Other Views of Creativity

Many recent works on creativity hypothesize, as does the investment theory, that multiple components must converge in order for creativity to occur.[21] Sternberg, for example, examined laypersons' and experts' conceptions of the creative person. People's conceptions contain a combination of cognitive and personality elements, such as "connects ideas," "sees similarities and differences," "has flexibility," "has aesthetic taste," "is unorthodox," "is motivated," "is inquisitive," and "questions societal norms."[22]

Amabile described creativity as the confluence of intrinsic motivation, domain-relevant knowledge and abilities, and creativity-relevant skills. The creativity-relevant skills include (1) a cognitive style that involves coping with complexities and breaking one's mental set during problem solving; (2) knowledge of heuristics for generating novel ideas, such as trying a counterintuitive approach; and (3) a work style characterized by concentrated effort, an ability to set aside problems, and high energy.[23]

Gruber and his colleagues proposed a developmental evolving-systems model for understanding creativity. A person's knowledge, purpose, and affect grow over time, amplify deviations that an individual encounters, and lead to creative products. Developmental changes in the knowledge system have been documented in cases such as Charles Darwin's thoughts on evolution. Purpose refers to a set of interrelated goals that also develop and guide an individual's behavior. Finally, the affect, or mood system notes the influence of joy or frustration on the projects undertaken.[24]

Csikszentmihalyi took a different "systems" approach and highlighted the interaction of the individual, domain, and field. An individual draws upon information in a domain and transforms or extends it via cognitive processes, personality traits, and motivation. The field, consisting of people who control or influence a domain (e.g., art critics and gallery owners), evaluates and selects new ideas. The domain, a culturally defined symbol system, preserves and transmits creative products to other individuals and to future generations.[25]

Gardner conducted case studies that suggest that the development of creative projects may stem from an anomaly within a system (e.g., tension between competing critics in a field) or moderate asynchronies between the individual, domain, and field (e.g., unusual individual talent for a domain).[26] In particular, Gardner analyzed the lives of seven individuals who made highly creative contributions in the twentieth century, each specializing in one of the multiple intelligences: Sigmund Freud (intrapersonal),

Albert Einstein (logical-mathematical), Pablo Picasso (spatial), Igor Stravinsky (musical), T. S. Eliot (linguistic), Martha Graham (bodily-kinesthetic), and Mohandas Gandhi (interpersonal). Charles Darwin would be an example of someone with extremely high naturalist intelligence.[27] Gardner points out, however, that most of these individuals actually had strengths in more than one intelligence, and that they had notable weaknesses as well in others (e.g., Freud's weaknesses may have been in spatial and musical intelligences).

Creativity, like intelligence, is essential for effective leadership. But leaders can be intelligent and even creative, but foolish. Why? What attribute do they lack? We believe the attribute they lack is wisdom.

Wisdom

When he was just starting out as an assistant professor, RJS had a student to whom he gave consummately bad advice concerning a career choice. She had two job offers. One was from an institution that was very prestigious but not a good fit to the kind of work she valued, which was teaching. The other institution was a bit less prestigious but was a much better fit to her values because it more valued teaching than did the more prestigious institution. RJS advised her to take the job in the more prestigious institution, telling her that if she did not accept the job there, she would always wonder what would have happened if she did. Bad advice: She went there and never fit in well. Eventually she left, and now she is at an institution that values the kind of work she does. In his late twenties, RJS gave advice that seemed right to him at the time, but that ultimately was foolish. He had not yet acquired the wisdom that a good mentor needs in order to do his or her job well.

Wisdom may be the most important attribute to seek in scholarship holders. People can be intelligent or creative but still not wise. People who use their cognitive skills for evil or even selfish purposes, or who ignore the well-being of others, may be smart—but foolish.

According to Sternberg's balance theory of wisdom, wisdom is defined as the application of intelligence and creativity as mediated by values toward the achievement of a common good through a balance among (a) intrapersonal, (b) interpersonal, and (c) extrapersonal interests, over the short and long terms in order to achieve a balance among (a) adaptation to existing environments, (b) shaping of existing environments, and (c) selection of new environments.[28]

Wisdom is not just about maximizing one's own or someone else's self-interest, but about balancing off various self-interests (intrapersonal) with the interests of others (interpersonal) and of other aspects of the context in which one lives (extrapersonal), such as one's city or country or environment or even God.

A person could be practically intelligent but use his or her practical intelligence toward bad or selfish ends. In wisdom, one certainly may seek good ends for oneself, but one also seeks common good outcomes for others. If one's motivations are to maximize certain people's interests and minimize other people's, wisdom is not involved. In wisdom, one seeks a common good, realizing that this common good may be better for some than for others.

Problems requiring wisdom always involve at least some element of all three interests—intrapersonal, interpersonal, and extrapersonal. For example, one might decide that it is wise to take a particular scholarship, a decision that seemingly involves only one person. But many people are typically affected by an individual's decision to go away to study—significant others, perhaps children, perhaps parents and friends. And the decision always has to be made in the context of the whole range of available options.

What kinds of considerations might be included under each of the three kinds of interests? Intrapersonal interests might include the desire to enhance one's popularity or prestige, to make more money, to learn more, to increase one's spiritual well-being, to increase one's power, and so forth. Interpersonal interests might be quite similar, except as they apply to other people rather than oneself. Extrapersonal interests might include contributing to the welfare of one's school, helping one's community, contributing to the well-being of one's country, serving God, and so forth. Different people balance these interests in different ways. At one extreme, a malevolent dictator might emphasize his or her own personal power and wealth; at the other extreme, a saint might emphasize only serving others and God.

Wisdom involves a balancing not only of the three kinds of interests, but also of three possible courses of action in response to this balancing: adaptation of oneself or others to existing environments; shaping of environments in order to render them more compatible with oneself or others; and selection of new environments.

There are five primary sources of differences directly affecting the balance processes. Consider, as an example, a teacher who has been instructed by a chairperson to spend almost all of his time teaching in a way that maximizes students' scores on standardized tests, but who believes that the chair is essentially forcing him to abandon truly educating his students.

1. *Goals.* People may differ in terms of the extent to which they seek a common good, and thus in the extent to which they aim for the essential goal of wisdom. They also may differ in terms of what they view as the common good. The teacher may believe that it is not in the students' best interest to engage in what he views as mindless drills for a test. The chair-

person, however, may have a different view. The teacher is thus left with the responsibility of deciding what is in the best interests of all concerned.

2. *Balancing of responses to environmental contexts*. People may differ in their balance of responses to environmental contexts. Responses always reflect the interaction of the individual making the judgment and the environment, and people can interact with contexts in many ways. The teacher may adapt to the environment and do exactly what the chair has told him to do, or shape the environment and do exactly what he believes he should do, or try to find some balance between adaptation and shaping that largely meets the chair's goals but also largely meets his own. Or the teacher may decide that the environment of the school is sufficiently aversive to his or her philosophy of teaching that he would prefer to teach at another school.

3. *Balancing of interests*. People may balance interests in different ways. The teacher must decide how to balance his own interests in good teaching with his interest in staying on good terms with the chairperson; with the student's interests in learning but also doing well on the standardized tests; with the parents' interests in having well-educated children; and so on.

4. *Balancing of short- and long-terms*. People may differ in their emphases. The teacher may believe that, in the long run, a proper education involves much more than preparing for statewide tests, but at the same time realize that, in the short run, the student's scores on the tests will affect their future as well as his future and possibly that of his chairperson and school.

5. *Values*. People have different values mediating their use of tacit knowledge in the balancing of interests and responses. Values may vary somewhat across space and time as well as among individuals within a given cultural context. The teacher's values may require him to diverge at least somewhat from the instructions of the chairperson. Another teacher's values might lead him to do what the chair says, regardless of how he personally feels.

Some people are intelligent and creative, but foolish. They lack wisdom. What are the characteristics of people who are smart, but foolish? We propose four characteristics.[29]

The first is *egocentrism*. Many smart people have been so highly rewarded in their lives that they lose sight of the interests of others. They start to act as though the whole world revolves around them. In doing so, they often set themselves up for downfalls, as happened to both Presidents Nixon and Clinton, the former in the case of Watergate, the latter in the case of "Monicagate."

The second characteristic is *a sense of omniscience*. Smart people typically know a lot. They get in trouble, however, when they start to think they know it all. They may have expertise in one area, but then start to fancy themselves experts in practically everything. At that point, they become susceptible to remarkable downfalls because they act as experts in areas where they are not knowledgeable and can make disastrous mistakes in doing so.

The third characteristic is *a sense of omnipotence*. Many smart people find themselves in positions of substantial power. Sometimes they lose sight of the limitations of their power and start to act as though they are omnipotent. Several U.S. presidents as well as leaders of other countries have had this problem, causing disasters on the basis of personal whims. Unfortunately, many corporate chieftains have also started to think of themselves as omnipotent, raiding the company's assets at will.

The fourth characteristic is *a sense of invulnerability*. Not only do the individuals think they can do anything; they also believe they can get away with it. They believe that either they are too smart to be found out, or, even if they are found out, they will escape any punishment for misdeeds. The result is the kind of disasters the United States has seen in the recent Enron, Worldcom, and Arthur Andersen debacles.

Other Views of Wisdom

There are other views of wisdom as well. Philosophical approaches have been reviewed by Daniel Robinson.[30] Robinson notes that the study of wisdom has a history that long antedates psychological study, with the Platonic dialogues offering the first intensive analysis of the concept of wisdom. He points out that in these dialogues there are three different senses of wisdom: wisdom as *sophia,* which is found in those who seek a contemplative life in search of truth; as *phronesis,* which is the kind of practical wisdom shown by statesmen and legislators; and as *episteme,* which is found in those who understand things from a scientific point of view.

Holliday and Chandler proposed five aspects to wisdom: exceptional understanding, judgment and communication skills, general competence, interpersonal skills, and social unobtrusiveness.[31] Sternberg reported a series of studies investigating people's conceptions of wisdom.[32] In one study, two hundred professors each of art, business, philosophy, and physics were asked to rate how characteristic was each of the behaviors obtained in a pre-study from the corresponding population with respect to the professors' ideal conception of an ideally wise, intelligent, or creative individual in their occupation. Laypersons were also asked to provide these ratings, but for a hypothetical ideal individual without regard to occupation. Six components of wisdom emerged: *reasoning ability, sagacity, learning from ideas and environment, judgment, expeditious use of information,* and *perspicacity.* These components can be compared with those that emerged from a similar scaling of people's implicit theories of intelligence, which were *practical problem-solving ability, verbal ability, intellectual balance and integration, goal orientation and attainment, contextual intelligence,* and *fluid thought.*

In both cases, cognitive abilities and their use are important. In wisdom, however, some kind of balance appears to emerge as important that does not emerge as important in intelligence in general.

Three kinds of factors—general person factors, expertise-specific factors, and facilitative experiential contexts—were proposed to facilitate wise judgments.[33] These factors are used in life planning, life management, and life review. Wisdom is in turn reflected in five components: (1) rich factual knowledge (general and specific knowledge about the conditions of life and its variations); (2) rich procedural knowledge (general and specific knowledge about strategies of judgment and advice concerning matters of life); (3) lifespan contextualism (knowledge about the contexts of life and their temporal [developmental] relationships); (4) relativism (knowledge about differences in values, goals, and priorities); and (5) uncertainty (knowledge about the relative indeterminacy and unpredictability of life and ways to manage). An expert answer should reflect more of these components, whereas a novice answer should reflect fewer of them. The data collected to date generally have been supportive of the model. These factors seem to reflect the pragmatic aspect of intelligence but to go beyond it, for example, in the inclusion of factors of relativism and uncertainty.

Some theorists have viewed wisdom in terms of postformal-operational thinking, thereby viewing wisdom as extending beyond the Piagetian stages of intelligence.[34] Wisdom thus might be a stage of thought beyond Piagetian formal operations. For example, some authors have argued that wise individuals are those who can think reflectively or dialectically, in the latter case with wise individuals' realizing that truth is not always absolute but rather evolves in an historical context of theses, antitheses, and syntheses.[35] Other theorists have viewed wisdom in terms of finding important problems to solve.[36]

Intelligence, creativity, and wisdom are important attributes of leadership. But for them to be useful as criteria in a scholarship or fellowship program, they need to be identifiable. How does one identify these attributes in individuals? Can they be measured? What we have found, in brief, is that the three constructs can be measured in a way so that one gets information that goes well beyond what one normally would acquire from standardized tests.

Research Base

Over the years, we have conducted research on intelligence, creativity, and wisdom that is designed to assess the usefulness of the WICS framework. So where does our consideration of the WICS framework leave us? What conclusions can we draw? Here are some of our main findings:

- Analytical, creative, and practical intelligence are three largely independent characteristics that can be measured distinctly. For example, someone can be analytically strong and creatively weak, or vice versa.
- Analytical, creative, and practical intelligence all predict school performance to some extent. In most programs, teaching emphasizes memory and analytical skills, so analytical tests will be the best predictors. But creative and practical skills matter too.
- Students who are taught in a way that is a better match to their patterns of memory, analytical, creative, and practical abilities outperform students who are taught in ways that are a poor match to their pattern of abilities.
- Practical tests predict job performance (e.g., as a manager, salesperson, professor, elementary school teacher) as well as, or better than, do analytical (IQ-based) measures; but they correlate minimally if at all with the analytical measures.
- Children from cultures other than developed Western ones need to be tested in ways that accommodate their special patterns of ability and developed skills. For example, rural Alaskan Eskimo children may not do so well on academic tests, but they do far better on tests of practical intelligence for their environment than non-Eskimos. In other words, people learn skills relevant to their environments, and we have to be careful about making generalizations about what skills are relevant in environments with which we are less familiar.
- Creativity is in large part a decision. Students can think more creatively when they are encouraged to do so and when given prompts to think creatively.
- Creativity involves elements of abilities, knowledge, styles of thinking, personality, motivation, and environment. Without an environment that supports creativity, many students with the abilities to be creative never show these abilities.
- We can teach even young children to think more wisely by encouraging them to understand other people's points of view and by helping them to use their intelligence and creativity for a common good.

We have argued in this essay that in selecting the leaders of tomorrow, three very important factors to consider are intelligence, creativity, and wisdom—synthesized so that they work together effectively. We are not claiming that these are the only attributes that matter. For example, motivation and energy are extremely important as well. We do believe, however, that motivation is partly (although not exclusively) situational, and that with the proper environment, anyone can be motivated to achieve.

We have concentrated in this essay on "tests" as measures of intelligence, creativity, and wisdom, but we believe that they represent only one of many ways of assessing these attributes. Interviews, questionnaires, letters of recommendation, and project work all can help in assessing these attributes.

We believe that scholarship programs should consider pooling their resources and developing a common model and common methods of assessment. By working separately, they fail to leverage their strengths and to share information regarding the best ways to make decisions. In essence, each program "reinvents the wheel." A consortium would be far more powerful than each program working on its own. WICS is one model that such a consortium might use.[37] Doubtless there are many others. The important thing is to work together toward a common good—toward devising the best ways to select students so as to maximize their positive future impact. We wish our scholarship students to show wisdom. We need to do the same.

Notes

1. Calvin Trillin, *Remembering Denny* (New York: Warner Books, 1994).

2. Amy Wallace, *The Prodigy: A Biography of William Sidis* (New York: E. P. Dutton, 1986).

3. Robert J. Sternberg, "The Theory of Successful Intelligence," *Review of General Psychology* 3 (1999): 292–316; Robert J. Sternberg, *WICS: A Theory of Wisdom, Intelligence, and Creativity, Synthesized* (in press); Robert J. Sternberg and Victor H. Vroom, "The Person vs. the Situation in Leadership," *Leadership Quarterly* 13 (2002): 301–23.

4. Robert J. Sternberg, *Successful Intelligence* (New York: Plume Press, 1997); Sternberg, "Theory of Successful Intelligence."

5. Arthur R. Jensen, *The g Factor: The Science of Mental Ability* (Westport, Conn.: Praeger/Greenwood, 1998); Charles Spearman, *The Abilities of Man* (London: Macmillan, 1927); Robert J. Sternberg and Elena L. Grigorenko, eds., *The General Factor of Intelligence: How General Is It?* (Mahwah, N.J.: Lawrence Erlbaum Associates, 2002).

6. Robert J. Sternberg and Wendy M. Williams, *Educational Psychology* (Boston: Allyn and Bacon, 2001).

7. Edwin Boring, "Intelligence as the Tests Test It," *New Republic*, 6 June 1923, 353–57.

8. See Robert J. Sternberg, ed., *Wisdom: Its Nature, Origins, and Development* (New York: Cambridge University Press, 1990); Robert J. Sternberg, ed., *Handbook of Perception and Cognition: Thinking and Problem Solving* (San Diego: Academic Press, 1994); and Robert J. Sternberg, ed., *Handbook of Intelligence* (New York: Cambridge University Press, 2000) for wide-ranging overviews of different ideas.

9. Spearman, *Abilities of Man*.

10. Louis L. Thurstone, *Primary Mental Abilities* (Chicago: University of Chicago Press, 1938).

11. Raymond B. Cattell, *Abilities: Their Structure, Growth and Action* (Boston: Houghton Mifflin, 1971).

12. James B. Carroll, *Human Cognitive Abilities: A Survey of Factor-Analytic Stud-*

ies (New York: Cambridge University Press, 1993); Jan-Eric Gustafsson, "Hierarchical Models of the Structure of Cognitive Abilities," in *Advances in the Psychology of Human Intelligence,* vol. 4, ed. Robert J. Sternberg (Hillsdale, N.J.: Erlbaum, 1988), 35–71; John L. Horn, "Theory of Fluid and Crystallized Intelligence," in *The Encyclopedia of Human Intelligence,* vol. 1, ed. Robert J. Sternberg (New York: Macmillan, 1994), 443–51; Philip E. Vernon, *The Structure of Human Abilities* (London: Methuen, 1971).

13. Howard Gardner, *Frames of Mind: The Theory of Multiple Intelligences* (New York: Basic Books, 1983); Howard Gardner, "Are There Additional Intelligences? The Case for Naturalist, Spiritual, and Existential Intelligences," in *Education, Information, and Transformation,* ed. J. Kane (Upper Saddle River, N.J.: Prentice-Hall, 1999), 111–31.

14. Robert J. Sternberg and Todd I. Lubart, *Defying the Crowd: Cultivating Creativity in a Culture of Conformity* (New York: Free Press, 1995); Robert J. Sternberg and Todd I. Lubart, "Investing in Creativity," *American Psychologist* 51, no. 7 (1996): 677–88.

15. Sternberg and Lubart, *Defying the Crowd.*

16. John Garcia and R. A. Koelling, "The Relation of Cue to Consequence in Avoidance Learning," *Psychonomic Science* 4 (1966): 123–24.

17. Robert J. Sternberg, *Beyond IQ: A Triarchic Theory of Human Intelligence* (New York: Cambridge University Press, 1985); Sternberg and Lubart, *Defying the Crowd;* Robert J. Sternberg and Linda O'Hara, "Creativity and Intelligence," in *Handbook of Creativity,* ed. Robert J. Sternberg (New York: Cambridge University Press, 1999), 251–72; Robert J. Sternberg and Wendy M. Williams, *How to Develop Student Creativity* (Alexandria, Va.: Association for Supervision and Curriculum Development, 1996).

18. Robert J. Sternberg and Elena L. Grigorenko, *Intelligence Applied,* 2nd ed. (New York: Oxford University Press, forthcoming).

19. John Dewey, *How We Think* (Boston: Heath, 1933).

20. Teresa M. Amabile, *Creativity in Context* (Boulder, Colo.: Westview Press, 1996).

21. Teresa M. Amabile, *The Social Psychology of Creativity* (New York: Springer, 1983); Teresa M. Amabile, *Creativity in Context;* Mihaly Csikszentmihalyi, "Society, Culture, and Person: A Systems View of Creativity," in *The Nature of Creativity,* ed. Robert J. Sternberg (New York: Cambridge University Press, 1988), 325–39; Mihaly Csikszentmihalyi, *Creativity: Flow and the Psychology of Discovery and Invention* (New York: HarperCollins, 1996); Howard Gardner, *Creating Minds* (New York: Basic Books, 1993); Howard E. Gruber, "The Evolving Systems Approach to Creative Work," in *Creative People at Work: Twelve Cognitive Case Studies,* ed. Doris B. Wallace and Howard E. Gruber (New York: Oxford University Press, 1989), 32–34; Howard E. Gruber, *Darwin on Man: A Psychological Study of Scientific Creativity,* 2nd ed. (Chicago: University of Chicago Press, 1981); Howard E. Gruber and S. N. Davis, "Inching Our Way up Mount Olympus: The Evolving-Systems Approach to Creative Thinking," in R. J. Sternberg, ed., *The Nature of Creativity,* 243–70; Howard E. Gruber and Doris B. Wallace, "The Case Study Method and Evolving Systems Approach for Understanding Unique Creative People at Work," in R. J. Sternberg, ed., *Handbook of Creativity,* 93–115; Michael D. Mumford and S. B. Gustafson, "Creativity Syndrome: Integration, Application, and Innovation," *Psychological Bulletin* 103 (1988): 27–43; David N. Perkins, *The Mind's Best Work* (Cambridge, Mass.: Harvard University Press, 1981); Dean K. Simonton, *Scientific Genius* (New York: Cambridge University Press, 1988); Dean K. Simonton, "Talent and Its Development: An Emergenic and Epigenetic Mode," *Psychological Review* 106 (1999): 435–57; Robert J. Sternberg, *Beyond IQ;* Robert J. Sternberg, James C. Kaufman, and J. E. Pretz, *The Creativity Conundrum: A Propulsion Model of Kinds of Creative Contri-*

butions (New York: Psychology Press, 2002); Sternberg and Lubart, *Defying the Crowd;* Robert W. Weisberg, *Creativity: Beyond the Myth of Genius* (New York: Freeman, 1993); Richard W. Woodman and Lyle F. Schoenfeldt, "Individual Differences in Creativity: An Interactionist Perspective," in *Handbook of Creativity,* ed. John. A. Glover, Royce R. Ronning, and Cecil R. Reynolds (New York: Plenum Press, 1989).

22. Robert J. Sternberg, "Implicit Theories of Intelligence, Creativity, and Wisdom," *Journal of Personality and Social Psychology* 4, no. 3 (1985): 607-27.

23. Amabile, *Creativity in Context* and *The Social Psychology of Creativity;* Mary A. Collins and Teresa M. Amabile, "Motivation and Creativity," in Sternberg, ed., *Handbook of Creativity,* 297-312.

24. Gruber, "The Evolving Systems Approach to Creative Work," and *Darwin on Man;* Gruber and Davis, "Inching Our Way up Mount Olympus."

25. Csikszentmihalyi, "Society, Culture, and Person."

26. Howard Gardner, *Creating Minds;* Emma Policastro and Howard Gardner, "From Case Studies to Robust Generalizations: An Approach to the Study of Creativity," in R. J. Sternberg, ed., *Handbook of Creativity,* 213-35.

27. Gardner, *Creating Minds* and *Frames of Mind.*

28. Robert J. Sternberg, "A Balance Theory of Wisdom," *Review of General Psychology* 2 (1998): 347-65; Robert J. Sternberg, "How Wise Is It to Teach for Wisdom? A Reply to Five Critiques," *Educational Psychologist* 36, no. 4 (2001): 269-72.

29. Robert J. Sternberg, "Smart People Are Not Stupid, but They Sure Can Be Foolish: The Imbalance Theory of Foolishness," in *Why Smart People Can Be So Stupid,* ed. Robert J. Sternberg (New Haven, Conn.: Yale University Press, 2002), 232-42.

30. Daniel N. Robinson, "Wisdom through the Ages," in R. J. Sternberg, ed., *Wisdom,* 132-34. See also Daniel N. Robinson, *Aristotle's Psychology* (New York: Columbia University Press, 1989), with regard to the Aristotelian approach in particular; and Gisela Labouvie-Vief, "Wisdom as Integrated Thought: Historical and Developmental Perspectives," in R. J. Sternberg, ed., *Wisdom,* 52-83, for a further review.

31. S. G. Holliday and Michael Chandler, *Wisdom: Explorations in Adult Competence* (Basel, Switzerland: Karger, 1986).

32. Robert J. Sternberg, "Implicit Theories of Intelligence, Creativity, and Wisdom"; Robert J. Sternberg, "Understanding Wisdom," in Sternberg, ed., *Wisdom,* 3-9.

33. Paul B. Baltes and Jacqui Smith, "Toward a Psychology of Wisdom and Its Ontogenesis," paper presented at the American Psychological Association, New York, August 1987; Paul B. Baltes and Ursula Staudinger, "The Search for Psychology of Wisdom," *Current Directions in Psychological Science* 2 (1993): 758-60; Jacqui Smith and Paul B. Baltes, "Wisdom-Related Knowledge: Age/Cohort Differences in Response to Life-Planning Problems," *Developmental Psychology* 26 (1990): 494-505.

34. Gisela Labouvie-Vief, "Beyond Formal Operations: Uses and Limits of Pure Logic in Life Span Development," *Human Development* 23 (1980): 141-61; Gisela Labouvie-Vief, "Dynamic Development and Mature Autonomy," *Human Development* 25 (1982): 161-91; Jean Piaget, *The Psychology of Intelligence* (Totowa, N.J.: Littlefield Adams, 1972).

35. Michael Basseches, *Dialectical Thinking and Adult Development* (Norwood, N.J.: Ablex, 1984); Patricia M. King, "Formal Reasoning in Adults: A Review and Critique," in *Adult Cognitive Development,* ed. Robert A. Mines and Karen S. Kitchener (New York: Praeger, 1986), 1-21; Karen S. Kitchener, "Cognition, Metacognition, and Epistemic Cognition: A Three-Level Model of Cognitive Processing," *Human Development* 4 (1983): 222-32; Karen S. Kitchener and H. G. Brenner, "Wisdom and Reflective Judgment: Knowing in the Face of Uncertainty," in R. J. Sternberg, ed., *Wisdom,* 212-

29; Karen S. Kitchener and Richard F. Kitchener, "The Development of Natural Rationality: Can Formal Operations Account for It?" in *Social Development in Youth: Structure and Content,* ed. J. Meacham and N. R. Santilli (Basel, Switzerland: Karger, 1981), 160–81; J. Pascual-Leone, "An Essay on Wisdom: Toward Organismic Processes That Make It Possible," in R. J. Sternberg, ed., *Wisdom,* 244–78; Klaus Riegel, "Dialectical Operations: The Final Period of Cognitive Development," *Human Development* 16 (1973): 346–70.

36. Patricia K. Arlin, "Wisdom: The Art of Problem Finding," in R. J. Sternberg, ed., *Wisdom,* 230–43.

37. The authors have engaged in many efforts to operationalize the WICS and related models. Several different student populations have been assessed, including a comparative study with Finnish, Spanish, and US students. The results are quite positive. More recently, RJS and a group of researchers have used these assessment tools to build a complement to the SAT examination. See Robert J. Sternberg, Elena Grigorenko, Michel Ferrari, and Pamela Clinkenbeard, "A Triarchic Analysis of an Aptitude-Treatment Interaction," *European Journal of Psychological Assessment* 15, no. 1 (1999): 1–11; Robert J. Sternberg, J. L. Castejón, M. D. Prieto, Jarko Hautamäki, and Elena Grigorenko, "Confirmatory Factor Analysis of the Sternberg Triarchic Abilities Test in Three International Samples: An Empirical Test of the Triarchic Theory of Intelligence," *European Journal of Psychological Assessment* 17, no. 1 (2001): 11–16; Robert J. Sternberg and the Rainbow Project Team, "The Rainbow Project: Augmenting the Validity of the SAT," paper presented to American Academy of Arts and Sciences, Boston, February 16, 2001; Robert J. Sternberg and the Rainbow Project Team, *The Rainbow Project: Enhancing the SAT through Assessments of Analytical, Creative, and Practical Skills* (New York: College Board, forthcoming); Todd I. Lubart and Robert J. Sternberg, "An Investment Approach to Creativity: Theory and Data," in *The Creative Cognition Approach,* ed. Steven M. Smith, Thomas B. Ward, and Ronald A. Finke (Cambridge, Mass.: MIT Press, 1995), 269–302; Sternberg and Lubart, "Investing in Creativity"; Sternberg and Lubart, *Defying the Crowd;* Robert J. Sternberg, "Nonentrenchment in the Assessment of Intellectual Giftedness," *Gifted Child Quarterly* 26 (1982): 63–67; Sheldon J. Tetewsky and Robert J. Sternberg, "Conceptual and Lexical Determinants of Nonentrenched Thinking," *Journal of Memory and Language* 25 (1986): 202–25; Robert J. Sternberg and Joyce Gastel, "Coping with Novelty in Human Intelligence: An Empirical Investigation," *Intelligence* 13 (1989): 187–97; Robert J. Sternberg and Joyce Gastel, "If Dancers Ate Their Shoes: Inductive Reasoning with Factual and Counterfactual Premises," *Memory and Cognition* 17 (1989): 1–10; Robert J. Sternberg, "Smart People Are Not Stupid"; Robert J. Sternberg, George B. Forsythe, Jennifer Hedlund, Joseph A. Horvath, Scott Snook, Wendy M. Williams, Richard K. Wagner, and Elena Grigorenko, *Practical Intelligence in Everyday Life* (New York: Cambridge University Press, 2000).

3 | Art and Science in Strengthening Scholarship Selection

Stanley J. Heginbotham

Most MAJOR NATIONAL FELLOWSHIP programs can make a *prima facie* case for having excellent selection processes because they choose quite extraordinary fellows. It is almost impossible not to be impressed by the caliber of each new crop of Rhodes, Marshall, Soros, Truman, Watson, or Woodrow Wilson scholars. A program that offers very prestigious and financially generous awards under reasonably liberal terms to a sizable part of the general American student body will undoubtedly attract extraordinary candidates. Such a program would have to have severely deficient selection processes in order *not* to select a truly impressive set of fellows. In such competitions, some individuals are such extraordinary standouts by a wide range of criteria that it is not a significant challenge to identify them.

The test of a selection process, however, is how well it discriminates among the next group of candidates. To what extent does it fill its quota of fellows with individuals who, with a reasonable degree of reliability, best reflect the program's authoritative selection criteria? I suggest in this chapter that many programs could do significantly better than they do because they not infrequently eliminate candidates who best reflect their selection criteria—and choose others that are impressive but less extraordinary than some who are rejected. This happens for several reasons:

- The program specifies inconsistent or ambiguous or contradictory selection criteria so that judges' disagreements often reflect different application of criteria rather than different evaluations of candidates against specific criteria.
- The program uses regional or institutional filters in ways that eliminate candidates in stronger areas or institutions who better meet the selection criteria than do candidates who are selected from weaker regions or institutions.
- The scoring system the program uses reflects differences in judges' standards as well as their assessments of different candidates, so that the true aggregate preferences of judges are not accurately tabulated.
- The scoring system is sufficiently imprecise that it fails to differentiate

accurately among judges' aggregate preferences of candidates at the margin of acceptance.

On the other hand, some who are unsympathetic to this line of argument make the following points:

- Inadequacies that a program might have are typically not obvious and are unlikely to be challenged by outsiders. Complaints can usually be addressed by minor fixes that don't seriously disrupt well-established processes. Major changes are likely to provoke concern and opposition from the many constituencies that claim some sense of ownership in well-established and prestigious programs. The maxim, "If it ain't broke, don't fix it," therefore, seems to many to provide useful guidance to program directors.
- The differences in quality among the excellent candidates who best meet a program's selection criteria and those that come close to that standard are relatively small. As long as they are all excellent, many argue, it doesn't really matter which among them receive awards and which do not.
- The art and science of prediction of future performance is sufficiently inexact that, within a group of excellent candidates, success is likely to be essentially random. So there is no point, some argue, in trying to make carefully refined choices at the margin.

The counterarguments to this view are, I believe, as follows:

- Major fellowship programs have a responsibility to be as fair as is reasonably possible. Since so much is at stake for the excellent candidates at the margin, the program should apply its selection criteria as rigorously as possible so that candidates who do, on serious consideration, seem best to meet those criteria are rewarded in favor of those who seem somewhat less excellent with respect to those criteria.
- Though prediction of future performance is an uncertain art, it still has considerable validity; so in the aggregate, rigorous care in selection at the margin will produce better results than a more casual approach.
- Selection design features and practices that seem reasonable but do not promote valid and reliable results are cumulative in their impact. Over time, a program that accommodates pressures for less-than-rigorous practices is likely to suffer a significant decline in the quality of its fellows relative to the quality of the pool from which it makes its selections.

Strengthening selection design and process for merit-based national fellowship competitions involves a combination of art and science. In many respects, the art is more important—and certainly more interesting—than the science; but it is best developed when informed by insights that come out of the social sciences, and especially the fields of sampling theory and psychological measurement. Thus, this chapter begins with some relatively simple notions on using statistical measures to enhance the reliability of selection before addressing several salient issues in the art of competition design.

In the section on scientific rigor, I argue that reasonably simple techniques of assessing levels of agreement among judges can be used to improve the reliability of competition results. The groups of judges that a competition typically engages to select fellowship winners are, in effect, a sample of some larger population of "experts" who have specialized knowledge or skills relevant to that specific fellowship's selection criteria. Calculating inter-judge agreement scores makes it possible to experiment with ways of improving levels of agreement—and thus the reliability of selection results— by phasing out judges whose judgments seem radically out of step with their peers, by refining and rationalizing the selection criteria and indicators of excellence that judges assess, and by assuring that the scores of judges are precisely and accurately tabulated. I argue that many programs introduce significant and quite unnecessary errors into the selection process through the use of inadequate procedures and measurement techniques.

In the section on the art of competition design, the chapter first argues that it is important for programs to forge and maintain strong "selection criteria chains." It seems self-evident that the program's selection criteria as stated to candidates should clearly and accurately reflect the funder's mandates; that the evidence about candidates that is collected via applications and interviews should provide valid measures of relative merit of candidates as specified by the selection criteria; and that judges should be clearly instructed to assess evidence about candidates against the same selection criteria as specified for candidates. In fact, however, the "chain" linking a funder's mandate to the criteria used by judges is often surprisingly ambiguous, inconsistent, and contradictory. As a result, judges often end up disagreeing with each other on what they are looking for, rather than on the relative merits of candidates with respect to well-defined selection criteria.

The second argument with respect to the art of competition design addresses the closely related problems of managing extremely large numbers of candidates and of meeting any goals the competition may have for the distributive characteristics—whether geographic or institutional or ethnic or gender or field of study or other—of its winners.

Issues of Scientific Rigor: The Importance of Reliability

Which of the more scientific considerations appropriately shape answers to the questions posed by the art of selection?

Social science methodologists worry about the validity and the reliability of their research. *Validity* addresses the question: Is what I am measuring an accurate reflection of what I am interested in? This is a central but very elusive question. Each program wants to identify and reward distinctive qualities and characteristics among candidates for its awards. Finding valid measures for competitions is very much an art, so I will defer validity issues to later in this chapter.

Reliability refers to the extent to which the results of research—or a selection process—are replicable or, at the other extreme, random. It is useful to think of the design and conduct of a competition as a kind of social science research project in which one seeks to identify the top X number of candidates as measured against a set of indicators reflecting selection criteria. If it were possible to conduct a competition multiple times, using different judges selected from a common pool of judges but the same candidates, a measure of reliability is the extent to which the results—that is, the identities of the winners of the competition—would be the same. Since it is manifestly impracticable to reproduce competitions, we all hope—and usually assume—that our processes are reasonably reliable and free of arbitrary or random results.

There are measures, however, that provide strong indicators of the extent to which the results of a competition are reliable. The first section of this chapter reviews a measure of inter-judge agreement as an approach to assessing the reliability of selection processes. Reliability can be enhanced by increasing the number of judges used in a competition and/or by taking steps that increase their agreement with each other. The second section examines the relative importance of these two factors. Finally, the third section discusses three techniques that can enhance selection reliability.

Inter-judge Agreement (or Correlation) as an Indicator of Reliability

Though it is impracticable to conduct multiple replications of competitions, it is possible to conduct a fairly basic test that provides strong indications of the reliability of a competition's results. It is helpful to use a survey research analogy. Survey research typically relies on drawing samples of a population to draw inferences about the population as a whole.

One can think of one's panel as a sample of some broader population of knowledgeable experts. When we read the results of a "scientific" survey that shows that 41 percent of a random sample of 640 members of a population report that they believe that candidate X is doing a good job, and we are told that the results are reliable within 4 percent, with 95 percent certainty, the pollsters have good reason to believe that, if the survey were repeated one hundred times using the same questions with one hundred different samples of respondents, in ninety-five or more of the repetitions, between 37 and 45 percent of respondents would report that candidate X is doing a good job.

How do they acquire "good reason" to believe this? By experience with populations that indicate how much variability there is within the population on questions being asked in the survey. If the question were "Is the world flat?" a random sample of one member of the U.S. population with college degrees would, with a very high degree of probability, provide an accurate reflection of the full population's beliefs. The greater the consensus within a population on the issue at hand, the smaller the sample one needs to provide accurate results with a high degree of probability. And the more precise and unambiguous the questions, the smaller the sample one needs.

In choosing fellowship winners, the test—though necessarily just as hypothetical—is similar: if a set of interviews of the same candidates, using different sets of seven panelists, were repeated one hundred times, how consistent would the selection results be? If the task were to select ten fellows, how many times out of one hundred would all ten be the same? How many times would nine be the same? How many times would eight be the same, and so forth? And how would the reliability of the results change if one used a sample of five panelists, or ten panelists, or fifteen panelists?

A simple test provides a useful indicator of the reliability of the results of a panel process. If twenty candidates are interviewed by seven panelists, one can ask each panelist to rank the twenty. Then one can calculate the degree of agreement among each pair of those seven panelists. If they all agree perfectly in their rankings, one could infer an extremely high probability that, in multiple repetitions of the panel process, the level of agreement across judges would be very high. On the other hand, if there were no agreement among judges, one could infer that the results were very close to random, and that multiple repetitions of the panel process using different panelists would produce quite different—indeed, almost random—results. The standard measure, the Spearman rank-difference coefficient of correlation, used to be rather burdensome to compute, but with computer spreadsheet functions, it is now quite simple.[1] Spearman rank-difference scores for two judges can range from 1.00—perfect agreement in rankings—to –1.00, where one judge gives the lowest rank to the candidate ranked highest by the other judge, second-lowest to the candidate ranked second-highest by the other judge, and so on. A rank-difference score of 0 reflects no relationship between the rankings of the two judges.

Inter-judge Correlations and Numbers of Judges: Two Ways of Improving Reliability

In general, the higher the inter-judge correlations, the smaller the number of judges one needs to achieve a given level of reliability. But how much difference do correlations and numbers of judges make? A useful approach is to think in terms of the number of errors a panel makes. We can assume that a "correct" panel result is one that would mirror the preferences of the full universe of individuals from which a panel would be drawn. One can construct a hypothetical set of 20 candidates, numbered 1 through 20, reflecting the ordered preferences of the universe from which the panelists would be drawn. Assuming that we want to assign 10 awards among the 20 candidates, a panel would have zero errors if its rank ordering of the top ten finalists included candidates 1 through 10, in whatever order. If a panel included candidate 11 but not 10, we would say it had one error. If it included candidate 12 but not 10, we would say it has two errors (it should have included candidates 10 or 11 in preference to 12).

Using random number techniques, one can create large sets of hypothetical panelists, each with her/his rankings of the candidates. One can then create hypothetical panels of any size. More specifically, one can create panels whose members agree with each other, on the average, at certain levels.

For purposes of illustration, I have constructed 15 hypothetical types of panels. They vary in the size of the panel and in the degree to which its members agree. Three panels have 7 members, three have 6, three have 5, three have 4, and three have 3. Among the three panels of a given size, the first has a high mean rank order correlation (approximately .667) among its members' rankings of the 20 candidates, the second has a moderate rank order correlation (approximately .500), and the third has a relatively low rank order correlation (approximately .333).

I generated 25 panels of each type, a total of 375 different panels. I numbered the candidates in order of their presumed ranking by the entire population and varied the rankings of individual panelists around that norm. I then averaged the rankings of the members of each panel and compared the results with the presumed rankings of the full population from which the samples of panelists were drawn. For example, Table 3.1 shows a reasonably typical result among the 25 panels of 5 members whose rank orders correlate at around the .333 level (candidates are listed in order of the average rankings of the five judges).

This panel ranked eight of the candidates 1 through 10 in the top 10, but moved 11 and 16 into that group as well, excluding candidates 6 and 10. So, it got 8 of 10 awards right and made the following errors:

gave award to 11 rather than 10	1 error
gave award to 16 rather than 6, 10, 12, 13, 14 or 15	6 errors
Total	7 errors

Following a parallel process for each of the 375 panels, I then calculated the average number of errors for panels composed of from three up to seven

Table 3.1

Hypothetical Rankings of Five Judges

Candidate	Judge A's Rankings	Judge B's Rankings	Judge C's Rankings	Judge D's Rankings	Judge E's Rankings	Avg Rank
1	1	5	6	1	3	3.2
2	6	7	3	3	2	4.2
3	9	1	9	5	5	5.8
5	12	2	8	9	4	7
9	7	9	2	2	17	7.4
8	8	12	13	4	1	7.6
4	13	8	5	8	6	8
16	3	4	1	16	19	8.6
11	2	6	11	11	14	8.8
7	15	3	10	12	7	9.4
12	10	15	4	7	16	10.4
10	5	11	18	6	13	10.6
6	17	10	7	10	9	10.6
14	4	14	14	14	12	11.6
20	11	20	19	13	8	14.2
13	18	17	12	15	11	14.6
15	14	16	15	18	15	15.6
18	16	13	16	19	20	16.8
19	20	18	20	17	10	17
17	19	19	17	20	18	18.6

members with inter-panelist correlations averaging .333 (low), .500 (moderate), and .667 (high).

The first of the following two charts shows how the average number of errors varied across panel size and inter-panelist correlation levels (chart 3.1). The second chart shows the probability that panels of different size and agreement would get at least 9 out of 10 awards correct (chart 3.2). What is striking in these graphs is the power of correlation levels in determining the reliability of a panel's results. Consider a program that used five panelists who, in a given year, had an average inter-panelist correlation of .333. In all probability, that panel would have made more than five errors in its judgments and had only about a 55 percent chance of reliably making at least 9 out of 10 awards correctly.

Chart 3.1

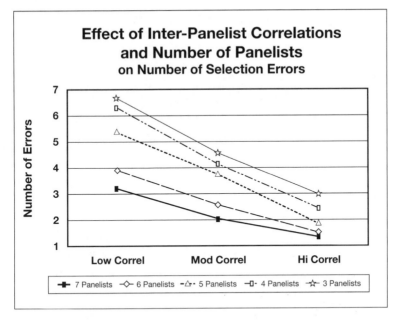

Chart 3.2

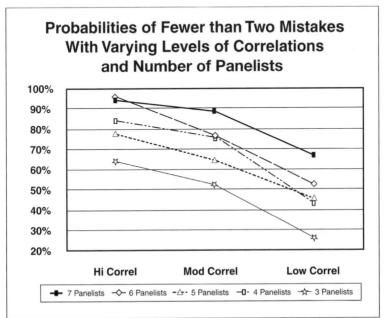

A manager who wanted to improve the reliability of his panel process could do so either by improving the level of agreement of his panelists, by increasing the size of the panel, or by a combination of both. Efforts that raised the inter-panelist correlation to about .667 without increasing the size of panels would reduce the average number of errors to below 2 and would increase the probability of getting at least 9 of the 10 awards right to over 80 percent. Increasing the panel size from five to seven, on the other hand, would only reduce the average number of errors to about three and would increase the probabilities of getting at least 9 of 10 awards right to about 67 percent. Even an improvement in average inter-judge correlations to .500 would have greater positive impact on the reliability of the panel's decisions than would adding two panel members.

Strategies for Strengthening Inter-judge Agreement

These facts suggest the value of some simple statistical analysis of the results of a competition's panel process. But this is true only if there are steps that one can practically take to improve inter-panelist agreement. Let me specify three steps that can be taken:

1. *Use correlation analysis in retention and release of panelists.* The easiest step is to look at the correlations of each individual panelist with her/his co-panelists. One can appropriately give serious consideration to the elimination in future years of a panelist who has a very low level of agreement on ranking of candidates with other panelists. In the 2002 Soros panels, for example, we reviewed the inter-panelist correlations for 28 panelists, which averaged .482. The average was substantially lowered by seven panelists with the lowest correlations, which averaged .222. A review of their performance as interviewers and in panel discussions confirmed the evidence that none of them seemed to have a firm grasp of the program and commitment to its selection criteria. All, consequently, are strong candidates for not being invited to return as panelists.

Of course, it is possible that a panelist with a low correlation may see things of importance about candidates that other panelists miss; or the same panelist may be a particularly stimulating interviewer. Such considerations can override correlation scores, but in my experience, this happens relatively rarely.

2. *Generate and maintain a solid, consistent, and unambiguous selection criteria "chain."* A central key to achieving good levels of agreement among judges is well-defined, carefully elaborated, and consistently articulated selection criteria that can effectively be assessed by competition judges. I think of this as a chain of interconnected links that ties the funder's goals to selection criteria, to language in program documents, to materials and presentations solicited from candidates, to instructions, to interactions among judges in order to achieve final judgments. Just as survey re-

search specialists devote a great deal of attention to finding the most reliable questions and sets of questions for tapping whatever they want to measure, competition professionals should devote a great deal of attention to designing their application materials, the data they elicit from candidates and references, the guidance they provide to judges, and the group process those judges use. I will discuss aspects of the art of specifying selection criteria in greater detail in the section on the art of selection, but for the purposes of this discussion, five points will suffice.

First, it is crucial to generate clear, precise, unambiguous, and consistent selection criteria. Judges need a clear focus for their consideration of the relative merit of the candidates. Though there are inevitably numerous aspects to those criteria, it is remarkably helpful when they are presented as components of a core selection criterion. The examples below suggest what I have in mind:

Example 1: We look for the individuals who have the greatest promise as scholars and teachers in humanistic disciplines.

Example 2: We seek to fund projects that will have the greatest impact on reducing excessive incarceration in the United States.

Example 3: We seek individuals who have shown extraordinary creativity and the greatest capacity to turn that creativity into sustained achievement.

Example 4: We seek students who have the greatest leadership potential and are committed to careers in public service. We seek to identify the individuals who are not only most talented but also most likely to translate this talent into actions that have a meaningful impact on the world.

In each of these cases, judges have a clear focus on the core criterion they should use in assessing the relative competitiveness of candidates for the program. In each case there are ambiguities—for instance, in example 1 do I value scholars more than teachers, or scholar-teachers more than either?—but they are relatively narrow and subject to further interpretation from the program managers.

Second, it is important to specify components—or indicators—of the core criterion that the program believes to be the most useful factors to be considered. It is then usually valuable to suggest which components the program believes to be of particular importance in considering candidates' merit with respect to its core selection criterion. Thus, the program may have concluded that a candidate's grades, extracurricular activities, presentation of self, writing ability, speaking ability, and social consciousness are the most significant indicators of a candidate's potential as a public sector leader (example 4).

A tempting, but I believe misdirected, approach is to specify the components that one believes to be important without articulating and relating them to the overarching goal. To say that a program's selection criteria are excellent grades, leadership in extracurricular activities, a commitment to public policy values, and moral character is to invite individual panelists to emphasize disproportionately the component or components that are most congenial to their thinking. When that happens, legitimate disagreements among panelists about the relative merits of candidates with respect to the overarching program goals can easily be dwarfed by disagreements that stem from differences in emphases on specific components. This is a formula for high levels of disagreement among panelists and results that are of unnecessarily low reliability.

Another misguided approach, I would argue, is to specify for the panelists the relative importance of the component considerations. Some programs might, for example, direct panelists to allocate 30 points to grades, 25 points to GRE scores, 20 points to leadership, 15 points to commitment to public policy values, and 10 points to moral character. This is particularly attractive to programs that feel they need to demonstrate their objectivity and lack of bias. The results may increase reliability, but at the expense of validity. In other words, little is achieved if, in increasing agreement across judges, you get them to agree on criteria that do not reflect the interests and goals of the program. The point is that grades, GRE scores, leadership, public policy values, and moral character are combined in distinctive mixes in different candidates. One seeks panelists who have the intuitive and experiential bases for effectively assessing how powerful the mix is in each individual for propelling the individual toward the goals of the program. To pre-assign weights is to deny them the opportunity to do so.

Third, scholarship managers must rigorously adhere to presenting the selection criteria in all program literature. Once a clear and concise statement of the core selection criterion and its components has been arrived at, it is important that that language be used consistently throughout the program's literature and in the training of panelists. It is tempting, in writing and updating brochures, guidance for judges, instructions for references, and application materials to try to help candidates and judges by providing more accurate and evocative language about what the program is really looking for. Often this is done to correct misperceptions that applicants and panelists seem to have developed from the existing language. We effectively say: "Let me explain what we are looking for in a different way" but typically leave the original way in the document as well. Every time the goals of the program or the criteria for selection are stated anew, however, an individual panelist is, in effect, invited to choose whichever version seems most congenial to him or her. The result is that different panelists apply different criteria, and disagreements in their rank orderings are magnified, not based on differing assessments of candidates, but rather based on the application of different criteria to the candidates.

Fourth, the application submissions should be tailored to the selection criteria. It is important to assess the materials in the application to assure that the information they generate corresponds to the components of the selection criteria. In order to assess a candidate against a set of components that are identified as relevant to the overall selection criterion, panelists need evidence that addresses, with as much validity as possible, each of the components. Programs have especially important choices in how they design essays, what information they solicit from references, and what guidance they provide panelists in how to organize and focus candidate interviews. I am often surprised by the lack of tight correspondence between selection criteria and data made available to judges.

Finally, judges must be trained. No matter how well-drawn a program's selection criteria are, there are bound to be interpretive ambiguities. Do we take a candidate's age into account? Would you prefer someone who will surely be very good, or someone who might be great but is a real risk? If a student's work is highly regarded within her discipline, but I think the discipline has become quite marginalized, do I apply the discipline's standards or my own? These kinds of issues are raised in panel discussions, and to the extent that the program managers have, or can evolve, clear answers to such questions, it is important that they be conveyed in an orderly way to panelists. Guidance documents usefully provide a set of answers to such frequently asked questions, but a discussion with panelists in advance of interviews almost invariably brings up new questions or reveals issues on which some panelists are reluctant to apply the guidance provided by the program.

3. *Solicit and record accurately and precisely the relative preferences of the screeners and panelists.* Though this recommendation seems self-evident, in my experience it is the most commonly violated. Many competition managers are inclined to believe that any one approach to scoring judges' preferences is likely to be as satisfactory—or valid—as another, and that in any case there is no real way of knowing which is better. A simple illustration should be adequate to disabuse readers of this view if they adhere to it. Consider two hypothetical procedures by which five judges might be asked to select the four best proposals from ten applicants (see Table 3.2).

In the first process, the program officer asks each judge to read all ten proposals and rank them, one to ten, in the order of their merit with respect to the program's selection criteria. When the results are submitted, the program officer announces that there is unanimity in the rankings: everyone agrees that among the seriously competitive proposals, the order of merit is: 1. Frank; 2. Betty; 3. Ian; 4. David; 5. Joan; and 6. Carol. So awards will be offered to Frank, Betty, Ian, and David. Joan and Carol will be the first and

Table 3.2
Comparative Judgments

Candidates

Judges	Frank	Betty	Ian	David	Joan	Carol	George	Allen	Eric	Harry
Adams	1		2	2			2	3		3
Barnes	1		1	2			2		2	3
Cooper		1		1	1	1	2		2	
Dunn	1	1			1	1		2	2	
Evans		1	1		1	1		2		2
Score	3	3	4	5	3	3	6	7	6	8

second alternates in the unlikely event that any of the first four declines an award. The remaining four candidates are eliminated.

In the second process—*in which the same judges read the same applications*—the program officer, reluctant to ask the judges to read all of the lengthy proposals, assigns six to each reader. Thus, every proposal is read by three judges, which seems an adequate basis for assessing them. Each judge is asked to grade each application according to whether it should *definitely be* funded (score a "1"), it should *definitely not be* funded (score a "3"), or the judge is *uncertain* (score a "2"). When the results are received, the program officer announces that the results are unambiguous. Four applicants received all "1"s (a total of 4 points) and should therefore receive awards. A fifth applicant received two "1"s and one "2" (5 points) and would be the first alternate, and a sixth received one "1" and two "2"s (6 points) and would be the second alternate. The results and the scores (adding the ratings of three readers) were as follows: Four awardees (3 points each): Joan, Carol, Frank, and Betty; alternates: Ian (4 points); David (5 points). Again, the remaining four candidates were eliminated.

What would, in the real world, almost certainly never be recognized, is that the two processes yield results that agree on only two of the applicants who should receive awards (Frank and Betty). Were the second procedure actually used, in all probability the errors it generated—that Carol and Joan, though very good, were not fairly judged to be among the four best candidates, and that Ian and David, though among the four best, would unfairly be denied awards—would never come to light.

Both processes *seemed* fair and reasonable, but in fact, in the second case, the expedient of using a three-point rating system and of having each application read by a subset of panelists, produced results that did not accurately reflect the true preferences of panelists.

The results, arrayed in this way and informed by the more fully elaborated results of the first process, show many unexpected outcomes. First, the results of the second process, though *consistent* with the results of the first process, provide far less detailed discrimination. Cooper, Dunn, and Evans, though they followed the instructions they received, had no impact on the judging because none of them registered an assessment of the relative merits of the only six candidates who, it turned out, were truly competitive. Second, the judges brought different *standards* to their readings. Though all five agreed about the relative merits of the applicants, Adams was the toughest grader among them, and Cooper, Dunn, and Evans were the most forgiving. Barnes was in between these extremes. The candidates—especially Joan and Carol, whose applications were assigned to the more generous judges (Cooper, Dunn, and Evans)—were therefore unfairly advantaged relative to those—especially Ian and David—whose applications were assigned to more demanding judges (Adams and Barnes).

Finally, a three-point rating system provides highly *ambiguous* results. Though the first process makes it clear that Cooper ranks David higher than Joan and Carol and that Evans ranks Ian higher than Joan and Carol, the second process completely hides these facts—to the clear disadvantage, as it turns out, of Ian and David.

But surely, one might argue, in the real world the panelists would discuss the candidates and correct these errors. A little reflection, however, reveals that this is not necessarily—or even likely—to be the case. Since the panelists, in fact, all agree as to the actual rank ordering of the candidates, any attempt by one panelist to persuade another panelist to change a rating can only result in a change that is divergent from, rather than more in consonance with, the views of the persuader. (It is also possible that a change in ratings will only result in a change in an individual judge's standards, which may or may not improve the results.) If Barnes persuades Cooper that David should really only be rated a 2, the result would be to shift Cooper's rating of David below his rating of Joan and Carol, quite the opposite of what Barnes would have intended if he had read those two applications.

The other point to be noted is that though it would be beneficial for the panelists to compare their relative rankings of sets of candidates ("Do you think David is better or worse than Joan?"), this becomes highly problematic when only subsets of panelists read each application. In the above example, no pair of candidates can be compared by all five, or even four, panelists. Nine percent of the possible pairs of candidates could be compared by three panelists and an additional 44 percent of all possible pairs could be compared by two panelists. The practical result is that each candidate effectively has to be discussed and rated separately, even though the critical issue is that candidate's merit relative to each other candidate.

But, one must ask, is this example at all realistic? In the real world, do competitions actually follow such rules? And do judges have such divergent standards? Unfortunately, the answer to both questions is yes. For many years the Fulbright faculty competitions administered by the Council on the International Exchange of Scholars used a comparable three-category rating system. Quite divergent standards brought to bear by panelists, combined with serious ambiguity in the ratings, led to numerous examples of panelist and staff confusion and misperception with respect to the true preferences of panels.

The Social Science Research Council (SSRC), in the first year of its integrated—that is, a single competition for all foreign areas—international dissertation fellowship program, used a similar system: in order eventually to select 53 fellows, it allocated applications from 134 finalists to be read by 16 panelists so that each of them would have to read only 35 applications. Panelists used a five-point rating system (1 reflected the best applications). When the preliminary scores of the panelists were tabulated, they showed that the mean ratings of the judges ranged from a high of 1.91 to a low of 3.32. (If one converts this to conventional grading scales, that would be the difference between a mean of B/B+ and a mean of C-.) Internal analysis showed that only 12 percent of this variation could be explained by differences in the qualities of the samples the panelists assessed. Thus, 88 percent of the difference was attributable to differences in the standards of the panelists.

In an analysis I did for SSRC, I corrected for the combined effects of differences in standards and the advantages of having one's applications read by disproportionately generous or tough graders.[2] I then divided the candidates into three groups, the top 39, who would be presumptive awardees; the next 14, who might plausibly win awards; and the remaining 81, who were unlikely to win awards. Of the top 39, the scoring system that SSRC had used relegated three to the middle category and two to the presumptive rejection category. Of the 14 who were appropriately in the middle category, three had been scored by SSRC as presumptive awardees and three as presumptive rejects. And of the 81 who were appropriately in the presumptive reject category, the SSRC system scored three in the middle category and two in the presumptive award category. There may have been other errors resulting from the ambiguity of the scoring system used by the SSRC, but there was no way to assess this source of possible error from the data.

Did the discussion materially correct for these sixteen errors in preliminary categorization of the finalists? There is no way of knowing for certain because there is no way of determining the extent to which changes in—or affirmation of—the preliminary categorizations resulted from changes in panelists' perceptions or corrections of the misrepresentation of their preliminary judgments. One would expect, nevertheless, that there would be significant realignment of the rankings of candidates consistent with the more rigorous scoring of preliminary ratings. It is telling, however, that fifteen of the eighteen erroneous preliminary categorizations were simply reaffirmed in the voting that followed the day-long discussions. Of the remaining three, all of the changes were in directions consistent with the more accurate preliminary assessments.

What lessons should we draw from this illustration? *First, in competitions, it is more reliable to ask judges to rank candidates relative to each other than to rate them relative to abstract categories.* This seems counterintuitive, in part because rating systems in the form of grades are such a ubiquitous feature of academic life. A rating system just seems to be the appropriate mechanism for measuring the relative merit of applicants in a competition. This is true even though we recognize the severe inadequacies of grades as valid and reliable measures of relative merit. First, ratings and grades reflect the toughness or leniency of a judge's standards as well as the judge's assessments of a student or candidate. Rankings reflect only a judge's sense of the relative merits of a given set of students or candidates. Second, ratings and grades are necessarily imprecise and ambiguous. Judges can only reliably assign applications among about seven abstract categories.[3] When ranking—comparing one application to another—however, they can make far more refined distinctions. This is especially important in highly competitive situations, where when judges give ratings, some will give all candidates who are plausible awardees the same high rating. Rankings distinguish relative quality of candidates at the margin.

And finally, ratings and grades are highly subject to inexorable pressures toward inflation. Judges who want to see a candidate rewarded can simply lower their standards, thereby raising the grade and improving the candidate's prospects. Inflation is not possible with rankings. There is only one top-ranked candidate and only one 5th-ranked candidates. Some judges try to inflate rankings by providing ties ("She's 5th, but I'll list her as tied for 1st"), but proper scoring systems correct for this (all five are scored as the arithmetic means of the 5, or as rankings of 2.5).

The point is that we need rating systems when we want to make even very approximate assessments of relative merit of performance of individuals who are not exposed to the same requirements assessed by the same judges. Grades provide us a metric for comparing an economics major at a California junior college with a history major at an Ivy League school. Knowledgeable observers use their contextual sophistication to discount the value of specific grades or GPAs. ("X is a much better school than Y, so a 3.5 GPA from X is more impressive than one from Y." "An 'A' in organic chemistry reflects much greater achievement than does one in athletic administration." "An 'A' from Professor Z is far more impressive than one from anyone else in her department.") This is at best, however, an approximate process and not something that is easily replicated in the context of judges' ratings in a competition.

The great strength of merit-based competitions, though, is that applicants are exposed to the same requirements, and they can be assessed by the same judges. This makes it feasible—and highly desirable—for those judges simply to rank candidates relative to each other, thereby avoiding the significant measurement errors inherent in rating—or grading—systems.

Second, when final rankings are to be made by one or more panels of judges, they should all *have read* all *of the applications—or interviewed* all *of the candidates—they are to discuss.* The essence of the discussion process is clear: First, identify candidates that all judges rank in the award range (1 through 6 if there are six awards available); second, identify candidates that all judges agree are not in the award range (7 through 20 if there are six awards available); and third, discuss the comparative views of the remaining candidates and rerank them.

A panel cannot conduct a rigorous comparative discussion and analysis of the candidates at the margin (those neither definitely in nor definitely out) unless all of the panelists have read all of those applications and can compare each pair. If a program is to award 30 to 40 fellowships, it faces a truly severe challenge if it takes this lesson seriously. This is the final expression of what I refer to as the Big Number Problem. I will discuss a range of solutions to this problem in the final section of this chapter.

A third lesson from merit competitions is, when screening large numbers of candidates, one should impose on the smallest possible number of judges to read the largest possible number of applicants. If you want each of 300 applications to be read by four judges, it is better to have each of twelve judges read 100 applications than each of twenty-four judges read 50 applications. The larger the pool each judge reads, the more likely it is to be representative of the whole pool and the more well-articulated the rankings across readers is likely to be.

A fourth lesson is, though it may seem implausible to ask a judge to rank order a hundred or more applications, several expedients provide much more reliable results than does a rating system. The Soros screening process, for example, uses benchmarks. We take several applications from the previous year for candidates that were judged to be at the margin between those who were invited for interviews and those who were not. We assign them scores of 5.0. We do the same thing for applications at the margin between finalists who did and did not receive awards and assign them scores of 6.0. We find that it is possible for screening judges to read several hundred applications and effectively rank order them by comparing them to the two sets of benchmarks. Since only about 8 percent of applicants receive interviews, it turns out to be unnecessary to rank order any applications in the bottom half. We periodically check our scores for consistency and then convert the scores to rank orders to compensate for the fact that one or the other of us may have become unduly generous or parsimonious over the several weeks of reading.

Applications that are seriously competitive are then read by specialist readers, who follow a similar scoring strategy. For each of the two of us who read all of the competitive applications, one used 13 ranking categories in discriminating among the candidates he ranked in the top 200, and the other used 18 categories. This provided a far more nuanced set of judgments than any rating system might have.

A fifth lesson is that assigning applications to be screened only by specialists in their fields is typically a mistake. If 300 applications fall neatly into six fields of study with 50 applications each, and one assigns four specialist readers to each field, one can rank order each field, but one has no way of interpolating the rankings across fields. Ratings provide the commonly accepted solution, but the results are likely to reflect different standards across fields as much or more than the relative merit of applicants across fields. In selecting judges, the key criterion needs to be breadth of perspective, so that individual judges can make reasonably authoritative judgments across fields, not just within them.

A final lesson is that mistakes made in designating awardees as a result of flawed scoring procedures are typically hidden. Evidence of error, moreover, is often unrecoverable. Judges who are asked to rate candidates, for example, do not provide precise rankings of applicants, so ambiguities cannot be resolved in retrospect. There is little incentive to seriously question results because judges, program officers, and funders typically feel assured that they have done a fine job in selection since the winners in their competition seem so great. Where resources are scarce, there is likely to be a surplus of highly qualified candidates; so the question of whether the *very good* were, in fact, *the best,* as judged with fairness, validity, and reliability, seems unnecessarily petty and pedantic. In my view, however, we ought to strive to select and reward the best, not just out of a concern for fairness, but also because good judges can presumably detect quite subtle differences in quality at the margins.

Issues in the Art of Competition Design

Two distinct challenges are central in the art of selection for major national fellowship competitions. The first challenge is the "selection criteria chain," which was discussed briefly in the previous section. In the multistage translation from the funders' goals to the considerations judges bring to bear in making their assessments of the relative strength of candidates, it is surprisingly easy for ambiguities and contradictions in selection criteria to emerge. The whispered game of telephone is an apt metaphor. We are repeatedly surprised by the extent of error in the process.

The second challenge involves two issues that are closely interrelated in major national competitions: how to cope with potentially impossible numbers of candidate; and how to assure the distributive characteristics of the winners that our funders, or we as program managers, want to achieve, without unduly sacrificing fairness and quality. The two problems are related because they can, and often are, both ameliorated by one device: the fragmentation or segmentation of competitions.

Building a Strong "Selection Criteria Chain"

Programs can often benefit from a systematic linking and adjusting of selection criteria components and the application submissions that the program requires. Not only should the selection components provide a coherent and reasonably comprehensive picture of the core selection criterion, but they should also be measured with reasonable accuracy by submissions in the application. Moreover, the various elements of the submissions should provide strong indicators of the components of the selection criteria. The lack of correspondence between the two elements is often surprising. Component criteria are often added or modified without adding or modifying submissions, and submissions are formulated without specific reference to the components of selection criteria.

A TECHNIQUE FOR ASSESSING A SELECTION CRITERIA CHAIN

It is helpful, in assessing a program's materials, to generate a table that lists components of selection criteria on a vertical axis and elements of submissions (including interviews) on the horizontal axis. One can then look at each submission element and determine which, if any, component of selection criteria the element measures, and how strong an indicator of that component it is. A strong chain has a close correspondence between the two dimensions, with some multiple indicators of key components.

In one such analysis of a major national competition, I found that judges were provided with six different sources of evidence—A through F—and were directed to consider a total of 28 different elements from those sources. I then assessed the extent to which each of these elements seemed to provide a measure of the five specific selection criteria that the program identified in its promotional materials. Using 5 as a strong measure of the criterion and 1 as a very weak measure, I found the pattern shown in Table 3.3, which suggests a relatively weak correspondence between stated selection criteria and the specific indicators that the submissions and the interviews tap. The point is not that the selection criteria are right or that the submission elements are wrong, but that there is not as much correspondence between the two as might be possible and helpful to judges.

In my experience, a lack of correspondence between selection criteria and the indicators provided to judges is often the result of one or more of three factors: First, disagreement among program staff (or board members) and incremental changes over time. Rather than reconcile disagreements about what the core selection criteria and their key components should be, it is easier to list multiple criteria. Second, when staff find that an important evaluative component is missing, it is easier to add a requirement for an essay or an evaluation without changing the selection criteria. And third,

Table 3.3
Degree of Correspondence Between Selection Criteria and Application Submissions

	A	A	A	B	B	B	B	B	B	B	B	C	C	C	C	C	C	D	E	F	F	F	F	F	F	F	F	F
	1	2	3	4	5	6	7	8	9	10	11	12	13	14	15	16	17	18	19	20	21	22	23	24	25	26	27	28
Criterion A	5	5	2	2		2	3		2		4			3	2		2	4	3	3	2			2	1	2	2	3
Criterion B								4					3			3					3	5						
Criterion C													3						3									
Criterion D					4																		5					
Criterion E																												

sometimes, as well, staff adopt another competition's formulation without assessing whether it provides data that correspond to their own program's selection criteria.

USEFUL PRINCIPLES IN BUILDING A STRONG SELECTION CHAIN

In assessing and thinking about modifying application materials, I find the following guidance helpful:

1. *Mine what you can find out about what candidates have done in the past.* Sternberg and Grigorenko (chapter 2 in this volume) wonderfully capture a basic truth of selection: "What better predictor of future creative work could one find than past creative work?" The same can be said for leadership or humanitarian service or entrepreneurship. Especially in essays, there is a predisposition to ask candidates to write about future plans. This leaves judges with agonizing questions about whether those promises will be fulfilled and throws discussion among judges into the realm of the speculative. It may be harder to dig out an understanding of the significance of what a person has done than to ask what they plan to do in the future, but it is likely to provide a more reliable indicator of future action.

Questions that ask candidates to reflect on what they have done are often quite revealing. In assessing future scholars, one wants to know how they think they came to a particular interest or research project, what struggles they had, how they overcame them, and what distinctive strengths they discovered in themselves. In assessing future public policy leaders, one wants to know how and why they got involved in organizations, what roles they have played, and what personal strengths, capabilities, and limitations they have discovered in the process. In assessing a future doctor, one wants to know how a candidate's interest in medicine arose, how she or he has pursued experiences that reveal an academic and/or personal capacity to practice and what the candidate has learned from the experience.

Letters of reference are often heavily discounted by judges. However, they can be extremely valuable if they are thought of as sources of verification and elaboration on past accomplishments. Though academics, especially, are predisposed simply to submit standard academic references that comment on a student's performance in class, it can be helpful to ask for specific reflections on a student's application essay as it reveals attributes that are central components of selection criteria. Judges can usefully learn if the candidate's contribution to a campus program really showed creative and determined leadership or was simply dedicated foot-soldiering or punching another extracurricular activity card. Did a research project demonstrate creative ingenuity and dedicated exploration, or was it simply implementing an aspect of the supervisor's own research enterprise? In many cases, references won't know or won't take the time to answer such questions. Others will answer such questions whether asked or not. I have been struck, however, that for students who turn out to be extraordinary, references will read the guidance materials carefully and, if asked to do so, will provide detailed evidence that speaks directly to what the program wants to know about the significance of what the candidate has achieved.

Finally, interviews are often misused as well. The path of least resistance is to ask candidates about their future plans or about their views of issues of interest to the judges. It is generally much more useful to use interviews to refine an understanding of the significance and meaning of what candidates have done in the past. Essays and references typically leave ambiguities that can be resolved, unstated personal reactions and lessons, implied but not explicit descriptions of roles and accomplishments. Sadly, however, at the conclusion of interviews, judges often retain significant misperceptions of the meaning or significance of an individual's accomplishments because they failed to pursue clues or ambiguities in the application materials.

2. *In exploring candidates' future plans, emphasize proximate next steps and the relationship of plans to past activities and interests.* Most programs want, at the same time, to select individuals who will continue to excel in whatever kinds of pursuits have characterized their past achievements. Asking for elaborate statements of long-term goals and ambitions generates far less valuable indicators in this regard than do tougher and more focused questions about "what next?" Does the candidate's proposed graduate study seem to build plausibly on past interest and activities? Has the candidate developed a realistic perspective on the best practicable educational programs? Has the candidate thought about and taken steps to pursue supplementary activities such as internships that will enrich future academic work?

3. *An iterative process should be followed in forging a strong selection criteria chain.* If a program uses an interview question that is highly evocative and helpful, it may make sense to reformulate one or more selection criteria components to better fit what you believe judges learn from reading the essays. If judges find it useful to assess a candidate's sophistication in evaluating the graduate programs they have applied to, consider incorporating that consideration into the selection criteria.

On the other hand, there is no point in articulating a selection criterion that you can't find a way to measure. It would be great to know how motivated a student is to become a leader or a teacher or a great scientist, but a program may be unable to come up with any measure of that motivation that it believes to be reasonably valid and reliable. If a program believes that one criterion is especially salient—past activities that demonstrated creative leadership, for example—it may be helpful to explore the possibility of developing multiple independent indicators of that criterion. An essay question, a specific question asked of referees, and a focused discussion in interviews may, in combination, provide a much richer story than would any single stimulus.

4. *Work to eliminate extraneous and inconsistent "hints" as to what the program's real selection criteria are.* Read the program documentation and note every case where there are implicit or explicit suggestions as to what the program is looking for. Then review the more formally stated selection criteria and work to establish a clear correspondence between the two. There should be a single and clear message.

ASSESSING STERNBERG AND GRIGORENKO'S PROPOSAL

In chapter 2, Sternberg and Grigorenko provide suggestions that a broad range of programs might use in revising their selection criteria. To what extent are these useful and practicable in thinking about the need to develop a strong selection criteria chain?

In attempting to produce insights that are useful to a broad range of competitions, they provide a useful general formulation for a core selection criterion: "individuals who are not only talented but most likely to translate this talent into actions that have a meaningful impact on the world." Individual programs may wish to substitute a different term for "talented," but the notion of identifying individuals who are most likely to translate their talent—or leadership, or creativity, or academic ability, or whatever—into actions that have a meaningful impact on the world seems to be of direct relevance to many major national fellowship programs.

To what extent, though, do Sternberg and Grigorenko provide practical, detailed guidance in building a strong selection criteria chain? As academic psychologists, they naturally focus their attention on the development of tests to measure successful intelligence, creativity, and wisdom. Such tests are typically of very limited utility in competitions. The greatest limitation of tests is that they are highly subject to "gaming." Were a major fellowship program to require that candidates take standardized tests that purported to measure successful intelligence, creativity, and wisdom, a market would very quickly develop that would offer guidance in the kinds of answers that would make candidates appear to be highly successfully intelligent, creative, and wise.

On the other hand, if one seeks other kinds of measures for the components of successful intelligence, creativity, and wisdom that Sternberg and Grigorenko suggest, the results seem much more helpful. One might develops essays, queries to referees, and interview foci that explore candidates' "talents" and how they have translated them into actions that have had a meaningful impact on their environments. One could then provide guidance to judges along the following lines. In assessing the candidates' demonstrated talents and the likelihood of translating those talents into meaningful impact, consider three aspects of what they have done in the past that are predictors of future effectiveness:

Creativity: Do they show

- an ability to question assumptions and redefine a problem?
- a willingness to sell ideas, take sensible risks, surmount obstacles, and delay gratification?
- a capacity for identifying and committing to something they love?
- personal courage?

Successful Intelligence: Do they show

- movement toward meaningful personal goals using analytical, creative, and practical abilities?
- a capacity to identify and compensate for weaknesses?

Wisdom: Do they show

- an ability to translate talents into activities that produce meaningful impact without excessive egocentrism, omniscience, omnipotence, and sense of invulnerability?

Indeed, using the existing Soros essay topics and core selection criteria, the guidance language suggested above could probably enhance the insights that judges bring to bear in assessing the relative "creativity and capacity to transform that creativity into meaningful achievement" that we hope to measure. Though many of Sternberg and Grigorenko's insights are susceptible to translation into useful criteria, other aspects of their schema are more difficult to operationalize (for example, the notion of balances as a sign of wisdom seems to be especially slippery in practice).

The Art of Processing Large Numbers of Candidates

Staff members of major national fellowship competitions are all familiar with the Big Number Problem. Of the thousand or so potential applicants for our highly remunerative and prestigious awards, how does one reliably discourage applications from those who are not likely to be competitive; exclude applications from the uncompetitive who do apply; select a number of finalists that is large enough to provide a reasonable size pool from which to select winners; and finally, devise a process that allows us reliably to determine the relative strengths of those finalists?

Both the promise and the threat of generous national fellowship programs is the large and potentially overwhelming number of candidates who would like to win the awards that the programs offer. A high ratio of applicants to awards is an attractive indicator of competitiveness; but the higher the ratio, the greater are not only the administrative headaches but also the potentially troublesome problems of eliminating the least competitive candidates and choosing from among those who seem highly competitive. Large numbers imply large opportunities for mistakes. Screening processes used by some programs—especially those that use large numbers of screeners and rely on rating systems—leave much to be desired in determining which candidates go forward into semifinalist and finalist status and which fall by the wayside.

All of us are also familiar with various forms of the distribution problem. We think of our competitions as based on merit, and indeed they are. But at the same time, virtually all major programs have distributive concerns, whether geographic (residence or school); demographic (gender, race, "minority," national heritage, etc.); institutional (elite vs. mass, research university vs. college, state vs. private, etc.); or intellectual (disciplinary, area studies, community). Some distributive mandates are included in the funders' statements of goals, others reflect the values of program managers, and still others are, I would argue, essential to the integrity of the program.

The hard reality is that there is typically a trade-off between achieving distributive goals and rewarding merit as defined by the program. We are very good at devising ways to disguise this trade-off, but I would argue that it is ubiquitous in merit-based competitions.

FRAGMENTATION AND SEGMENTAL FILTERS

The Big Number Problem and distributive problems are related in major national competitions because fragmentation of competitions and the use of filters can be, and often are, used to help solve both problems. *Fragmentation* refers to the process of creating multiple competitions out of one. The Social Science Research Council until recently fragmented its foreign area dissertation competition by allocating to each of several area studies committees the selection of fellows proposing to do research in its area of jurisdiction. The American Rhodes Scholar program fragments its competition into eight separate regional competitions, each of which yields four scholars annually. In both cases, the results of any one competition have no impact on the results of any other. The results assure a fixed distributive pattern across the spheres of the separate competitions—foreign areas of study in the case of SSRC, regions of the United States in the case of the Rhodes. In both cases, as well, the Big Number Problem is reduced by a factor of about eight.

Segmental filters refer to separate screening mechanisms that assess applicants within different components of the applicant pool. A number of programs, for example, use college or university committees to screen and sometimes rank applicants from among their students. Those not screened out are then forwarded to a subsequent selecting authority, where they compete with students from other colleges and universities. Again, distributive goals are typically achieved—the process helps the program assure that no one institution or small group of institutions achieves greater dominance in the competition than seems appropriate, and the problem of large numbers is simplified. Institutions may simply not forward less competitive applications, or they may indicate to the selecting authority which applications they should take very seriously and which they can reasonably ignore.

Segmental filters can be relatively weaker or stronger, depending on the extent to which they screen out less competitive applicants and on the decision rules that the selecting authority uses. The Mellon Humanities program, for example, uses regional committees as strong filters. Those committees submit the applications of highly competitive finalists to a national selection committee, which exercises some discretion in selection but which is highly attentive to equitable distribution among districts and to the priorities expressed by the district committees. Thus, even with a very large body of applicants and a very sizable number of awards to be made—about 85 annually—the national selection committee has a manageable task in making final judgments because the choices it faces are highly structured. Similarly, the Watson program uses small liberal arts colleges as relatively strong filters. It both limits eligibility to students at fifty such institutions and limits schools with fewer than 1,000 students to two nominees and those with between 1,000 and 3,000 students to four nominees. Thus, as many as 50 fellows can be selected from approximately 200 nominees.

Larger programs can use multiple segmental filters and/or fragmentation both to shape distributional characteristics and to facilitate management of large numbers of candidates. Again, the Rhodes competitions provide a striking example. Applications are submitted to college and university committees, which filter out the least competitive applications and provide indicative rankings of others. In the case of large universities, most of whose applicants would be applying to a single state committee, this constitutes a strong filter; however, a smaller college might not filter at all if no more than one or two of its students wanted to apply to any one state.

State committees provide a second strong filter. They identify the top applications among those nominated by colleges and universities and interview perhaps 10 to 20 candidates, of whom a small number are recommended to the regional committee as finalists. Each state is assured of a manageable-sized pool of candidates from a diverse set of institutions, and each regional committee is assured of a manageable-sized pool of finalists that includes the most promising candidates from each state in the region.

Each regional committee is the ultimate source of decision for four Rhodes Scholars.

The advantages of such a system are substantial. Both at the state and the regional levels, it is quite possible for one small committee to judge all applications relative to each other and arrive at carefully considered rankings. The system also provides for intensive use of interviews, which, arguably, are likely to be more reliable at the university and state levels as predictors of success at the regional level than would be assessments of application materials only.

The trade-offs between distributive goals and overall merit in such a multi-tier filtering and fragmenting system are intense, however. Programs that are tempted to use such systems should be fully aware of the trade-offs. If they choose to use filtering and/or fragmenting devices, they should design systems that have as few unintended consequences as possible. Let me suggest some of the aspects of the challenge. First, a goal of more or less equal distribution of awards across regions or states clearly advantages students from smaller regions or states and disadvantages those from the larger regions or states. If a system were to fragment competitions so that a student from each state received an award, students from the four smallest states would likely have competition less than 1–50th as intense as that faced by students from California, and those from the next eight smallest states would likely have competition less than 1–25th as intense. Regional strategies generally yield patterns of unequal opportunities that are less extreme, but they can still be considerable.

A second issue involves whether students should compete against others from their state of residence or the state in which their undergraduate institution is located, or whether they should have a choice. In part, this judgment is shaped by program goals. Where the focus is on diffusion of winners across geographic space, the state of residence seems more relevant; where the focus is on diffusion across undergraduate institutions, the state in which that institution exists makes sense. The argument for a choice seems primarily to be a pragmatic one—the candidate can reduce travel time and cost to the interview site by choosing the location that makes sense logistically.

Dual choice produces troubling dilemmas, however. Thus, in a competition based on state-level screening, a student from California who studies at Berkeley is likely to face a situation that is about seventeen times more competitive than a California student who studies at the University of Nevada at Las Vegas and chooses to submit an application to Nevada. The dual eligibility also means that students' likely success can be affected by their sophistication in gaming the selection process: a Yale student from New

York has to decide whether to apply from Connecticut where, if students all apply from their home states, the competition would likely be only about a third as intense as in New York, or to apply in New York, where he or she would not be competing with other Yalies who chose to apply to Connecticut.

A third issue arises when college and university filters are combined with state or regional competitions or filters based on residence. In such cases, institutions that have geographically diversified student bodies have significant advantages over those—especially state universities—that have primarily in-state student populations. Thus, if institutions are limited to five nominees to a program, Berkeley—with about 93 percent in-state students—might be able to nominate only five students to the California state or region. Harvard, on the other hand—with a highly geographically diversified student body—would be able to nominate highly credible students to a broad range of state panels or regional committees. The military service academies—West Point, Annapolis, and the Air Force Academy—are especially well-positioned for a competition such as the Rhodes. Because their students are nominated by members of Congress, they are assured of having significant numbers of students from each state in the union.

A fourth issue is the composition of regions. Geographic propinquity is clearly desirable, as is cultural similarity, so that students are competing against others from roughly comparable educational environments. If regions are combined with state filters, the problems become especially complex. Combining states of roughly equal size reduces the extent to which students from larger states are compared. But a program may wish to compensate for the disadvantages of students from large states by putting them in regions with smaller states. One can also affect opportunities by varying the numbers of states in each region. The nominees from a state in a region with four states have twice the opportunities for awards than the nominees from a state in a region with eight states if both regions are allocated the same number of awards or finalists.

Not surprisingly, in practice, it is virtually impossible to achieve all of a program's desired distributive goals and avoid significant unintended distributive consequences. Cultural clustering almost inevitably involves combining big and small states in the same district. And cultural regions don't neatly group themselves into consistent numbers of states. Thus, any program that operates separate regional competitions or uses regions as strong filters faces major challenges in constructing regions that reasonably achieve its distributional goals without excessive unintended unfairness.

For programs that are grappling with such issues, the following points are important to consider. First, distributive mandates are surprisingly difficult to implement. Fragmentation of competitions and the use of segmental filters have definite distributive impacts and can greatly ameliorate the Big Number Problem, but they typically also produce significant patterns of unfairness. Most of us find it hard, I think, to accept the fact that a student from California should have one-fiftieth the chance of winning a "merit" award as a student from Vermont or Alaska, but that is implied in state competitions. Managing actually to design a competition that accurately carries out this mandate is extremely difficult. Conducting multiple regional competitions or using strong regional filters produces a credible, but not trouble-free, approach for programs whose mandates include distributive equity across regions of the United States.

Fragmentation and segmental filters inevitably favor candidates in weaker fragments or segments of the population over candidates who are more highly qualified in stronger fragments or segments. This not only raises issues of fairness but also means that use of fragmentation and segmental filters has a negative effect on the overall quality of the fellows in a program. This is entirely justifiable when a program's goals mandate such distribution, but it is truly unfortunate when it is the unintended product of fragmentation and segmental filters designed to simplify a program's Big Number Problem or achieve other goals.

Perhaps the most dramatic example of this phenomenon is the Faculty Fulbright Program administered by the Council on International Exchange of Scholars. I was asked to look at its selection process some years ago, in part to see if the apparent decline in the prestige and quality of the program's scholars might be rectified. What I found was a system of fragmentation of competitions by country that has been compounded by requests— or demands—from USIA field offices to provide scholars who met very narrowly drawn selection criteria tailored to the needs of local universities. These were unexceptional goals, but the result was that CIES was conducting over 500 distinct competitions, for which, in most cases, it had none, one, or two candidates. Overall quality cannot help but suffer dramatically under such circumstances.

Second, fragmenting competitions or creating segmental filters just for the purpose of facilitating management of the Big Number Problem should therefore be looked at with skepticism. As I will argue in a subsequent section, it is possible to design quite manageable and reliable unitary competitions that don't rely on segmental filters.

Finally, fragmentation and segmental filter strategies, once implemented, are difficult to unravel and abandon because they generate their own constituencies. Some years ago, the Social Science Research Council fragmented its foreign area dissertation fellowship program into about seven regions, with a number of untoward consequences. As vice president, I was charged with implementing a mandate from the Mellon Foundation to reestablish a single competition that would make it possible to select the most promising candidates, irrespective of the region or regions of the world in which they wanted to study. The area studies committees of the SSRC and the national area studies associations united in opposition to this effort. Even the partisans of areas that were likely to benefit from a unitary competition objected, both because they lost power over the process and because they lost the predictability of a known number of fellowships each year. It took several years and a new council administration before the opposition was finally overcome.

CHALLENGES IN A NON-FRAGMENTED AND NON-SEGMENTED COMPETITION: THE PAUL AND DAISY SOROS CASE

In contrast to most national fellowship program benefactors, Paul and Daisy Soros, the benefactors of the Soros Fellowships for New Americans, have specified that they want to fund the thirty applicants who best meet the fellowship's eligibility and selection criteria irrespective of what part of the United States they come from, what college or university they attend, or what their ethnic background is.[4] Paul Soros made it clear that if the thirty best people the program could find were all from the same state or university or field of study or ethnic background that would be fine with him.

This posed a serious Big Numbers Problem for the program's managers. Fragmenting the program into several regional or state competitions was inconsistent with the Soroses' mandate. It was tempting to ask colleges and universities to nominate candidates, but the program's selection criteria are sufficiently unusual and different from those typically emphasized by college and university faculty—creativity and accomplishment more than grades and GREs—that it seemed likely to be counterproductive to delegate preliminary screening to students' academic institutions. It was also very unclear where the most creative and accomplished New Americans were likely to be found, so it seemed inappropriate to eliminate some institutions or to limit the number of nominations from others.

In the absence of a way of dividing the competition, the challenge was to select thirty fellows from among over a thousand candidates without fragmentation or segmental filters. An early decision was that interview panels could effectively interview twelve candidates in a day and that seven days of interviewing—a total of 84 finalists—would provide an adequate basis for selection of thirty.

Thus, the central problem has been to identify the top 84 candidates from among a thousand or more applications. The solution during the first six rounds has been to make intensive use of two judges (the program director and the author of this paper), each of whom reviews approximately 700 applications over a five week period. Each judge typically does a first read of about 500 applications, finds about 300 that are clearly not competitive, scores the remaining 200, and sends them to the other judge for a second reading. Since it would be impossible to directly rank the plausibly competitive applications from 1 to 400, the judges use a set of benchmarks to provide indirect rankings. Applications from the preceding year that were on the margin of being in the top 84 (i.e., candidates who ranked 82nd to 86th) are assigned scores of 5.0. Applicants who were on the margin of being in the top 30 are assigned scores of 6.0. Judges then assign scores to applications based on their merit with respect to appropriate benchmark applications. Thus, a candidate interested in law school might be compared to benchmark applications in law from the preceding year that received scores of 5.0 and 6.0. Calibrating the new application's merit relative to the two benchmarks, the judge would assign it a score between 4.0 and 7.0. Though this approach does not provide a complete rank ordering, the judges find that they are able, in making paired comparisons of candidates as they proceed, to establish between 13 and 17 graduated scores between 5.0 and 7.0. When the two scores are added together, this provides a highly differentiated set of scores.

Specialist readers—in science, engineering, medicine, law, the arts, humanities, social sciences, and business—are then retained to provide a third reading for applications in their field deemed by one of the preliminary readers to be in the competitive range (usually scored 5.0 or above). The scores of each reader are then ranked within specialized fields to achieve overall rankings within fields, and the rankings of the two preliminary readers are used to calibrate rankings across fields to arrive at the identification of approximately one hundred most highly ranked candidates. Those who at least two readers agree are in the top 84 are then identified as presumptive finalists. The readers then reconsider applications ranked in the top 84 by one reader but not the other two, and the quota of 84 finalists is then completed after a final reranking of these applications.

Having 84 finalists for 30 fellowships poses a second challenge. The program initially determined that it is not reasonable to expect any one external panelist to serve for more than one day. Thus, the 84 finalists are effectively allocated among seven interview days of 12 finalists each. Each set of 12 is ranked 1 through 12 by the panels of their day. If the finalists are assigned reasonably randomly across days, it is extremely unlikely that fewer than two of the top 30 finalists would be among those interviewed on any one day. Thus, the top two finalists from each day are typically selected as fellows. Similarly, there is a very low probability that any of the finalists ranked 9th through 12th in a given day would be among the top 30. Therefore, at the end of each day four finalists are typically eliminated from further consideration.

This leaves the following problem: none of the regular panelists can compare candidates across clusters, so there is no direct way, using the normal panel process, of identifying the best 16 from among the 42 remaining finalists—those ranked 3rd through 8th on each day.

The program has managed this problem by engaging three individuals associated with the program—the director, this author, and a son of the funders—to attend interviews of all candidates. Using the rankings of each day's panels, they follow an iterative process of selecting the highest ranked candidate from the seven highest ranked remaining candidates from each day until the remaining pool has been completed. In practice, the three judges select 11 to 13 fellows and 6 to 10 alternates. Information on the alternates is then submitted to the program's Board of Trustees, whose members choose the final three to five fellows and three ranked alternates.

The Soros formula for managing the Big Numbers Problem seeks to not disadvantage any student because of the locus of his home or the type or location of her undergraduate institution. Primary reliance for preliminary screening on two readers maximizes consistency in the criteria applied and in the rankings of candidates, and assumes, with reasonably good evidence, their diligence and reliability. Nevertheless, an impartial observer might be concerned about the extent to which these two individuals can bring an adequate breadth of perspective, even when their judgments are combined with those of a much more diverse set of specialist readers. Moreover, when the two judges do disagree significantly about individual cases, the process has an element of arbitrariness in the screening.

The Soros process, furthermore, relies exclusively on analysis of the submitted applications in determining the 84 finalists to be interviewed. This is in clear contrast to competitions that use segmental filters. The Rhodes process, for example, may involve 500 or more interviews at the state level—not to mention campus interviews—as a basis for determining which candidates will go forward to the final regional selection.

The reliance on the same two individuals who conduct the screening, supplemented by the donors' son, to make the critical judgments across the seven days of interviews also lends an element of arbitrariness to the process when there are significant disagreements among the three.

Finally, the process violates a rule that many consider a *sine qua non* of procedural fairness for merit-based competitions: that screening and selection should be conducted by disinterested experts who are independent— that is, not part of the administrative or governance structure of the administering organization. Both of the two screening judges are paid employees of the program; the same two individuals and a son of the Soros family make a number of final judgments in comparing finalists across interview days; and the Board of Trustees, part of the governance structure who were not present at any interviews, make the most difficult final marginal judgments based on the paper applications and staff recommendations.

Notwithstanding the mandate from Paul and Daisy Soros to avoid considerations of distributive equity of any kind, the closely related issue of a candidate's background quickly arose in deliberations. The program's selection criteria emphasize "extraordinary creativity manifest in a pattern of extraordinary sustained achievement." Screening and interviewing applicants in the first round highlighted the fact that *extraordinary* creativity and achievement is highly context-sensitive. What might be more or less routine for a student from a privileged background might be truly extraordinary for someone raised in a preliterate tribal setting in the Amazon jungle or the Laotian highlands. Judged by conventional standards of academic achievement, standardized test results, and scale of achievements, the latter applications would not have been competitive. The program decided, however, to take context seriously and hit on the notion of "trajectory" as a device for distinguishing relative extraordinariness among individuals from radically different backgrounds. The following excerpt from guidance to screeners and panelists characterized the program's thinking:

> We have found that the most helpful conceptual device for approaching comparable treatment of two applicants [from radically different backgrounds] is the notion of "trajectory" or "distance traveled." If one considers the background factors in the two lives, which candidate demonstrates a more promising—or a steeper—trajectory? We seek the individual who has, given her/his background, both demonstrated extraordinary creativity and achievement and shows promise of continued growth in the fostering of her/his creativity and in achievements that are informed and encouraged by her/his continuing education.
>
> The notions of trajectory and distance traveled are helpful to screeners in our efforts to give appropriate weight and significance to the following kinds of background characteristics:
>
> (a) sophistication and supportive qualities of applicants' cultural backgrounds;
>
> (b) educational sophistication, occupational experience, economic status, and value structures of their parents;
>
> (c) age at which and the circumstances under which they and/or their parents came to the United States;
>
> (d) age at which and the circumstances under which they learned English;
>
> (e) cultural, educational, and economic opportunities afforded them in this country;
>
> (f) discrimination and/or disadvantages they may have encountered;
>
> (g) "fit" or "conflict" between their personal interests and goals and those pressed on them by familial or community forces;
>
> (h) their age.

This instruction makes it clear that judges should interpret "extraordinary" in terms that are highly sensitive to the contexts of candidates' lives: their families, their cultures, their immigrant experience, their exposure to hostile or supportive environments, their use of opportunities, and their stage in life and in educational experience. In other words, the notion of trajectory incorporates critical elements of distributive justice in the selection criteria, thereby reducing the need to impose distributive considerations in ways that undermine reliance on merit.

To illustrate how screeners and panelists might think about merit relative to trajectory, I have characterized, in impressionistic charts, the trajectories of four very different types of candidates (see Chart 3.3). The horizontal axis reflects age, and the vertical axis reflects some measure of past and future achievement. The dotted lines suggest a range of possible future achievements.

One candidate is from a preliterate Southeast Asian Tribal community. Her family escaped a genocidal campaign by Laotian communists, spent five years in Thai refugee camps, and was unceremoniously dumped in the United States. When she seemed to be doing well in school and started to talk about going to college, her father arranged her marriage to a boy from another tribal family. She had her first child at 17 and her second at 19, but still got to community and junior college and then to UCLA. She became a leading figure in efforts to accommodate the police and her tribal community in a Central Valley county of California. She will clearly benefit from getting a law degree, although she will probably never achieve national standing. But what an amazing trajectory, and what potential for leadership among the 20,000 members of her community in this country and the many others who encounter its members! My image of her chart (top left) shows her at rock bottom when she was married off and put on the tribal "mommy path," amazing ascent for ten years of community college and UCLA work and finding a career, and some plateauing as that career establishes itself. Law school provides the opportunity for new growth (the dotted lines indicate a range of potential trajectories, and the solid line is my estimate of where she is likely to go with the fellowship). She may well plateau again, but it will have been an extraordinary and inspiring journey.

On the bottom left is a young man whose father got a medical degree from the American University of Beirut and did post-doctoral research at Harvard Medical School. The young man went to the best schools, won a Marshall Scholarship, and is now at Harvard Medical School. He has published numerous scientific papers and seems clearly to be heading toward major scientific discoveries in medicine. Looking at the chart, one can argue that the ascent has not been spectacular, but one does have to allow for the

Chart 3.3

FOUR TRAJECTORIES OF CREATIVITY AND ACCOMPLISHMENT

Southeast Asian Tribal Family

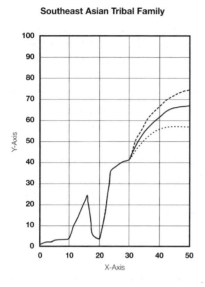

Bosnian Mixed Academic Family

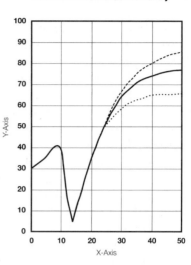

Middle Eastern Medical Family

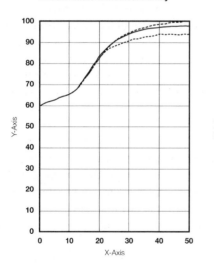

East African Educator Family

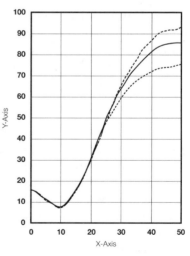

ceiling effect. Within his cohort of privileged 24-year-old future physician-scientists, he is still exceptional.

At the top right is a young woman from a mixed Serbian-Muslim family from Bosnia. Though she had an advantaged upbringing within that society, her family was effectively decimated by the outbreak of the war. Her intelligence and linguistic skills allowed her—while in her mid-teens—to obtain a volunteer and then a paid position as an interpreter for the UN staff and eventually, while still a teen, for the senior general in the British sector. This visibility, however, made her again vulnerable to agents of ethnic cleansing; so she escaped, on asylum status, to a small, little-known Midwestern college. Though she was first in her college class academically and in terms of leadership, her immigration status greatly limited her medical school admissions possibilities. She ended up at a highly respectable but not top-ranked institution. The spread between the two dotted lines suggests that I think this is a real risk, but my sense is that this person, though she will never reach the heights of the Middle Eastern medical-scientist-to-be, will draw on the toughness and insight that were forged in the crucible of civil war to produce remarkable achievements.

Finally, at the bottom right is a young woman who was born in East Africa. Her parents were products of village tribal communities, but both received good educations and won scholarships to a first-rate U.S. university. The family lived in Harlem, but she was picked up by a program called "Prep for Prep," won a full scholarship to a top-flight boarding school, attended Columbia University, and is now in her second year at the Harvard Medical School. The trajectory looks similar to that of the girl from Bosnia, but note that the real take-off came about ten years earlier in her life, and her level of achievement was much higher at the time of the competition. Her potential is probably greater, and the risk inherent in funding her is probably less.

The incorporation of trajectory in assessing creativity, accomplishment, and potential, then, provides a strategy for getting at merit that relies in only a limited way on academic record and standardized tests. For the Southeast Asian woman, just graduating from UCLA was an extraordinary achievement; her grades seemed only marginally relevant. It was a foregone conclusion that her LSAT grades would be uncompetitive. Most standard fellowship programs wouldn't have touched her, and the program director informed law schools that she had impressed the Soros panel with her poise, determination, and self-knowledge. The Middle Eastern man's grades and MCAT scores were superlative, but it was his research, his ability to articulate the significance of what he was doing, and the thoughtful and enthusiastic letters from his advisors, including a Nobel laureate, that set him apart from others with comparable grades and standardized test scores. The Bosnian woman's story was wonderfully compelling, and details she added in her interview reinforced a sense that this was a person of stature and great leadership potential, notwithstanding a somewhat diffident presentation of self. Her grades, place-in-class ranking, and MCAT scores were very important, though, because they validated her academic potential, which was important, given the unknown quality of the college she attended. And finally, for the woman from East Africa, it was the institutional trajectory that was so impressive. Her grades and test scores were consistent with that trajectory, but they were not in and of themselves determinative.

There are, of course, limitations and inadequacies in a trajectories approach to determining relative merit. Much of the information judges rely on is produced by the candidates themselves. The approach depends on the fact that the two required essays often provide rich contextual evidence about the circumstances that surrounded the evolution of a candidate's creativity, the challenges and sources of support that she or he mobilized in transforming that creativity into meaningful and sustained achievement, and the plausibility and maturity of the candidate's educational and career planning. References are specifically asked to validate or otherwise reflect on the significance and dynamics of the candidate's creativity and achievements, and their insights are often complemented by exhibits that the candidates can include in their applications. The approach would be much more difficult to implement if the application's written materials were heavily focused on future academic or research interests and plans.

Understanding these differences imposes a special demand on judges to interpret the significance of background characteristics. How does one assess the consequences of being a Mien woman when most judges will never even have heard of such a tribal group? We think of someone from Haiti as coming from an extremely impoverished background, but clearly there is a Haitian elite, and children from that subculture may have arrived in this country with significant educational and cultural advantages. Having spent four years in India, I am reasonably good at drawing inferences about the subcultural backgrounds of different candidates from the Indian subcontinent, but I am much less adept at understanding differences among candidates from Vietnamese or Chinese or Jamaican or Nigerian backgrounds. These judgments require psychological sophistication on the parts of judges in assessing the relationship between background, motives for particular kinds of achievement, and prospects for continuing productivity or high-slope trajectories.

Nevertheless, this approach provides judges with basic interpretive tools that make it possible to take into account and compensate for the differential impact of a broad range of background characteristics. It is arguably a better-grounded approach than one that focuses exclusively on the race, minority status, or region of residence of a candidate, or the type of academic institution she or he attends. Contextual analysis provides strong evidence of the degree to which skin color, cultural characteristics, family dynamics, language acquisition, and educational opportunity at different levels are, for individual candidates, impediments or aids in that individual's efforts to find expression of creative urges and transform those urges into meaningful and sustained achievement.

One might reasonably ask about the distributive consequences of running a program that, on the one hand, rejects regional fragmentation or other efforts to achieve a particular distributive composition of the Soros classes of fellows but, on the other hand, tries to use the notion of trajectory to compensate for background characteristics in determining the relative extraordinariness of creativity and achievement. Comparisons with other programs are problematic because the pools of eligible students are different. Soros candidates are New Americans and are disproportionately drawn from states and institutions where immigrant communities are strong, and the appeal of the elite schools—especially Harvard—and prestigious occupations—especially medicine and law—are particularly strong for immigrant families.

Nevertheless, comparison with a program that has a strong emphasis on fragmentation and segmental filters is suggestive. I compared the successful Soros Fellows over the past two years with American Rhodes Scholars for the same period. Notwithstanding the Soros emphasis on trajectory, students from elite institutions were far more prominent among Soros than among Rhodes winners. Forty-three percent of Soros Fellows, as opposed to 25 percent of American Rhodes Scholars, were from six elite private institutions (Harvard, Yale, Princeton, Columbia, MIT, and Stanford). Harvard alone accounted for 25.4 percent of the Soros awards but only 7.8 percent of the American Rhodes scholarships.

These statistics lend plausibility to the accusation that the Soros program is highly elitist. Perhaps those involved in the selection process are unduly impressed by elite institutions. However, examination of the background characteristics of the Soros students from elite institutions—and especially Harvard—provide impressive evidence of the ability of those institutions to identify and attract extraordinary individuals from very modest and often quite disadvantaged backgrounds. California stood out as well in the differences between the two programs. While 22 percent of Soros Fellows were from California and 13.5 percent from that state's public university system, only 3 percent of American Rhodes Scholars were from California, and none were from the state's public university system. These data reflect some combination of three phenomena: the disadvantage of students from large states in competitions that filter by state and region, the particular disadvantage of students at state universities in competitions that filter by university and state, and the strength of the New American population in California.

Whereas 12.5 percent of American Rhodes Scholars were from the military academies, Soros has had only one finalist and no winners from the academies. These data may reflect some combination of the following: the disinclination of New Americans to apply to military academies; the advantage of academy students—who are systematically selected for their residential diffusion across the 50 states—in a system that combines university filters with state filters; and the fact that the academies select for and train students in leadership, which is more central to the Rhodes selection process than that of the Soros program.

Approximately 37.5 percent of American Rhodes Scholars, compared to about 10 percent of Soros Fellows, are from Gulf and Midwestern states. This may in part reflect the relatively small numbers of New Americans in these regions of the country, but clearly it is also a product of the fact that the fragmentation of the Rhodes process mandates that three-eighths of their scholars should come from these regions.

Though the Soros selection criteria do not provide a clear mandate for doing so, its emphasis on trajectory does clearly promote distributive goals. If the dominance of students from Harvard were to begin to threaten the integrity of the program—that is, if students from other institutions were to begin to decide that it wasn't worth their while to apply—the rankings generated in the screening process would make it possible to construct a finalist pool that contained the 84 most exceptional candidates consistent with a specified maximum number of students from Harvard. The ranking of finalists would, if then necessary, also make it possible to select the most exceptional 30 fellows, consistent with a specified maximum number of students from Harvard. This approach provides a more precise mechanism for achieving many distributive goals—especially involving minorities, women, and students at different types of academic institutions—than do fragmenting or segmental filter strategies.

The design—or more often modification—of selection processes is largely an art form. A grounding in sampling theory and psychological measurement techniques can, however, provide useful guides to making changes that improve rather than complicate selection processes. This chapter highlights a number of principles that can be useful in assessing selection processes:

- It is both possible and valuable to assess the extent to which competition judges agree with each other.

- Improving levels of agreement by judges can significantly improve the quality of the candidates selected for awards, especially when making judgments at the margin between the barely in and the barely out.
- Inter-judge agreement measures can provide a useful indicator as to whether or not individual judges are making significant contributions to the evaluative process.
- Clarity, focus, and consistency in the statement and application of selection criteria are extremely important in fostering reasonable levels of inter-judge agreement and in strengthening the quality of judgments of the relative merit of candidates, again, especially at the margin.
- Rating systems, in which judges are asked to place candidates in conceptual categories, are far less precise and reliable than are ranking systems, in which judges are asked to compare candidates against each other. This is true even when it is not possible to have all of a group of judges read all of a set of applications.
- A strong selection criterion chain is important; the indicators that we solicit through applications and interviews should be closely tied to more formally stated selection criteria. It is a useful exercise to modify both in order to achieve greater correspondence between the two.
- In evolving selection criteria and indicators, eliciting and carefully assessing the past actions and achievements of candidates probably provides better predictors of future action than focusing on candidates' future aspirations.
- Distributive goals are present in almost every competition. They typically involve a trade-off with the overall quality of the individuals we select, so those goals should be pursued with care and precision.
- The threat of too many candidates to deal with cost-effectively is endemic to major national competitions.
- Fragmenting competitions—that is, conducting separate and independent competitions by geography or scope of applications—simplifies the Big Number Problem and can, if well designed, also achieve funder-mandated distributive goals.
- Using segmental filters—that is, multiple screening groups to eliminate candidates within a specific geographic or institutional segment of the candidate population—can also, if well designed, achieve both simplification of the Big Number Problem and distributive goals.
- Both of these strategies, however, are almost certain to reduce access of some highly qualified candidates to the final rounds of competition and so should be used only when they directly address and advance distributive goals of the program. If management of a Big Number Problem is the only goal, there are usually better solutions.
- Adjusting, through such concepts as "trajectory" or "distance traveled," for background factors in assessing the extent to which candi-

dates are extraordinary provides a means of promoting distributive justice without many of the discriminatory consequences of fragmentation, segmental filters, and quotas or quota-substitutes based on ethnicity, minority status, gender, and some other demographic characteristics.

Notes

1. The formula for the coefficient of correlation for two judges requires the calculation and then the squaring of the difference between the ranking allocated to each candidate by the two judges. Those squares are then summed and multiplied by six. That number is divided by the total number of candidates multiplied by that number squared minus one, and the resulting number is then subtracted from one to obtain the coefficient. Using a Lotus 123 spreadsheet, this is accomplished in a single, relatively simple calculation because the calculating, squaring, and summing of the differences in rankings is accomplished by a single function: @SUMXMY2. For 20 candidates whose rankings by two judges are recorded in cells C48 through C67 and D48 through D67, the coefficient of correlation is generated by the formula:

$$(6* @SUMXMY2(C\$48..C\$67,D\$48..D\$67)/(20*(20^2-1))$$

2. In an unpublished paper, "Measurement Error and Questionable Recommendations in a Peer Review Competition: A Methodological Assessment and Case Study," December 3, 1997. A later report to SSRC assessed changes made in the selection process in the subsequent year's competition.

3. The classic reference for this finding is G. A. Miller, "The Magical Number Seven, Plus or Minus Two: Some Limits on Our Capacity for Processing Information," *Psychological Review* 63, no. 2 (March 1956): 81–97.

4. Eligibility for the Soros fellowships is limited to "New Americans": students who are naturalized citizens or resident aliens or who are the children of naturalized citizens.

4 | The Evaluation of Scholarship Programs

Michele Lamont

I<small>T IS</small> E<small>STIMATED</small> that six thousand nationally competitive scholarships are available to Americans annually and that a conservative estimate would bring their annual direct expenditure to over 400 million dollars. Yet fellowship programs and their awardees remain vastly understudied topics, both from the perspective of scholarly research and from an evaluative point of view. Few foundations conduct regular evaluations of their funding programs, and scholars working on the reviewing process can be counted on one hand. Moreover, few foundations follow their awardees to document what they have done with their lives.[1]

This chapter is only an introduction to the subject of evaluation. Before drawing general conclusions concerning how efficient these scholarship programs are, we need more systematic information about specific programs. Here I suggest a platform of questions for the evaluation of fellowship programs and raise a few issues that we may use to guide our inquiry into the topic.

This chapter is based on reports that fellowship programs have provided about themselves.[2] My remarks also draw on my work as consultant to foundations (the Paul and Daisy Soros Fellowships for New Americans, in particular) and on my own experience as a panel member. In addition, I draw on available studies of fellowship recipients, such as Berger's study of the Westinghouse Prize winners and Zuckerman's study of Nobel Prize winners.[3] Finally, I refer to my own research on various fellowship programs, which includes a study of the "presentation of self" among the 1994 Presidential Scholars, an analysis of letters of recommendation written for Woodrow Wilson Fellows in the 1950s and the late 60s, and an ongoing NSF-sponsored study on definitions of excellence used in funding panels in the social sciences and the humanities.[4] This last study draws on observation of, and interviews with, scholars serving on panels for the following funding agencies: the American Council for Learned Societies; the Women's

Studies Fellowship program of the Woodrow Wilson National Fellowship Foundation; the Social Science Research Council and ACLS International Dissertation Field Research Program; a Society of Fellows at a major research university; and an anonymous foundation in the social sciences and the humanities.

My discussion focuses on American programs. Apart from the excellent review of the early ERASMUS Scholars Program,[5] I did not have access to systematic information concerning other European and international programs (e.g., the Deutscher Akademischer Austauschdienst [DAAD], other programs of the Academic Cooperation Association of the European Union, and Commonwealth Fellowships.) Moreover, the Gates Cambridge Trust, the Nelson Mandela Trust, and the Ford Foundation International Fellows Program are so new that there are no studies of their effectiveness.

The fellowships under discussion here have a variety of goals in their mission. Chief among these is to support scholarly work after the baccalaureate degree. Some scholarships focus on graduate degrees (e.g., Gates Cambridge, Commonwealth, Paul and Daisy Soros), while others support and reward promising academic research conducted by Ph.D. candidates and confirmed scholars (DAAD, Howard Hughes, Open Society Institute). Among the post-bachelor's fellowships, some programs will support candidates specializing in almost any subject, while others support only projects in the sciences (Howard Hughes) or in the humanities (Mellon). Moreover, a number understand the development of individual creativity and leadership as an essential objective (Watson, Rhodes), while other programs profess larger public purposes in addition to investment in the individual (Fulbright, Truman, Rhodes, Ford-IFP).

Evaluation of the various types of fellowship programs often raises different questions, concerning the selection of panelists, for instance. Whereas decisions concerning academic or research fellowships are generally made by top scholars who draw on their expertise to select awardees and do not require special training in selection, decisions concerning general post-bachelor's fellowships can be made by various categories of people who are not specifically trained for this purpose (e.g., former awardees).[6] In the case of academic competitions, the process of panel deliberations is highly institutionalized and generally agreed upon, given that peer review consumes a large portion of the working lives of academics. In contrast, in the case of general post-B.A. competitions, the more heterogeneous group of panelists often does not have the benefit of clear expectations. The former awardees or the members of various professional elites that often make up panels for general and post-B.A. competitions often share little beyond their common stellar status.

Four Questions

Despite these differences, similar questions can be asked when evaluating fellowship programs. I have identified four sets of questions that may provide scholars and administrators analytical leverage in understanding the world of evaluation. They pertain to (1) the framework for evaluation; (2) organizational mechanics; (3) the cultural determinants of success of competitions (more specifically, what are the "taken-for-granted" assumptions about excellence among applicants and panelists); and (4) the structural determinants of the success of awardees (and by extension, of the competitions themselves).

One may begin by considering the *appropriate framework for evaluation*. More specifically, what are the goals of the program? Are these goals precise enough for experts to determine whether they are achieved? Moreover, when is it appropriate to evaluate the success of a program?

A second set of questions has to do with the *organizational mechanics of the program* and whether they generate maximum results. These include the marketing of the program to the appropriate pool of applicants; the selection, preparation, and evaluation of screeners and panelists; the panel deliberations and the decision-making process; and the types and amount of resources made available to awardees during the fellowship. These aspects are often within the control of the funding organization and can be acted upon to improve the performance of the program.

A third set of questions concerns the *cultural determinants of success* of fellowship competitions, that is, the taken-for-granted assumptions about excellence at work in the process of fellowship application and selection. We are concerned here with the cultural assumptions of potential applicants (concerning what one should do to win a competition, for instance) and the cultural assumptions of panelists (concerning how to recognize originality, for instance). These topics would not figure in evaluation research as it is generally practiced, in part because they concern assumptions that cannot be acted upon by funding organizations. They are largely implicit and part of a broader cultural environment that provides superseding context for each organization. But they undoubtedly affect the outcome and success of nationally and internationally competitive scholarships.

A fourth set of questions has to do with the *structural determinants of success* for the awardees, factors that are also beyond the control of the organization. These include the kinds of resources that awardees have access to throughout their careers, the characteristics of the internal labor market in which their careers proceed, the limitations created by gender discrimination in the workplace, and so on. These factors have a direct impact on the success of fellowship competitions that aim at identifying people who perform superlatively in their field of choice.

Before addressing these four sets of questions, I want to make a last, important preliminary comment. To the extent that it is conducted, the assessment of fellowship programs is often framed as follows: Are programs successful in identifying talent? Do awardees live up to their promise? How successful are they? The tacit assumption here is that fellowship programs make awards to talented people with the hope that the fellowship will help them become "all they can be." Accordingly, an important psychological literature relevant to our topic privileges the impact of individual talent or skills on success. Cognitive psychologists and organizational behavior specialists working on multiple intelligence, creativity, and leadership have been central to developing this individual-centered approach.[7] The literature, reviewed in part in the interesting chapter written by Sternberg and Grigorenko (chapter 2 of this volume), is concerned with the development and identification of success, intelligence, or creativity, instead of analyzing how they come to be defined as such. Hence, this literature is more focused on excellence itself, and on its development within the individual, than on the social process of production of excellence and its constraints, which is the dimension of the problem that has captured my interest. This line of work is illustrated, for instance, in the work of Ericsson on the acquisition of expert technical performance in the arts, science, sports, and games, which examines the role of talent versus deliberate practice in the acquisition of expert skills.[8] The literature on gifted children—how to identify them and what to do with them—is another example of this line of work.[9]

In this chapter I frame the question slightly differently and perhaps somewhat counter-intuitively. I build on insights offered by research in the sociology of science, arts, and literature that has been concerned with analyzing the social process by which contributions come to be defined as original and significant, instead of presuming that they are or can be intrinsically important. Instead of focusing solely on the trajectory of the brilliant individual or the brilliant contribution, this literature considers the interplay between the "producer," his/her contribution, and the environment in which it is produced, diffused, and evaluated. The point of focus is not the genius accomplishing great things, but the system that makes his or her work possible and that makes it likely that it will be viewed as path-breaking or exceptionally significant.

This approach is illustrated by Bruno Latour's influential book on Louis Pasteur, which shows that this scientist was able to enlist the assistance of human and nonhuman actors to turn microbes into a hard fact and to ensure the diffusion of this finding.[10] He was also able to institutionalize microbes as a reality through an "alliance" with the French social hygienist movement that was engaged in public health reform in nineteenth-century France. Similarly, in her book *The Glory of Van Gogh,* Nathalie Heinich shows that the crystallization of Van Gogh's reputation required the production and diffusion of an ideology of the isolated genius—an ideology of artistic singularity—among critics and artistic publics.[11]

In my article "How to Become a Dominant French Philosopher: The Case of Jacques Derrida," I show how the influential work of this French theorist was framed very differently in France than in the United States, so as to fit the specific definitions of intellectual sophistication and important work that prevailed among French philosophers and American literary critics in the 1960s and 70s.[12] This study, illustrative of what could be called an environmental approach to the riddle of success, also showed that the context of production, evaluation, and reception is as important as the cultural product itself in understanding its success. This success depends largely on intersubjective conventions and criteria of evaluation that escape the control of individual producers.[13] Applied to our topic, this environmental approach would emphasize factors such as institutionalized definitions of success and of the "ideal self" adopted by applicants and panelists.

The environmental approach, with its focus on constraints, and the individual-centered approach, with its focus on particular performances, are somewhat at odds with one another in how they approach the riddle of excellence. But they are also complementary, since each is concerned with elements that are essential to solving this riddle. Although I will refer to individual processes herein, the bulk of my discussion will center on the social mechanisms at work—mechanisms that may be less salient than individual factors in the everyday life of the administrators of fellowship programs. I want to bring these mechanisms to the reader's attention with the hope that they will shape the thinking about particular fellowship programs: What are their goals, and who do these fellowships want to reward? Throughout, I have included a discussion of how to maximize the diversity of the pool of selection and awardees, since at a time when a few highly prestigious universities produce the majority of our nation's leaders, this is one of the criteria by which many programs measure their own success.[14] I have a hunch that all the programs represented in this volume have wrestled with the issue of how to avoid the monopolization of awards by graduates of a few elite institutions. With this goal in mind, I turn to the four sets of considerations mentioned above.

Appropriate Framework of Evaluation

The first consideration in any evaluation is, of course, the goals of the program. Are they defined in such a way that it is possible to determine whether they have been attained? The improvement of international understanding is certainly a laudable program objective, but it may be very difficult to reach a definite conclusion concerning whether a specific program has achieved it. To frame the question somewhat more concretely, it is useful to survey the goals of the various programs represented in this volume. According to Appendix 1, "Opportunities for Competitive Scholarships," the majority of these programs aim at rewarding "superior standards of intellectual ability," "exceptional ability," "exceptional promise," "academic performance," and the like. Several, such as the Ford Foundation International Fellowship Program, combine standards of academic excellence with other standards pertaining to leadership, character, or other virtues. (For instance, in Ford's case, the focus is on "exceptional individuals" from previously underrepresented groups who will become leaders in their fields while furthering development in their country and economic and social justice worldwide.) Other program objectives include "acquiring critical skills," "redirecting career objectives," "encouraging public service," "sustaining creativity," "furthering international mobility," and "developing global or national perspective or affinity." I will concentrate my attention on programs that aim to identify people with exceptional or superior ability, since this goal seems to be the common denominator shared by the majority of the programs under study here. Regardless of overall purpose, all programs use "exceptional or superior ability" as the usual criterion in choosing finalists from among the many worthy candidates who have applied (although "identifying leaders and creative people" and "developing elites" are strong competitors in programs such as Rhodes, DAAD, and Fulbright).

With this focus in mind, a second consideration from the individual-centered perspective is: How much time should elapse between the making of an award and the evaluation of its success? How long does it take to determine whether recipients with exceptional ability live up to their promise? Should we wait until they are dead? Should we focus on the date of production of their first major contribution, their best contribution, or their last contribution?[15] The answers to these questions probably vary with the field of achievement. Indeed, we know that on average, mathematicians produce their best work earlier than astronomers and medical researchers.[16] Moreover, the level of expectations generated by the award should certainly influence the timing of the evaluation.

A third consideration is how to *measure* whether a recipient has lived up to his/her promise. For academic fellowships, should productivity be measured by absolute figures such as citation counts? By formal criteria, such as holding of leadership positions in one's field? Or more relationally, by comparing an awardee with other members of his/her cohort? I don't have one answer to offer. Decisions probably have to be made case by case.

A last consideration is how and when to evaluate a program as a whole, as opposed to the success of specific awardees. One should certainly wait until it has been operating for a substantial amount of time before trying to determine whether it has borne fruit. Some programs have existed for a long time and have yet to be evaluated. This lacuna is somewhat puzzling in a field where superior performance is so highly valued. Is it that the entire organizational field of fellowship programs shares the assumption that identifying talent is an art more than a science? That it requires a good nose for potential but little else? That selection is based on trust, faith, and luck and cannot be bureaucratized? Sociologists of organization would explain this phenomenon by "mimetic isomorphism" (organizations that do similar things tend to mimic each other in their practices) and would predict that evaluation will spread across organizations once they come to believe that it makes the other organizations in their field more rational and efficient.[17]

Organizational Mechanics of the Program

Drawing on my own experience as a consultant and on the evaluative reports I had access to, I have created a platform for evaluating the organizational mechanics of funding programs. It includes a longish list of questions that I believe may be helpful for the evaluation of scholarship programs. This list is not exhaustive, but it covers most of the relevant organizational components.

IDENTIFICATION OF CANDIDATES

How are candidates found? By publicizing the program? By sending "talent scouts" or "truffle hounds" (Robert Merton's term)? Through anonymous or acknowledged nominations? Should programs have a systematic marketing plan that targets institutions (e.g., universities) or groups whose populations have been underrepresented among finalists in the past?

POOL OF SELECTION

What is a sufficient pool? How can one avoid tapping only advantaged populations (e.g., students who attend elite institutions that publicize available fellowships)? How does filtering by universities and program staff limit diversity? How can bias be remedied? Could personal training make program staff sensitive to the importance of encouraging applicants from traditionally underrepresented institutions, if that is the program's goal? How much does it cost per applicant to create a sufficient pool? In 2001, I have been told, the cost-per-applicant to the Paul and Daisy Soros Foundation Program was $593. Is that too high? Average? Too low?

SELECTION OF SCREENERS AND PANELISTS

These can be chosen from various pools. As suggested above, they can be academic experts or former awardees. They can also be people who have distinguished themselves in their own fields and who are identified by program officers through informal consultation with specialists in the field. In some cases, they may not have any special competence that qualifies them as panel members (e.g., personal contacts of program personnel, friends of trustees, people who "owe you one"). In all cases, consistent and, as far as possible, universalistic criteria of selection should be used, both to maximize outcomes and to protect the legitimacy of the program.

One of the main challenges raised by the selection of evaluators pertains to the composition of the panel. How can one ensure that the panel is sufficiently diverse in expertise, age, gender, race, region, and type of institutional affiliation and that the panel members complement one another? How many years should evaluators serve? How much continuity should there be from one year to the next? What percentage of each panel should be renewed every year? These questions are also relevant to the selection of screeners, those individuals who do the preliminary winnowing of likely prospects from the large number of people who usually apply. The literature does not provide answers to these questions; and again, my research suggests that program administrators are working out responses tailored to the specific needs of their program and not on the basis of some recognized "best practice."

My current project on the evaluation of excellence in academic fellowship competition suggests that program officers play a central role in the selection of screeners and panelists and that they have pretty clear views concerning who is a good screener or panelist. They define a good screener by the ability to provide thorough, informed, and balanced written evaluations in a timely manner. A good panelist combines common sense, social skills, negotiating abilities, and expertise. She/he should also be thorough, thoughtful, prepared, open, and willing to defer when arguments are substantively justified.[18] Program officers spend considerable time in informal consultation to identify good screeners—and more important, good panelists. In the case of academic fellowships, the consultation has to be broad enough to ensure that program officers are not exclusively tapping within a few academic networks, hence privileging one set of criteria or research style over others. Here again, diversity and universalism are the key to legitimacy.

FORMATION AND EVALUATION OF SCREENERS AND PANELISTS

Depending on the mode of selection of panelists and screeners, they may require training. In most cases, evaluators will draw on their accumulated expertise and on knowledge gained from past experiences as panel members. But panelists rarely if ever receive formal training in the evaluation of proposals. Generally they receive information concerning the goals of the competition and perhaps a list of past awardees. The program officer may also provide clear information about what is being evaluated (the individual or the project), the criteria of selection to be used (e.g., how to assess originality and significance), and the weight to be given to each criterion (e.g., standards of excellence vs. geographic distribution of awardees), or the officer may leave these to the discretion of the evaluators. In general, the more recognized as expert the panel members are, the more likely the panel is to be given full sovereignty over decision making.

After the panel deliberations are completed, program officers assess the session and reach conclusions about whether the panel members are to be asked to serve again. They rarely provide panelists with information that would assist them in evaluating and improving their own performance as judges (e.g., on their own strengths and weaknesses or on the performance of the awardees they selected in previous panels). To the extent that such evaluation is conducted, the information remains in the hands of the fellowship program. On a personal note, I should add that academics are confronted annually with whether or not our departmental graduate admissions committee does "a good job" because we get to teach the new cohort and form opinions concerning their potential. In contrast, we are never confronted with the outcome of the work we do as panel members. We cannot be held accountable for what awardees do with their lives, but we should certainly be reminded of the impact that getting (or not getting) a fellowship has on people.

THE WORK OF SCREENERS AND PANELISTS

The job of screeners consists generally in weeding out proposals of unpromising applicants working within their area of expertise and in shaping the list of finalists that will be discussed by the panel. Screeners generally have a reasonable amount of time to perform these tasks, and there is wide variation in the care they put into them (for instance, in the extent to which they provide detailed written comments on proposals to panelists).

The task of panelists consists in evaluating the finalists, in building cases in favor of or against candidates, in discussing their cases with other members of the panel, and in making recommendations concerning recipients. This job requires many important skills. In the case of the academic fellowship competitions that I am studying, panelists are asked to read and rank from 30 to 80 proposals. They have to study their applications and accompanying material in sufficient depth to be able to formulate convincing arguments and to justify their ranking. They also have to learn to make a persuasive case for or against proposals. We have found that they often adopt a pragmatic stance in their attempt to convince one another, with the result that disciplinary differences in the types of arguments evoked are much weaker than the literature would have predicted.[19] Panelists use a wide range of criteria and mix and match from repertoires of arguments, depending on what they believe will do the trick in a particular case. For instance, an anthropologist who favors a hermeneutic approach may promote a proposal in the name of its positivistic soundness, while a political scientist who tests quantitative models in his own work may point to the cultural sensitivity demonstrated by a proposal to have it funded.

The work of academic panelists requires enormous intellectual breadth and the ability to bridge disciplinary boundaries and understand what is at stake in fields far removed from their own. It also requires enough self-confidence to be able to make rapid judgments on a large number of proposals while absorbing the new information that is pouring in from the other panelists. Hence, making awards is certainly less a science than an art, especially given the time constraints under which panels generally conduct their business and the fact that panelists may not be consistent in the criteria they use. A general question is whether panels would reach wiser and better-informed decisions if more time were made available for deliberation. Unfortunately, we do not have systematic information on the average time devoted to the assessment of each proposal across competitions. I suspect that these figures would be surprising to many.

MATERIAL PROVIDED TO SCREENERS AND PANELISTS

The evidence on which screeners and panelists base their judgment normally includes some or all of the following: biographical sketches, personal statements, essays/publications/portfolios, grade transcripts, and letters of recommendation. The program should consider whether this evidence is useful, targeted, and sufficiently exhaustive. Letters of recommendation are now largely being disregarded (except those written by friends, colleagues, and acquaintances!) because of their general inflationary character. Is there a good alternative? Programs should also consider whether screeners should provide written comments to panelists on proposals, and what this information should consist of.

INTERVIEW OF CANDIDATE

An interview with a candidate is often part of the evidence provided to panelists to help them make an assessment. This aspect of the process raises a number of questions: Why is the interview being conducted (e.g., to give candidates a general look-over? To evaluate their "presentation of self"? To assess verbal skills and class-based cultural capital?[20] To get answers to specific questions)? How is the decision concerning whom to interview reached? How much preparation do candidates receive? Is coaching available? How much time is allotted to each person? How much time does the panel set aside to discuss candidates after their interviews? Are the procedures for discussing candidates the same across panels? How is uniformity ensured? Do interviews have negative, unintended consequences, for instance, favoring candidates whose own sociodemographic characteristics are similar to those of the panelists?[21] The work of Goldin and Rouse on the impact of blind auditioning (i.e., the use of a screen) for female musicians underscores the importance of minimizing information about the ascribed characteristics of applicants.[22]

THE DYNAMICS OF PANEL DELIBERATION

Panel deliberations are greatly influenced by the behavior of the chair and the program officer during the meeting. There are important variations in how directive people in these positions are. They play a crucial role in setting the tone and in shaping the "group culture." They also determine whether the panel's decisions will be based on consensus or will require voting. Moreover, the program officer and the panel chair are the ones who have to manage overbearing personalities (the sure sign of a poor panelist), excessive alliances and allegiances, or strong disagreements. They have to do "repair work" when a panelist feels slighted (perhaps his/her expertise is not given proper recognition, or perhaps she/he believes that another panelist is not showing proper respect for a field or a topic).[23] To succeed at these various tasks, both the chair and the program officer need to have the respect of the other panelists. Respect may be granted because of professional status, knowledge, experience, or competence. Age, gender, race, and institutional affiliation (in the case of panel chairs) also have an impact. Indeed, much could be learned from studying age, race, and gender dynamics on panels. They would constitute fertile terrain for conversation analysts studying the gendered patterns of interruptions in group conversations,[24] as well as the gendered distribution of power and status within small groups.[25]

More generally, panel deliberations are also affected by the amount of information that panelists have about one another before the meetings. Do they know of their respective scholarly reputations? Have they read each other's work? Do they share friends or acquaintances? Do they come from the same institution, the same geographic area, or institutions with similar (or different) prestige levels? These factors influence feelings of proximity and differences as well as the extent to which one panelist is likely to defer to another's judgment beyond purely substantive reasons. Of course, one cannot entirely discount matters of intellectual taste (e.g., whether one panelist dislikes the type of scholarship that another panelist is associated with). Nevertheless, with only two exceptions, the interviews I have conducted with more than seventy-five panelists suggest that they all buy into a "culture of excellence" that prevents them from framing the outcome of the deliberations as a reflection of cronyism.

A last consideration concerning panel deliberations is whether they are binding on the program. In some cases, program administrators are allowed to "edit" the outcome of the panel deliberations to ensure that they reflect the program's objectives. We may consider the pros and cons of this practice for diversity and quality of awards.

RESOURCES PROVIDED TO AWARDEES DURING TENURE

Presumably, effectiveness of fellowship programs depends on what kind and amount of resources are provided to recipients. They generally include some or all of the following: tuition, stipend, housing, health insurance, travel, moving expenses, research funds. Are these sufficient to cover the full costs of the program/education that the fellowship is meant to support? The resources should be extensive enough so as not to exclude candidates from less-privileged backgrounds. The suitability of the size of the award should be assessed by considering average time to completion as well as the total cost of completing the program. Finally, administrators should consider the total cost by awardee and whether the program itself is cost-effective. We may discuss various available procedures for establishing cost-effectiveness.

Another type of resource provided by fellowships includes orientation sessions, seminars, and workshops where awardees can meet each other and develop relationships. Does the fellowship program put together a structure that makes it possible for awardees to develop into a peer group? What informal and formal knowledge and experience do fellowship holders gain from such a group? Are the groups only social? If so, do they strengthen the qualities that the program wants to strengthen? Finally, are awardees put in contact with potential mentors? Do they have access to advisors while in the program? And is there any follow-up after their completion of the program? These are all questions that are rarely considered in the evaluation of fellowship programs but that deserve consideration.[26]

EVALUATION OF THE PROGRAM

The last relevant dimension of the organizational features of programs is the mechanisms they have put in place to evaluate themselves. How do they assess whether they have identified the types of candidates they wanted to identify and achieved their objectives? How do they assess whether their program really makes a difference? The challenge, of course, is to disentangle the impact of an award on a career without having information concerning what the career would look like if the recipient had not benefited from the award. We also need to parcel out the impact of the award and that of broader social factors that facilitate or limit achievement. There is no easy answer to these questions, but a first step could consist in collecting narratives on awardees' life courses at regular intervals (e.g., five, ten, and twenty years after receiving the fellowship). Fellowship recipients could be asked to address questions such as: What has the fellowship allowed you to do that you would not have done otherwise? Has it opened doors to you that increased not only your performance but your access to other resources such as prestigious jobs and other fellowships? What kind of network has it allowed you to develop? What has been the impact of mentorship and cohort support on your trajectory? What are the factors that stopped your progress? Background questions could include whether awardees have received assistance from their extended family networks, including family friends.

Beyond identifying whether programs have an impact on individual awardees, organizations may also consider additional types of impact that may be relevant to their mission. In the case of the Social Science Research Council fellowship programs, the relevant types of impact have been identified as including Production of Knowledge, Capacity Building (including for leadership), Public/Policy Impact, Network Creation/Promotion, and Infrastructure. Other funding programs may follow in SSRC's footsteps in developing a specific framework of analysis for estimating success across a range of dimensions.

Again, programs have control over much of what goes on under the nine headings that were reviewed in this section. But they have no control over awardees beyond making resources available to them, boosting their confidence by selecting them, and affecting their identity by altering their life course. This is why it is important to turn to the two last dimensions of our inquiry, the cultural and structural determinants of success of fellowship competitions.

Cultural Determinants of Success: Taken-for-Granted Frames of Excellence

I focus specifically on the United States to describe the "cultural determinant" part of the equation. The "cult of excellence" is part of the American national character and of how other societies define American distinctiveness.[27] "Being number one," competition, and rankings are thought to have a special appeal for Americans. The competitive frenzy that surrounds standardized testing and college admission are only among the most visible expressions of this orientation.[28] University and college administrators are not immune from it: their ranking in *U.S. News and World Report* is of great concern to them and they strategize to maximize their relative position, being aware that it will affect their ability to attract students and faculty and to command the loyalty and generosity of their alumni.[29] Hence, rankings have a strong impact on many aspects of the higher education system.[30] They participate in defining a broad culture of excellence that shapes many aspects of the fellowship allocation process. I focus on this culture's impact both on the potential applicants and on the criteria that panelists use to assess candidates.

Let us first consider applicants, concentrating our attention on the students who are most likely to apply for a post-B.A. fellowship. It does not seem unreasonable to assume that many of the most competitive students have attended an elite college or university, and before that, either an elite private high school or one of the two hundred star American public high schools, which are located in towns such as Newton, Massachusetts, and Princeton, New Jersey, that have an exceptionally high local tax basis.[31]

Students who attend such high schools are often confronted daily and for several years with an environment that highly values achievement and entices them to perform. At the same time, they are under pressure to define their niche and figure out what will distinguish their college application from that of similarly high-performing and privileged youth.[32] These pressures often lead to a certain homogenization among young adults.

This phenomenon is described in a paper titled "The Best of the Brightest: Definitions of the Ideal Self among Prize-Winning Students," which documents and explains characteristics of the "ideal self" rewarded by the American educational system as defined and projected by high school students who have been selected as Presidential Scholars in a national academic competition sponsored by the Department of Education and a White House Commission.[33] Drawing on analysis of competition essays and interviews with awardees, we identified how these students implicitly and explicitly define the ideal self and what they do to demonstrate that they embody the characteristics of the self they perceive as rewarded by the American educational system. The data show that "morality" is the most salient dimension of the ideal self displayed by Presidential Scholars and that they define it in relation to self-actualization, authenticity, and interpersonal morality. They often resemble one another in the stress they put on self-actualization and on "being true to yourself" and "doing your own thing."

A growing number of teachers, scholars, and journalists have come to similar conclusions concerning the cultural homogeneity of college students and the unintended consequences of the hoop jumping they are subjected to, including at my former institution, Princeton.[34] Students understand that admission into a top college translates into lifetime advantages.[35] They learn to develop a flexible self, adapted to the imperatives of a growing competition for admission to highly selective colleges.[36] In one of the most cynical and familiar manifestations, many of them have come to view volunteering as an essential résumé component in college admission and the pursuit of awards. While they might profess belief in the motto "to thy own self be true," few of them engage in risk-taking behavior that would challenge cohort beliefs concerning what will give them "success," whether defined as admission to an Ivy League university or as a Rhodes or Marshall Scholar. For instance, Steinberg mentions a student who chose not to write her college admission essay on her passion for corresponding with death-row inmates for fear that it would reduce her chances.[37]

Although more empirical work is needed to establish the extent of the cultural homogenization process, it is certainly important to keep it in mind when evaluating fellowship programs, and particularly post-B.A. fellowship programs. Most likely, this process determines whether programs reach their objectives. Those judged the best performers may be the most conformist, or students who can demonstrate the greatest ability to jump through the hoops presented to them. If this is indeed the case, fellowship programs need to step back and reflect on whether this ability is what they really mean to reward. Such cultural assumptions are embedded in much wider belief systems about what defines the "modern self," which, according to Meyer is subjected to a highly institutionalized set of rules that includes an obligation to search for self-esteem, to be efficient and individualistic, and to develop an internal locus of control.[38] Fellowship administrators may be able to limit the impact of these cultural assumptions and maximize the diversity of winners by becoming attuned to the fact that some of these virtues (especially that of self-actualization) are class-specific and distinguish American upper-middle-class culture from American working-class culture and French upper-middle-class culture, among others.[39] Against this background, a successful competition would be one that rewards not only high performance, as it is conventionally defined, but also individuals who "think out of the box" and "trump the game." Many panelists consider great instrumentalism incompatible with the true originality that should define a culture of excellence. Instead of having to establish minute distinctions between candidates who resemble one another on quantitative and, increasingly, on qualitative measures, it may be preferable to attempt to enlarge the pool of candidates who have not been "prepped" for success but who may have impressive potential. Asking applicants to provide a narrative concerning how the project they proposed emerged, who helped them in developing it, and whether and how it is similar to the work of their mentor could be helpful in identifying the most original applicants.

Taken-for-granted frames of excellence also shape the work of evaluators. The implicit definitions of excellence shared by people who serve on fellowship panels is also a topic that remains largely understudied and one on which we are trying to shed some light, in the case of academic fellowship panels in particular.[40] For instance, Guetzkow and colleagues have found that the evaluation of originality proceeds at three levels. First, panelists assess the substantive contribution of a project on the basis of their expert knowledge of the field. Their expertise allows them to locate the project within available knowledge and approaches and to identify precisely whether and how it distinguishes itself from the rest. Second, discussions of originality are largely framed in moral terms and concern the character of the author and his/her work. A computer-assisted content analysis of forty-two interviews conducted with panelists reveals that winning applicants and their work were deemed courageous, ambitious, risk-taking, independent, curious, and intellectually honest. They were also characterized as "challenging the status quo" and as "exhibiting a passion for ideas." Likewise, the vocabulary used by panelists for describing lack of originality had a clear moral tone. Those at the losing end of the competition were deemed to lack ambition, energy, or creativity. The terms used by panelists to describe them include: complacent, tired, hackneyed, "rehashing," "spinning their wheels," traditional, "gap-filling," or alternatively, trendy and facile. Third, we find that discussions of originality are largely framed in emotional as opposed to cognitive terms. Respondents describe as "original" proposals that excite them. By comparing how panelists across a wide range of panels make explicit their criteria of evaluation when they are asked to explain or justify specific decisions in an interview situation, we may be able to reach a better understanding of how excellence is defined in academic and post-B.A. fellowship competitions. It is interesting to note that among the academics we interviewed, there seems to be a widely shared agreement that intellectual excellence exists, that the process of allocating fellowships is largely universalistic, and that "the cream rises to the top" (as opposed to being constructed by panelists).[41] Such assumptions appear to be a crucial feature of the cultural structures within which evaluations are conducted, and we need to gain better purchase on them if we are to truly understand the cultural determinants of the success of fellowship programs.[42]

Structural Determinants of Success

Some of the fellowship programs discussed in this volume have as a goal to alter life courses. Receiving a competitive fellowship certainly increases an individual's chances of success considerably, if only because it makes it more likely that she/he will be selected for other fellowships, following the principle of the Matthew Effect ("those who have will get") proposed by Merton.[43] Drawing awardees from a more diverse background would certainly increase the chances that such programs would reach their goals. In chapter 3, Heginbotham develops the notion of "trajectory" to assess the success of a competition, by considering the awardees' point of departure and social destination. A similar concept has been used by sociologists studying social reproduction and social mobility. It may be useful to revisit briefly what they have to tell us about the structural determinants of success, that is, the factors that make some individuals more likely than others to rise to the top of their field. Again, we need to recognize that the work of awardees may have a limited impact on the success of fellowship programs, and that this success also depends on social mechanisms that deserve consideration.

Perhaps the most important contribution to this topic to be made in recent years was that of the late Pierre Bourdieu, the influential French sociologist with whom I studied when I was a graduate student in Paris in the early 1980s. Bourdieu's reputation was first based on his writing with Jean-Claude Passeron on social reproduction.[44] In this book the authors argued that individuals from different social classes have access to very different resources (economic, cultural, and social capital), which they can mobilize in their pursuit of success. For instance, children of professionals and managers are exposed from a very early age to the middle-class culture that is valued by the educational system. In contrast, students from less-privileged backgrounds have to gain familiarity with this culture while at school. Thus, they have to accomplish more than middle-class students to reach a comparable level of performance, and as such, they are being "overselected" by the educational system. Consequently, they are likely to do less well and to sort themselves, or to be tracked, into the less-competitive educational programs that offer the lowest payoffs (vocational programs, for instance).

A large literature has applied Bourdieu's work to the United States and has shown how the transmission of privilege works in the American context, including through the educational system.[45] Along different lines, a long tradition of stratification and mobility research has examined the relationship between social origin and destination and has established time and time again that people with the most advantages get the greatest rewards.[46] Also of relevance are studies of the social processes such as racism and sexism that discriminate against specific groups, of the direct role played by economic advantages in securing better educational and professional opportunities, and of the cumulative advantage of background and social position at every stage of the development of the individual.[47]

Applied to the selection of fellowship recipients, these literatures can help us understand how, compared to less privileged people, individuals from middle- and upper-middle-class backgrounds are better able to mobilize their own and their family's economic, social, symbolic, and cultural capital in their pursuit of success. For instance, due to a lack of economic capital, children of disadvantaged backgrounds often cannot volunteer because they frequently have to work or take care of siblings. This may handicap them in the selection process. Their family is less likely to provide them with relevant social capital—in this case, ties to distinguished endorsees whose letters of recommendation have most impact on selection panels. Lack of social capital also reduces the likelihood that they will know about available fellowships and how to maximize one's chances of obtaining one. Moreover, their lower symbolic, cultural, and social capital is likely to influence their presentation of self on the application, their performance in the interview, and the likelihood that they receive a fellowship. These are factors that panelists should be mindful of if they want to avoid rewarding primarily those whose social background prepares them best to land prestigious fellowships of various sorts.

The large literature on the social determinants of the careers of professionals and managers and of elite school graduates is relevant to assessing whether awardees live up to their promise.[48] Here, I will focus on one study on the effects of having children on the lives of top-level women financial executives. The author, Mary Blair-Loy, has interviewed women in their thirties, forties, and fifties to identify the factors that led them to abandon full-time employment to raise children. She shows that the younger generation is considerably less likely than the older generation to work part-time after having children, both because their partners share more of the housework and because they have babies at an older age, at a time when they are further along, and more invested, in their careers. Older women were more likely to become homemakers after childbirth, in large part because their husbands tended to have all-consuming careers and did not share responsibility. Or else the older women were more likely to forgo childbearing and to divorce or remain single. Such factors are relevant for our purpose because they influence whether women who are fellowship recipients are as likely as their male counterparts to live up to their promise.[49]

Being a leader in one's field often results from the constant and incremental accumulation of achievements and rewards of various size and prestige over a long period of time.[50] Small, repeated divergences in the paths taken result in large, macro-patterns of inequality in the academic world and elsewhere.[51] Consequently, perhaps receiving a prestigious scholarship is likely to have the biggest impact on the trajectory of those who do not have all it takes to succeed: the award will be more likely to redirect this individual's trajectory and to open doors that would have been closed otherwise. From this proposition, it follows that the most successful programs are not necessarily the ones that produce the largest number of stellar leaders and exceptional individuals, but are the ones that increase substantially the likelihood that individuals with great creative potential are put on a substantially different trajectory. But then again, the success of a program has to be assessed not only in terms of its impact on individuals but also in terms of the program's distinctive objectives, including its broader social impact.

The evaluation of fellowship programs is an important topic to those who award fellowships, to scholars who study social processes, and to fellowship recipients and non-recipients alike. From the perspective of administrators, the efficacy of programs is an obvious concern, since their challenge is to make programs work! For scholars, the evaluation of fellowship programs raises all kinds of fascinating substantive issues (about competing definitions of scholarly quality, for instance) that remain largely unexamined. For recipients, a well-administered program can have a multilevel impact on their professional and intellectual trajectory by making resources available and prompting a redefinition of their self-concept and aspirations. For non-awardees, the mere process of applying for a fellowship can be an important source of inspiration and learning. Moreover, it is crucial that fellowship programs be perceived as equitable and effective by recipients and nonrecipients alike if the programs are to maintain their ability to establish meaningful symbolic distinctions between what is exceptional and what is not.

This chapter has argued that the effectiveness of fellowship programs requires consideration of four sets of questions pertaining to the *appropriate framework of evaluation,* the *organizational mechanics of programs,* the *cultural determinants of success,* and the *social determinants of success.* Organizational objectives and mechanics are only one part of the equation, and the only part over which programs have control. The success of awardees depends on many environmental factors that are far beyond organizational control. The effectiveness of a program is to be assessed on a number of criteria, but these should include minimizing the impact of cultural and structural determinants of success and ensuring that winners are chosen from a culturally and socially diverse pool of applicants.

Notes

1. In contrast, there is a sizable literature on what happened to graduates of elite high schools and to college students. See Karen D. Arnold, *Lives of Promise: What Becomes of High School Valedictorians—A 14 Year Study of Achievement and Life Choices* (San Francisco: Jossey-Bass, 1995); Heran A. Katchadourian and John Boli, *Cream of the Crop: The Importance of Elite Education in the Decade After College* (New York: HarperCollins, 1994); Robert Klitgaard, *Choosing Elites* (New York: Basic Books, 1985).

2. The Danforth and Kent Fellowships of the Danforth Foundation; the ERASMUS

Scholars Program administered by the European Commission of the European Union; the Fulbright Scholars Program administered by the Council for International Exchange of Scholars; the Graduate Fellowship and Israel Fellowship Programs of the Wexler Foundation; the International Dissertation Field Research program of the Social Science Research Council and the American Council for Learned Societies; the Markle Scholars' program; the Predissertation Fellowship Program of the Social Science Research Council; the Thomas J. Watson Fellowships; and the Women's Studies and the former Woodrow Wilson Fellows Program administered by the Woodrow Wilson National Fellowship Foundation.

3. Joseph Berger, *The Young Scientists: America's Future and the Winning of the Westinghouse* (Reading, Mass.: Addison Wesley, 1994); Harriet Zuckerman, *Scientific Elite, Nobel Laureates in the United States* (New York: Free Press, 1977). See also chapter 5 in this volume.

4. Michele Lamont, Jason Kaufman, and Michael Moody, "The Best of the Brightest: Definition of the Ideal Self among Prize-Winning Students," *Sociological Forum* 15, no. 2 (2000): 187–224; Angela Tsay, Michele Lamont, Andrew Abbott, and Joshua Guetzkow, "From Character to Intellect: Changing Conceptions of Merit in the Social Sciences and the Humanities," *Poetics* 36 (2003): 23–51; Joshua Guetzkow, Michele Lamont, Marcel Fournier, Gregoire Mallard, and Roxane Bernier, "Evaluating Creative Minds: The Assessment of Originality in Peer Review," paper presented at the symposium on Creativity, International Sociological Association Meetings, Brisbane, Australia, July 2002.

5. Ulrich Teichler, "Student Mobility in the Framework of ERASMUS: Findings of an Evaluation Study," *European Journal of Education* 2 (1996): 153–79.

6. Post-B.A. fellowship programs that focus only on the sciences or the humanities (Hughes, Mellon) are likely to employ panelists who are themselves experts.

7. Mihaly Csikszentmihalyi, *Creativity: Flow and the Psychology of Discovery and Invention* (New York: HarperCollins, 1996); Howard Gardner, *Intelligence Reframed: Multiple Intelligences for the 21st Century* (New York: Basic Books, 1999); Daniel Goleman, Richard Boyatzis, and Annie McKee, *Primal Leadership: Realizing the Power of Emotional Intelligence* (Boston: Harvard Business School Press, 2002).

8. K. Anders Ericsson, "The Acquisition of Expert Performance: An Introduction to Some of the Issues," in *The Road to Excellence: The Acquisition of Expert Performance in the Arts, Sciences, Sports, and Games,* ed. K. Anders Ericsson (Mahwah, N.J.: Lawrence Erlbaum Associates, 1996), 1–50.

9. See websites: www.tip.duke.edu and www.aagc.org/main.html.

10. Bruno Latour, *The Pasteurization of France* (Cambridge, Mass.: Harvard University Press, 1998).

11. Natalie Heinich, *The Glory of Van Gogh: An Anthropology of Admiration* (Princeton, N.J.: Princeton University Press, 1996).

12. Michele Lamont, "How to Become a Dominant French Philosopher: The Case of Jacques Derrida," *American Journal of Sociology* 93, no. 3 (1987): 584–622.

13. Howard Becker, *Art World* (Chicago: University of Chicago Press, 1983).

14. Michael Useem and Jerome Karabel, "Pathways to Top Corporate Management," *American Sociological Review* 51 (1986): 184–200.

15. Dean K. Simonton, "Creative Expertise: A Life-Span Developmental Expertise," in *The Road to Excellence,* ed. K. Anders Ericsson, 227–54.

16. Ibid., 241.

17. Paul J. DiMaggio and Walter W. Powell, "The Iron Cage Revisited: Institutionalized Isomorphism and Collective Rationality in Organizational Fields," *American Sociological Review* 48 (1983): 147–60.

18. Gregoire Mallard, Michèle Lamont, and Joshua Guetzkow, "The Pragmatics of Evaluation: Beyond Disciplinary Wars in the Assessment of Fellowship Proposals in the Social Sciences and the Humanities," paper presented at a conference of the Theory Section on "Sociological Theory and Empirical Research," American Sociological Association Meetings, Chicago, August 2002.

19. Ibid.

20. Pierre Bourdieu, *Distinction: A Social Critique of the Judgment of Taste* (Cambridge, Mass.: Harvard University Press, 1984.)

21. Rosabeth Moss Kanter, *Men and Women of the Corporation* (New York: Basic Books, 1977).

22. Claudia Goldin and Cecilia Rouse, "Orchestrating Impartiality: The Impact of 'Blind' Auditions on Female Musicians," *American Economic Review* 90, no. 4 (September 2002): 715–41.

23. Harold Garfinkel, "Studies of the Routine Grounds of Everyday Activities," in *Studies in Ethnomethodology* (New York: Prentice Hall, 1967), 35–75.

24. Peter Kollack, Philip Blumstein, and Pepper Schwartz, "Sex and Power in Interaction: Conversational Privileges and Duties," *American Sociological Review* 50 (1985): 34–46.

25. Cecilia L. Ridgeway, "Interaction and the Conservation of Gender Inequality," *American Sociological Review* 62 (1997): 218–35; Joseph Berger, Murray Webster Jr., Cecilia Ridgeway, and Susan J. Rosenholtz, "Status Cues, Expectations, and Behavior," in *Social Psychology of Groups: A Reader,* ed. Edward J. Lawler and Barry Markovsky (Greenwich, Conn.: JAI Press, 1993), 1–22.

26. Julian Wolpert, "The Wexner Foundation's Graduate Fellowship and Israel Fellowship Programs: A Tenth Year Evaluation," unpublished report, Woodrow Wilson School, Princeton University, 1997.

27. Richard M. Huber, *The American Idea of Success* (New York: Pushcart Press, 1971); Seymour Martin Lipset, *American Exceptionalism: A Double-Edged Sword* (New York: Norton, 1996).

28. Nicholas Lemann, *The Big Test: The Secret History of the American Meritocracy* (New York: Farrar, Straus and Giroux, 1999); Bill Paul, *Getting In: Inside the College Admission Process* (Reading, Mass.: Addison Wesley, 1995).

29. Wendy Nelson Espeland and Mitchell L. Stevens, "Peculiar Symbols: The *U.S. News and World Report* Rankings of Colleges and Law Schools," paper presented at the American Sociological Association Meetings, Chicago, August 2002.

30. Wendy Nelson Espeland and Michael Sauder, "Fear of Falling: How Law Schools Respond to Media Rankings," paper presented at the American Association of Law Schools, New Orleans, January 2001.

31. Jay Mathews, *Class Struggle: What's Wrong (and Right) with America's Best Public High Schools* (New York: Random House, 1998). We know that parents are attracted to these towns in part because they want to increase the chances that their offspring will receive high quality education and gain admission to a top college (although attending such schools may, in fact, reduce the likelihood of being admitted, according to Paul Attewell, "The Winner-Take-All High School," *Sociology of Education* 74, no. 4 (2001): 267–95. These schools seem like a reasonable alternative to paying the high tuition fees associated with private education.

32. Jacques Steinberg, *The Gatekeeper: Inside the Admission Process of a Premier College* (New York: Viking, 2002).

33. Michele Lamont, Jason Kaufman, and Michael Moody, "The Best of the Bright-

est: Definition of the Ideal Self among Prize-Winning Students," *Sociological Forum* 15, no. 2 (2000): 187–224.

34. David Brooks, "The Organization Kid," *Atlantic Monthly* 287, no. 4 (2001): 40–54.

35. Linda Loury and David Garman, "College Selectivity and Earnings," *Journal of Labor Economics* 13 (1995): 289–308.

36. Elizabeth Duffy and Idana Goldberg, *Crafting a Class: College Admissions and Financial Aid, 1955–1994* (Princeton, N.J.: Princeton University Press, 1998).

37. Steinberg, *The Gatekeeper.*

38. John W. Meyer, "Self and Life Course: Institutionalization and Its Effects," in *Institutional Structure: Constituting State, Society, and the Individual,* ed. George M. Thomas, John W. Meyer, Francisco O. Ramirez, and John Boli (Beverly Hills, Calif.: Sage Publications, 1987), 242–61; John Meyer and Ronald L. Jepperson, "The Actor and the Other: Cultural Rationalization and the Ongoing Evolution of Modern Agency," *Sociological Theory* 18, no. 1 (2000): 100–120.

39. Michele Lamont, *Money, Morals, and Manners: The Culture of the French and American Upper-Middle Class* (Chicago: University of Chicago Press, 1992); Lamont, Kaufman, and Moody, "The Best of the Brightest," 187–224.

40. Unlike the few available studies of the peer review process, e.g., General Accounting Office, *Peer Review: Reforms Needed to Ensure Fairness in Federal Agency Grant Selection: Report to the Chairman,* Committee on Governmental Activities, U.S. Senate (Washington, D.C.: GAO 1994). This study aims less at assessing the fairness of the process than at analyzing the substance of how quality is assessed. On grant-making processes, see Donald Brenneis, "New Lexicon, Old Language: Negotiating the 'Global' at the National Science Foundation," in *Critical Anthropology Now,* ed. George Marcus (Santa Fe, N.M.: School of American Research Press, 1999), 123–46.

41. Guetzkow, Lamont, Fournier, Mallard, and Bernier, "Evaluating Creative Minds."

42. William Sewell Jr., "A Theory of Structure: Duality, Agency, and Transformation," *American Journal of Sociology* 98 (1992): 11–29.

43. Robert K. Merton, "The Matthew Effect in Science," *Science* 159 (1968): 56–63.

44. Pierre Bourdieu and Jean-Claude Passeron, *Reproduction in Education, Society, and Culture* (Beverly Hills, Calif.: Sage, 1970).

45. David Karen, "Toward a Political-Organizational Model of Gatekeeping: The Case of Elite Colleges," *Sociology of Education* 63 (1990): 227–40; Annette Lareau, "Invisible Inequality: Social Class and Childrearing in Black Families and White Families," *American Sociological Review* 67 (2002): 747–76; Annette Lareau, *Inside Families: The Importance of Social Class in Children's Daily Lives* (Berkeley: University of California Press, 2003); P. McDonough, *Choosing Colleges: How Social Class and Schools Structure Opportunity* (Albany: SUNY Press, 1997); Michele Lamont and Annette Lareau, "Cultural Capital: Allusions, Gaps and Glissandos in Recent Theoretical Developments," *Sociological Theory* 6, no. 2 (1988): 153–68.

46. For cross-national purposes, see Robert Erikson and John H Goldthorpe, *The Constant Flux: A Study of Class Mobility in Industrial Societies* (Oxford: Oxford University Press, 1992).

47. David B. Grusky, *Social Stratification: Class, Race, and Gender in Sociological Perspective,* 2nd ed. (Boulder, Colo.: Westview Press, 2001).

48. Randy Hodson and Teresa A. Sullivan, *The Social Organization of Work* (Belmont, Calif.: Wadsworth, 1990); William G. Bowen and Derek Bok, *The Shape of the*

River: Long-Term Consequences of Considering Race in College and University Admission (Princeton, N.J.: Princeton University Press, 1998).

49. Mary Blair-Loy, *Competing Devotions: Career and Family among Women Financial Executives* (Cambridge, Mass.: Harvard University Press, 2003).

50. Lamont, "How to Become a Dominant French Philosopher."

51. Jonathan Cole and Burton Singer, "A Theory of Limited Differences: Explaining the Productivity Puzzle in Science," in *The Outer Circle: Women in the Scientific Community*, ed. Harriet Zuckerman, Jonathan Cole, and J. T. Bruer (New York: W. W. Norton 1991), 277–310 and 319–23.

5 | Pathways to Prominence

Explaining Contours of Career Hierarchy of American Rhodes Scholars

Ted I. K. Youn and Karen D. Arnold, with Mandy Savitz and Susan Legere

Winners of the U.S. Rhodes Scholarship competition are chosen as potential national leaders and are very likely to join American professional elites. For example, current and former positions held by the thirty-two members of the Rhodes Class of 1968 include a president of the United States; cabinet and subcabinet secretaries; federal judges; elected state and city officials; professors at Harvard, Princeton, Cornell, the University of Virginia, and other leading universities; influential research scientists; high-ranking military officers, corporate executives, and CEOs; a prominent arts administrator; senior partners in leading law firms; the former Washington Bureau chief of *Time* magazine; the president and general manager of the *Washington Post*; and a prize-winning senior reporter for the *Chicago Tribune*. The more recent Rhodes Class of 1982 is equally prominent, including several congressmen and an elected mayor, a Pentagon liaison officer to the National Security Council, State Department diplomats, professors at leading research universities, and an executive editor of *Nation*. What explains such attainment of status and influence in contemporary society? What role do educational institutions play in producing the next generations of elites?

Relatively little is known about how higher education shapes American society through choosing, socializing, and legitimating prominent national leaders. Over the past fifty years increased access to higher education; the civil rights, feminist, and gay rights movements; and the enlargement of American political participation have all moved in the direction of expanding social equality. The impetus for democratization has also led to widening participation by women and ethnic minorities among leadership groups.[1] The appearance of diversity is paradoxical, however. For example, upper-class cultural capital still matters profoundly in elite membership. Nearly all top national leaders continue to be wealthy, white, Christian males from the upper third of the social ladder.[2] It has been argued that the diversity forced upon the traditional power elite from external pressures may actually have helped to strengthen it by giving the elite "buffers, ambassadors, tokens, and legitimacy."[3] Furthermore, a handful of highly prestigious universities in American higher education continue to produce the majority of our nation's leaders.[4]

Have American elites become increasingly diverse in their social and educational backgrounds? Are educational pathways to prominence becoming broader and more profuse? Cultural and historical perspectives are needed to trace the role of higher education in generating social elites. This chapter reports findings from the first phase of a project on the higher education and careers of American Rhodes Scholars. Based on the data from a national survey of American Rhodes Scholars, the chapter focuses on the relationship of social origins, cognitive ability, educational credentials, and career attainment of elites from 1966 to 1992.

Higher Education and Social Reproduction of American Elites

Social science research in social stratification points to a well-established proposition: educational attainment has a significant effect on career achievement.[5] Distinctive college character, family and educationally conferred cultural capital, and cumulative advantage through prestigious credentials are theorized to account for the relationship between educational background and social stratification. The general theoretical framework of the growing importance of refined distinctions among educational credentials was advanced by Max Weber in *Economy and Society* as early as 1900. Prestigious educational credentials have a profound impact on careers of elites. Such credentials, according to Weber, support their "holders' claims to the monopolization of socially and economically advantageous positions."[6]

A series of studies in recent decades investigated the relationship between undergraduate institutions and graduates' occupational success. Research has demonstrated the importance of higher education institutions' general organizational character, especially as it relates to status, on the development of individuals and their likelihood of exceptional career achievements.[7] Taken together, these studies support the powerful influence of highly selective coeducational and single-sex liberal arts colleges in producing prominent graduates.

Along with distinctive socialization within certain colleges, the advantages conferred by prestigious baccalaureate credentials relate to the role of particular institutions in the greater society. All socializing organizations recognize the importance of the relationship with their social setting. One major effect of educational institutions as socializing organizations is the symbolic redefinition of graduates as possessing special qualities and skills associated with attendance. Colleges and universities vary in the kinds of individuals they are expected to produce and the kinds of changes in individuals that they can legitimately expect to effect. This social characterization occurs independently of whether or not actual changes in competency have occurred among students. The redefinition of the products of an organization, a validating process granted by societal constituents, is referred to as organizational "chartering."[8]

Like the idea of "institutional charters," screening theories dispute the existence of direct relationships between schooling and labor market success.[9] Screening and credential theorists argue that schooling itself is not productive in labor markets but that it simply sorts individuals by family origins, affective behavior, or ability. The main function of schooling is screening, with employers more likely to prefer graduates of highly selective colleges and universities. Given the tenuous connections between educational level, actual skills, and work requirements, "cultural credentials" in the form of prestigious college degrees serve as certification of ability, high educational quality, and "trainability."[10] A handful of prestigious institutions preserve their power and privilege in the status hierarchy by maintaining their gatekeeping function.[11]

The idea that a few highly visible organizations are chartered to produce elites raises profound implications about social relations among educational organizations. It invites the possibility of cultural gatekeeping organizations in the educational system in which a few schools might monopolize pathways into leadership roles.[12] When these gatekeeping organizations create an elaborate institutional field to govern cultural markets, other organizations mimic them in search of cultural legitimacy. Postsecondary schooling may construct a variety of "ritual structures" in order to dramatize the importance of high selectivity and exclusivity among its organizational members.[13] Such structures include formal curriculum, residential life, and an emphasis on intensity of relationship among participants.[14] These ritual structures help communicate deeper meanings of collective identity among students and validate the "charter" of an elite-forming institution.

The general thesis that institutional origins affect career success was reinforced by Robert J. Merton's well-known "Matthew Effect" in science careers. Merton argued that there is a continuing interplay between the status system, based on honor and esteem, and the academic prestige system, based on different life chances, which locates scientists in different positions within the opportunity structure of science. Those scientists who work with famous mentors, practice at prestigious institutions, or receive public recognition through grants and awards tend to be rewarded with further advantages. An important point is that, without deliberate intent, the

Matthew Effect operates to penalize creative but unknown individuals, thereby reinforcing the already unequal distribution of awards in the status system. Baccalaureate prestige, according to this notion, would result in differential chains of opportunities that would intensify inequality.[15]

Contemporary cultural theorists provide a theoretical understanding of the ways in which schooling reproduces social stratification through ostensibly meritocratic institutions. For example, Pierre Bourdieu sees the educational system as the principal institution governing the allocation of economic and symbolic status and privilege in contemporary societies. Schools, according to Bourdieu, offer the primary institutional setting for the production, transmission, and accumulation of various forms of cultural capital. Even though Western societies have expanded opportunities for education and democracy, glaring inequalities in wealth, income, and status hierarchies persist. The educational system continues the function of reproducing social class relations, reinforcing rather than redistributing the unequal distribution of cultural capital. By consecrating particular cultural heritages, schools and colleges also legitimate the status order among institutions. In spite of formal meritocratic rules, educational institutions actually enhance social inequalities rather than attenuate them.[16] Most importantly, as Bourdieu elaborates, a form of "the cultural arbitrary" is often manipulated by dominant groups in society, and they in turn establish the specific cultural content that defines what it means to be meritorious.[17] An example of this specific cultural content might easily be traditional forms of educational credentials or admission processes of highly prestigious institutions that represent the institutional embodiment of elite cultural attributes. The importance of cultural capital is underscored by findings of the importance of upper-class social background in many studies of contemporary elites.[18]

Generations of American Rhodes Scholars

Rhodes Scholars offer an ideal population for the investigation of higher education's role as a screen in producing members of professional elites. This analysis is part of a larger study of five historical cohorts of American Rhodes Scholars involving survey, interview, and archival data. The study traces American Rhodes Scholars in the last half of the twentieth century in order to determine how changing dynamics of merit, sponsorship, and democratization affect elite membership, socialization, occupational structures, and perceptions of leadership. Since 1903, thirty-two American Rhodes Scholars have been chosen annually for a two- to three-year fellowship for Oxford study and associated travel. Students compete during or soon after their final year of undergraduate study. The criteria for the scholarship are intellectual and scholastic excellence, exemplary character, potential for leadership in public service, and physical vigor.[19] Recipients of one of the preeminent honors in the United States, the nearly 1,700 living Rhodes Scholars are a strong presence among American elites.

The study began with the hypothesis that social democratization since World War II would result in greater diversity among American elites.[20] An important indicator of such democratization would be increased diversity over time in the number, type, and prestige of colleges and universities producing Rhodes Scholars. An earlier analysis, therefore, investigated the numbers of Rhodes Scholars from different institutions since the beginning of the scholarship.[21] We then concentrated on patterns of baccalaureate origins in four cohorts of Rhodes Scholars: immediate post-war (1947–49), civil rights era (1967–69), affirmative action era (1977–79), and Reagan/Bush era (1986–89).

In our previous paper, we reported that the presumption of increased baccalaureate diversity among Rhodes Scholars since World War II did not hold true for postsecondary background.[22] Tallies of undergraduate institutions revealed that just three universities have produced nearly one in five Rhodes Scholars since 1903. Since the beginning of the scholarship in 1903, graduates of Harvard, Princeton, and Yale have received 513 of the 2,812 Rhodes Scholarships given. The dominance of these three institutions has increased since midcentury. Beginning in the 1960s, the three leading institutions have produced one in three Rhodes Scholars. The "Big-Three" Rhodes schools produced two to four times as many Rhodes Scholars as the next most prolific institutions.

The Current Study

Having established a pronounced association between three prestigious universities and the Rhodes Scholarship, the study now turns to the ways elite baccalaureate credentials interact with pre-college cultural capital and cognitive ability to shape distinctive career outcomes. We seek to understand the joint and independent contributions of social class, ability, and educational background on career attainment of American elites since the Vietnam conflict and tumultuous cultural revolution of the mid-1960s.

If rewards come from participation in prestigious status cultures, then upper-class affiliations and credentials from high-status colleges should result in tangible career benefits. As many as 1,200 applicants compete for the 32 annual American Rhodes Scholarships.[23] Considering the formidable selection standards, it is very possible that these two elements—prestigious education and upper-class origins—would lead Rhodes Scholars into gateways to leadership roles. On the other hand, American society has undergone a process of democratization since the middle of the twentieth century. We wondered whether Bourdieu's contention that schooling reproduces existing social inequality holds true in post–Vietnam conflict America. Increased access to higher education, the civil rights movement, affirmative action, and the women's movement have all been forces for democratization in the United States. If the membership of American elites has indeed become more democratic, we would expect greater diversity among Rhodes Scholars and decreased prominence of social origins in determining career success. By the same token, greater undergraduate competition and diversity might increase the importance of cognitive ability in determining career prominence. The thesis of the importance of increasing democratization would also presume that the baccalaureate-career relationship would change over time in the direction of greater baccalaureate diversity, with the possibility of increased effects of cognitive ability and less importance of institution in determining professional attainment.

Research Question

With the spread of equality of opportunity in the last fifty years, how does the Rhodes Scholarship illuminate the relationship between higher education and career distinction? Is undergraduate education the definitive turning point in eventual career attainment? Does cognitive ability predict social mobility? Under what conditions do individuals fail to capitalize on Ivy League baccalaureate degrees or, conversely, do they rise to eminence from nonselective colleges? These questions are vital in uncovering whether higher education opens or closes opportunity for Americans.

Cultural capital theory leads us to hypothesize that individuals with the most cultural resources will attain the most valued educational credentials. The combination of privileged social origins and prestigious scholastic capital will lead to career prominence, according to this formulation, but cultural capital alone will also relate directly to occupational distinction. These relationships might change over time, however, as American society becomes more philosophically and practically egalitarian.

The central research question of the current study, therefore, is as follows: *What patterns of social background, ability, and baccalaureate credentials affect the career prominence of three generations of American Rhodes Scholars?*

We have avoided directional hypotheses because models of cultural capital and historical democratization make different assumptions that imply different hypotheses. For instance, a cultural capital view might anticipate upper-class individuals as more likely to select and be admitted to top baccalaureate institutions but also as more likely to achieve prominence regardless of university background. A focus on democratization would expect increasing diversity over time in Rhodes Scholars' social and baccalaureate origins and no particular link between social origins, educational prestige, and career attainment. Does ability play the chief role in determining opportunities in a competitive meritocracy? Does an increased degree of democratization enhance such chances among high-ability individuals? These are the central issues of this chapter.

Data Source and Sample

The population for this study included three cohorts of Rhodes Scholars from 1966 to 1992. Total population size was 570. (Several scholars died soon after their Oxford study and were omitted from the analysis.) Sample size will be reported for each analysis. Specifically, cohorts included: post–Civil Rights and Vietnam Era (n = 215): Rhodes classes of 1966 to 1972; Affirmative Action Era (n = 220): classes of 1976 to 1982; and Reagan/Bush Era (n = 218): classes of 1986 to 1992. Each class included 32 Rhodes Scholars.

We chose these three cohorts for two reasons. Most importantly, they represent key benchmark periods of distinct social change. Each period also represents an expansion of democratic institutions, including dramatic expansion of higher education and enlargement of social equality.[24] For example, the civil rights movement, anti-war uprisings, and youth culture all pointed to a democratizing impetus in society that might differentiate later cohorts from their predecessors. The second period was also marked by social upheavals associated with affirmative action policy. Women were first allowed to compete for the Rhodes Scholar class of 1977. Second, the choice of these three cohorts was made because both SAT and ACT scores were available for these classes.

The data for this chapter come from our recent survey of Rhodes Scholars and from public information about them. Survey data were collected in Spring 2001 from 874 U.S. Rhodes Scholars in five historical cohorts (an 85 percent response rate). The 40-minute survey was a structured questionnaire designed by the researchers and pretested and administered orally over the telephone by trained interviewers from the National Opinion Research Center at the University of Chicago between January and March 2001. The data on social origins, including father's education and father's occupation, were included in the survey. The chapter's analyses also use data from biographical print and electronic sources. Chief among these sources is *Who's Who.* Inclusion in *Who's Who* was determined from a name-by-name search in the Wilson Biographical and Genealogical Index, an on-line database including the family of *Who's Who* publications. We also drew from the *Register of Rhodes Scholars, 1903–1995* for the names of Rhodes Scholars' high schools. Finally, we received college entrance examination scores from the Educational Testing Service and the American College Testing program.

Analysis Procedures

Former Rhodes Scholars preside over many governmental, economic, and cultural institutions in contemporary society, leaving profound marks in major social institutions. Their pathways to prominence in society reflect contemporary contours of career hierarchies, potentially illuminating complex processes of how American society selects and sponsors individuals for public leadership positions. What patterns of social background, ability, and educational credentials shape prominent leaders? Our analytic model includes the following variables.

INDEPENDENT VARIABLES

Social Origins: High school background, father's education, father's occupation, and appearance in the *Social Register* comprised the measure of social origins. These variables correspond with social origin variables used in previous studies of elites.[25]

1. High School: Prestigious preparatory school attendance, according to the literature on elites, reflects inherited cultural capital and builds social capital in the form of useful connections to privileged classmates and their families.[26] More recent work argues that certain public high schools located in wealthy areas serve as feeders to prestigious universities and national elites by providing exceptional academic and social advantages to the top tier of their student populations.[27] We therefore investigated the relative effect of high school type, including famous preparatory schools, elite public schools, and other private and public secondary schools. Using high school information provided in the *Register of Rhodes Scholars, 1903–1995,* we classified each Rhodes Scholar as follows: (1) top preparatory school; (2) "elite public" high school; (3) other private, non-parochial school; (4) military academy; (5) Catholic high school; (6) non-elite public high school. We created a continuous variable for high school rank corresponding to this list, ranging from preparatory school at the top to unranked public school at the bottom.

2. Father's occupation and education: These are standard measures of social origins. Data for these variables came from the telephone survey. We ranked the occupations according to the Hollingshead Two-Factor Index of Social Prestige, a measure of vocational level that incorporates education, occupational prestige, and income.[28] The Two-Factor Index ranks occupations on a continuous 7-item scale ranging from major professional to unskilled laborer.

The co-authors independently ranked the father's occupations and then resolved discrepancies in discussion. When insufficient information was available, for instance to judge whether a businessman was a minor or major executive, we systematically varied conservative and liberal rankings.

3. *Social Register:* This is an upper-class index that lists members of families considered to be at the highest echelons of society in twelve major metropolitan areas.[29] Professional accomplishments alone are insufficient for *Social Register* listing; rather, inclusion is determined by peers through the ascribed status of one's family.

To determine whether Rhodes Scholars grew up in a family of social prestige, we searched *Social Register* volumes for fathers' names in the years and locations corresponding to the Rhodes Scholar's high school period. A dichotomous variable indicated *Social Register* family appearance (1); or no appearance (0).

Educational Background: Based on the Rhodes Scholarship dominance of Harvard, Princeton, and Yale that we had previously uncovered, we used a dichotomous variable to indicate baccalaureate origins. All scholars possessed an undergraduate degree as a requirement of the Rhodes Scholarship. We coded Rhodes Scholars as having received an undergraduate degree from Harvard, Princeton, or Yale (1); or having received a baccalaureate elsewhere (0).

Ability Measure: To determine the effect of ability on career prominence, we added SAT or ACT scores of Rhodes Scholars of these three cohorts to the analysis. Separate SAT verbal and SAT quantitative scores were used as a continuous variable.[30] ACT scores were converted to comparable SAT concordance measures according to the standard algorithm provided by the American College Testing Program (ACT).[31]

DEPENDENT VARIABLES

Career prominence, the outcome of interest in the current analysis, was measured by inclusion in *Who's Who. Who's Who in America* and associated *Who's Who* texts by field, region, and ethnicity are compilations of biographies based on the reference value of an individual's professional position and/or noteworthy career achievement.[32] *Who's Who,* according to Baltzell, is a "nationally recognized listing of brief biographies of the leading men and women in contemporary American life."[33] There are many limitations of this index as a full and accurate depiction of career achievement, including the voluntary provision of information by those selected by career achievement criteria rather than automatically included by virtue of official position. Still, as Baltzell states, "Whatever its inadequacies, *Who's Who* is a universally recognized index of an American elite" and has been used extensively in studies of eminence and elites.[34] *Who's Who* listings were obtained from the Wilson Biographical and Genealogical Index electronic data base and coded dichotomously: biographical listing appearing in national, regional, or field-specific *Who's Who* (1); and no biographical listing appearing (0).

ANALYSES

The analyses reported in this chapter include the last three cohorts of the larger Rhodes Scholar study, spaced around the turn of the decade in 1970, 1980, and 1990. We began the analysis with descriptive statistics characterizing the social origins, education, and prominence of the sample. This phase of analysis included some comparisons by cohort and gender. We also examined bivariate relationships among college prestige, father's occupation and education, and so forth.

After this descriptive phase, we constructed a logistical regression model, a multivariate technique for estimating the probability that an event occurs. Family background, ability scores, and educational background were entered in forced blocks as joint predictors of the likelihood of career prominence. This is an appropriate way to predict the probability of being listed or not listed in *Who's Who*.[35] Both the dependent variable, and one of the independent variables (baccalaureate prestige) are dichotomous variables. Assumptions of multivariate normality in ordinary least-squares regression and linear discriminant analysis do not hold for such 2-level variables, nor does ordinary regression result in predicted values that can be interpreted as probabilities. Logistic regression directly estimates the probability of being in *Who's Who* from the continuous and dichotomous independent variables. The parameters of the model are estimated using the maximum likelihood method. Logistic regression technique enables a test of how well the overall model fits the data, the relative contribution of each variable to predicting the odds ratio of *Who's Who* listing, and the effects, if any, of interactions between independent variables.[36]

Descriptive Findings

Social Origins of Rhodes Scholars

American Rhodes Scholars came primarily from middle- and upper-middle-class backgrounds. Overall, 50 percent of the group had professional or executive fathers; an additional 24 percent had fathers who were managers; 12 percent, administrative staff; 6 percent worked in clerical and sales; and 7 percent as skilled or unskilled laborers (see Table 5.1).

One-way analysis of variance showed no statistically significant differences among the three cohorts in the level of father's occupation, attendance at prestigious high schools, or appearance in the *Social Register*. Our assumption of increasing democratization in American society in the two decades following World War II led us to expect that later Rhodes Scholars would come from less privileged origins than earlier groups. This was not the case. Although all cohorts represent similar social backgrounds, it is notable that no cohort is solely dominated by upper-class members. It is also suggestive that the number of Rhodes Scholars with fathers employed in the lowest three categories, though small, decreased over the period associated with these cohorts. At the same time, the percentage of the two higher categories of occupation has steadily increased from Vietnam era to the 1990s.

Are Rhodes Scholars from Harvard, Yale, and Princeton children of upper-class families? Among Vietnam-era Rhodes Scholars, 34 percent of those identified from upper-class professional fathers attended the Big-Three institutions, and that increased modestly in the 1990s cohort (see Table 5.2).

Baccalaureate Origins of Rhodes Scholars

A previous paper described changes in baccalaureate origins of Rhodes Scholars since World War II.[37] Three institutions have come to play a dominant role in the production of Rhodes Scholars. From the first half-century of the Rhodes Scholarship (1903–46) to the present, Harvard, Princeton, and Yale have moved from producing one in five Rhodes Scholars[38] to supplying one in three today. The three cohorts in the current analysis document this trend. The "Big-Three" universities accounted for undergraduate degrees of just under a third of the entire sample. A closer examination shows that 25 percent of the post–World War II cohort received Big-Three baccalaureates; whereas 32 percent of the Cold War group, 36 percent of the Vietnam-era, 37.2 percent of the Affirmative Action-era, and 37 percent of the Reagan/Bush-era cohorts hold Big-Three undergraduate degrees.

The social origins of Rhodes Scholars play a role in baccalaureate credentials. Attending Harvard, Princeton, or Yale is modestly associated with a high-ranked high school and a professional father (r's = .15–.26, p<.01).

Ability

The early versions of both the SAT and ACT were viewed as a form of intelligence test. Since the initiation of the ACT Assessment test in the late 1950s, both the SAT and the ACT have been used to assess verbal and mathematical reasoning abilities that indicate potential college performance.[39] In the absence of standardized cognitive ability measures (i.e., an IQ test), we employed these test scores for the statistical models as measures of ability.[40]

In *The Shape of the River*, Bowen and Bok report that SAT scores continue to have some independent effect on advanced degree attainment as

Table 5.1
Father's Occupation by Cohort

Father Cohort	Higher Professional	Manager & Lesser Prof.	Administrative Staff	Clerical Sales	Skilled Unskilled	Total
Vietnam Era N = 180	43%	30%	12%	6%	9%	100%
Affirm Action Era N = 184	55%	19%	12%	6%	7%	100%
Reagan/Bush Era N = 206	52%	27%	11%	5%	5%	100%
Total	50%	25%	12%	6%	7%	100%

Table 5.2
Father's Occupations among Rhodes Scholars of Big-Three Graduates

Father Cohort	Higher Professional	Managers & Lesser Prof.	Administrative Staff	Clerical Sales	Skilled Unskilled
Vietnam Era N = 180	34	42	32	20	6
Affirm Action Era N = 184	36	15	32	19	23
Reagan/Bush Era N = 206	39	26	24	11	18

well as graduation rate and rank in class among those who were admitted to colleges by the race-sensitive admissions policy. They argue that SAT scores are useful in predicting advanced degree attainment and successes in college. Furthermore, they find that SAT scores are quite consistent predictors of high earnings for both men and women college graduates. The relationship between SAT scores and earnings, however, flattens out when the analysis moves to include the highest SAT levels, though even at this level, the differences in earning between men and women persist. It is interesting to note, as Bowen and Bok point out, that when selectivity of high school and social status were added to the model, high school prestige influences chances for attending a highly selective college.[41]

In the case of Rhodes Scholars, however, distinctions based on level of SAT score should not be overplayed among an extraordinarily high-achieving student population. In fact, over three-quarters of Rhodes Scholars received graduate degrees (83.5 percent). In view of the generally high academic standing of the entire Rhodes population, one should not be too surprised to see that a substantial number of those at the lower level of these SAT distributions went on to earn advanced degrees such as M. D.s, J. D.s, and Ph.D.s.

Table 5.3 illustrates the distribution of the mean SAT Verbal and Quantitative scores among the three featured cohorts of Rhodes Scholars.

Adult Prominence of Rhodes Scholars

Rhodes Scholars are not distributed evenly across national elites. The emphasis on higher education in Rhodes Scholar selection and Oxford study means that scholarship winners cluster in intellectual professions. Our preliminary analysis indicates that Rhodes Scholars are strongly represented in academia, law, government and public administration, the military, and journalism. Medicine, research science, and corporate leadership are reasonably well represented. As members of professional elites, Rhodes Scholars are underrepresented among artists, entertainers, entrepreneurs, labor leaders, and athletes.

As Table 5.4 shows, the Vietnam-era cohort is extremely well-represented among elites as measured by inclusion in *Who's Who*. This cohort has had time to reach the peak of their careers. The middle cohort graduated from college between 1976 and 1982 and is currently in their mid- to late-forties. This group is also strongly represented in *Who's Who,* even though their highest-level career achievements might occur within the next twenty years. The most recent cohort is currently in their early- to mid-thirties, and only five have already been listed in *Who's Who.* The timetables of their careers, including two to three years at Oxford and almost universal further graduate study, means that they are just beginning full-time professional

Table 5.3

Mean SAT Scores of Rhodes Scholars from the Big-Three and Other Institutions

Three Cohorts

Cohort		SAT Verbal	SAT Math
Vietnam Era	Big Three	680	689
N = 181	Non-Big Three	663	664
	All	669	673
Affirm Action	Big Three	686	689
Era N = 203	Non-Big Three	656	666
	All	666	673
Reagan/Bush	Big-Three	689	690
Era N = 211	Non-Big Three	636	665
	All	654	674
Total	Big-Three	686	690
3 Cohorts	Non-Big Three	650	665
	All	662	673

work. It is perhaps notable that any of this group has already been distinguished enough to be already listed in a biographical collection of prominent Americans.

Logistical Regression Analysis

The central question of the Rhodes Scholar study has to do with the conditions that lead to professional attainment and public leadership in adulthood. Appearance in *Who's Who* serves as the outcome measure for assessing professional prominence. We therefore conducted a logistical regression analysis of the relative contribution of social origins, ability, and educational background on the likelihood of appearance in *Who's Who*. As described previously, these were measured by father's education, father's oc-

Table 5.4
American Rhodes Scholars Included in
Who's Who by Cohort

Cohort	%
Post WWII	47
Cold War	51
Vietnam Era	39
Affirmative Action Era	19
Reagan/Bush Era	2.5

cupation, high school prestige, SAT verbal and SAT mathematics scores, and Big-Three baccalaureate versus all others. Table 5.5 shows the results of the logistical regression, conducted for the 570 cases in the Vietnam, Affirmative Action, and Reagan/Bush cohorts.

As Table 5.5 shows, the model fits modestly with chi-square = 17.060 with 6 degrees of freedom at $p = 0.009$, leading us to reject the null hypothesis and conclude that the overall model of social origins, ability, and educational prestige does predict the likelihood of professional prominence better than chance. Although the model is significant, the Cox and Snell and Nagelkerke R^2 statistics indicate that the amount of variability in *Who's Who* accounted for by the independent variables is quite modest. Similarly, a classification table derived from the model was not effective in predicting whether a Rhodes Scholar would be listed in *Who's Who*.

For each variable, Table 5.5 indicates logistic regression coefficients, standard errors, Wald statistics, degrees of freedom, and significance of the Wald statistics. Two variables contributed significantly to the overall model fit: SAT verbal score and baccalaureate prestige. Social origins and high school prestige did not contribute directly to the eventual likelihood of becoming prominent.

We conducted an analysis of residuals, considering the 13 outliers with standard residuals above 2 who had biographies listed in *Who's Who* but were mistakenly predicted as not appearing there. As compared to the larger Rhodes Scholar group, the outliers included a disproportionate number of African Americans and were concentrated in the Vietnam Era cohort. These students reported particularly positive undergraduate experiences. As adults, they were twice as likely as other Rhodes Scholars to be appointed to public office, were unusually well-connected to people of influence, and

Table 5.5
Logistical Regression Analysis of Social Class, High School Quality, SAT-V, and Baccalaureate Origin
on *Who's Who* (N = 570)

	Chi-Square	df	Significance
Model	17.060	6	.009

Cox & Snell R^2		.031
Nagelkerke R^2		.050
-2 Log likelihood		514.519

Variable	ß	S.E.	Wald Stats	df	Sig.	Odds Ratio
Fa Ed	-.163	.147	1.232	1	.267	.849
Fa Occ	-.036	.140	0.067	1	.796	.965
HS Prest	.203	.197	1.062	1	.303	1.225
SAT-V	.004	.002	4.046	1	.044	1.004
SAT-Q	.000	.002	0.012	1	.914	1.000
BA Prest	.506	.239	4.462	1	.035	1.658
Constant	-4.432	1.263	12.304	1	.000	.012

were highly involved in prestigious professional associations and political organizations.

Our research attempts to understand the career contours of a uniquely situated group of American elites. Logistical regression findings support an interaction between meritocracy and social reproduction explanations for the effects of schooling in which highly able individuals are eventually finely sorted on the basis of cultural capital.[42] Privileged social origins alone do not lead directly to the top levels of careers. Rather, upper-middle-class children are more likely to attend prestigious colleges. Attending Harvard, Princeton, or Yale then yields direct effects on professional prominence. The conversion of family cultural capital into occupational status is realized via the institution of higher education. Our data suggest that an important mechanism for this conversion occurs through the medium of verbal ability.

It should first be noted that Rhodes Scholars are all enormously accomplished. Their SAT scores are extremely high and narrowly distributed. Certainly, the group fits a meritocracy argument that only high-ability students become eligible for such high-status roles as Rhodes Scholars.

The high, narrow range of ability measures, social origins, and adult occupational positions is an indication of merit but also a problem in differentiating Rhodes Scholars as adults. It is therefore unsurprising that the overall logistic regression model is fairly weak, and it is perhaps also surprising that it does differentiate significantly among this extraordinary population. Even among these high-achieving individuals, attaining public prominence is significantly enhanced by the possession of prestigious credentials, specifically baccalaureate degrees from Harvard, Yale, and Princeton. The positive career effects of Big-Three degrees differentiate among Rhodes Scholars with similar ability or from varied social origins. As argued by Bourdieu, Collins, Useem and Karabel, and others, the prestige of credentials as a form of cultural capital makes a difference.[43] To extend Bourdieu's thesis further, we conclude that higher education contributes to the maintenance of unequal social rewards by privileging holders of cultural capital while disadvantaging others.

The point raised here leads us to consider the importance of structural features of undergraduate curriculum and a variety of ritualized forms of activity in different institutional settings. One of our previous analyses found that Rhodes Scholars were full-time, residential undergraduates engaged in academically intensive liberal arts study.[44] As undergraduates, these students participated in small seminars featuring discussion and writing, developed personal relationships with faculty, wrote senior honors theses, and participated extensively in extracurricular activities. They also benefited from the reputation of their college, earning a high-status credential that could be converted to additional educational opportunities and subsequent occupational entry. As Bourdieu observed in the French system of higher education, type and prestige of higher educational institution attended are critical to later careers and to reaching public prominence.

The role of verbal ability in converting academic talent into career prominence also supports Bourdieu's cultural capital analysis. Basil Bernstein argued that "status groups may be distinguished by their forms of language use" developed within the family, prior to the school years, as a result of class-based linguistic practices. Bernstein found that the very structure of intelligence was intimately related to socialized language use.[45] Bourdieu, like Bernstein, argues that language performance is the key to educational achievement. Cultural capital that is characteristic of dominant groups in society, such as verbal facility, knowledge about high-status institutions, and preference for so-called high culture forms of art and leisure, results in ways of perceiving and presenting oneself ("habitus") that are rewarded in formal education. In particular, a certain style of fluent speaking and writing is highly valued in schools. Students' social origins also determine their expectations about what they are likely to achieve and therefore shape educational and professional aspirations. Students from privileged social backgrounds are able to exchange their cultural capital for high grades, superior verbal SAT scores, prestigious educational credentials, and, ultimately, entrance into high-level professional circles.

In addition to bearing out the idea of verbal ability as embodied cultural capital, the importance of verbal SAT scores in the analysis supports the role of liberal arts education in preparing elites.[46] The Rhodes competition itself requires the highest degree of written and oral language ability. The Rhodes Scholar selection process requires written essays, intensive interviews by a group of former Rhodes Scholars, and a mandatory cocktail party. Surviving this gauntlet calls for verbal fluency, general cultural knowledge, social poise, and precisely the right level of assertiveness.

The historical period represented by the three focus cohorts began with an unprecedented broadening of access to higher education and expansion of the postsecondary sector. The huge baby boom generation swelled the number of college-age youth at the same time that more and more young men were choosing higher education as an alternative to the military draft. Women entered higher education in great numbers, eventually constituting the majority of American undergraduates. The story of the late 1960s and early 1970s points to inflation of educational credentials. It also suggests that the very top universities are acting increasingly as key gatekeeping institutions in supplying national professional leaders. The Big Three, particularly Harvard, are playing a crucial role of differentiating groups that are aspiring to gain access to credentials leading to membership in power elites. Harvard, Princeton, and Yale appear to serve much the same function in producing American elites as do Oxford and Cambridge in Great Britain. Not only are these three institutions producing highly disproportionate numbers of Rhodes Scholars, but their share of scholarship winners has increased over the past twenty-five years. Furthermore, the Rhodes Scholars with Big-Three degrees are more likely to become professionally prominent. It is clear, however, that prestigious higher education dwarfs the effects of upper-class background in determining graduates' entrance into professional leadership groups.

It is also apparent that the Rhodes Scholarship continues to be a highly effective institution in the preparation of prominent individuals. As with prestigious education, more research is needed to understand the interplay between selection and socialization in the Rhodes Scholarship success. The larger study currently in progress will gather data from interviews, telephone surveys, and campus site visits to help address this crucial question.

Notes

This paper is a fully collaborative effort by these authors. We would like to acknowledge helpful comments made by Caroline H. Persell, Michele Lamont, and David Swartz on our earlier version. We are also grateful to Larry H. Ludlow for his valuable advice in the methodological section. This research is supported by the Spencer Foundation's Major Grant Program and the Andrew W. Mellon Foundation.

1. Richard D. Alba and Gwen Moore, "Ethnicity in the American Elite," *American Sociological Review* 47, no. 3 (1982): 373–83; K. H. Jamieson, *Beyond the Double Bind: Women and Leadership* (New York: Oxford University Press, 1995); Richard L. Zweigenhaft and G. William Domhoff, *Diversity in the Power Elite: Have Women and Minorities Reached the Top?* (New Haven, Conn.: Yale University Press, 1998).

2. See Zweigenhaft and Domhoff, *Diversity in the Power Elite.*

3. Ibid., 191.

4. Ted I. K. Youn, Karen D. Arnold, and K. Salkever, "Baccalaureate Origins and Career Attainments of American Rhodes Scholars: A Test of Cultural Capital Theory," paper presented at the annual meeting of the Association for the Study of Higher Education, Miami, Florida, 1998; Michael Useem and Jerome Karabel, "Pathways to Top Corporate Management," *American Sociological Review* 51 (1986): 184–200.

5. Gary Becker, *Human Capital* (Chicago: University of Chicago Press, 1964); Peter Blau and Otis Duncan, *The American Occupational Structure* (New York: John Wiley and Sons, 1967); W. H. Sewell and Robert M. Hauser, *Education, Occupation, and Earnings* (New York: Academic Press, 1975).

6. Max Weber, *Economy and Society* (Berkeley: University of California Press, 1978), 999–1000.

7. Burton R. Clark, *The Distinctive College: Antioch, Reed and Swarthmore* (Chicago: Aldine, 1970); C. H. Fuller, "Ph.D. Recipients: Where Did They Go to College?" *Change* 18, no. 6 (1986): 42–51; R. H. Knapp and J. J. Greenbaum, *The Young American*

Scholar: His Collegiate Origins (Chicago: University of Chicago Press, 1953); R. H. Knapp and H. B. Goodrich, *The Origins of American Scientists* (Chicago: University of Chicago, 1952); M. Elizabeth Tidball, "Baccalaureate Origins of Recent Natural Science Doctorates," *Journal of Higher Education* 57 (1986): 606–20; M. Elizabeth Tidball and Vera Kistiakowsky, "Baccalaureate Origins of American Scientists," *Science* 193 (1976): 646–52; Lisa E. Wolf-Wendel, "Models of Excellence: The Baccalaureate Origins of Successful European American Women, African American Women, and Latinas," *Journal of Higher Education* 69 (1998): 141–86.

8. David Kamens, "Colleges and Elite Formation: The Case of Prestigious American Colleges," *Sociology of Education* 47 (1974): 354–78; J. W. Meyer, "The Charter: Conditions of Diffuse Socialization in Schools," in *Social Processes and Social Structures: An Introduction to Sociology,* ed. W. Richard Scott (New York: Henry Holt, 1970).

9. Ivar E. Berg, *Education and Jobs: The Great Training Robbery* (Boston: Beacon Press, 1971); Barry R. Chiswick, "Schooling, Screening, and Income," in *Does College Matter? Some Evidence on the Impacts of Higher Education,* ed. Lewis C. Solmon and Paul J. Taubman (New York: Academic Press, 1973); Joseph E. Stiglitz, "The Theory of 'Screening,' Education, and the Distribution of Income," *American Economic Review* 65 (1975): 283–300; Paul J. Taubman and T. Wales, *Earnings: Higher Education, Mental Ability, and Screening* (Philadelphia: University of Pennsylvania Press, 1972).

10. See Berg, *Education and Jobs;* Randall Collins, *The Credential Society* (New York: Academic Press, 1979); Lester Thurow, *Generating Inequality* (New York: Basic Books, 1995).

11. See Collins, *Credential Society.*

12. D. Karen, "Toward a Political-Organizational Model of Gatekeeping: The Case of Elite Colleges," *Sociology of Education* 63 (1990): 227–40.

13. David H. Kamens, "Legitimating Myths and Educational Organization: The Relationship between Organizational Ideology and Formal Structure," *American Sociological Review* 42 (1977): 208–19; Kamens, "Colleges and Elite Formation."

14. K. A. Feldman and Theodore Newcombe, *The Impact of College on Students* (San Francisco: Jossey-Bass, 1969); Kamens, "Legitimating Myths and Educational Organization"; Peter W. Cookson Jr. and Caroline Hodges Persell, *Preparing for Power: America's Elite Boarding Schools* (New York: Basic Books, 1985).

15. Robert K. Merton, "The Matthew Effect in Science," *Science* 159 (1968): 56–63.

16. Pierre Bourdieu, "Cultural Reproduction and Social Reproduction," in *Knowledge, Education, and Cultural Change,* ed. Richard Brown (London: Tavistock House, 1973); Pierre Bourdieu, "The School as a Conservative Force: Scholastic and Cultural Inequalities," in *Contemporary Research in Sociology of Education,* ed. John Eggleston (London: Methuen, 1974).

17. Pierre Bourdieu, *Distinction: A Social Critique of the Judgment of Taste* (Cambridge, Mass.: Harvard University Press, 1984).

18. Cf. Pierre Bourdieu, *Homo Academicus* (Stanford, Calif.: Stanford University Press, 1988); D. Karen, "Toward a Political-Organizational Model of Gatekeeping"; Patricia M. McDonough, *Choosing Colleges: How Social Class and Schools Structure Opportunity* (Albany: SUNY Press, 1997); Useem and Karabel, "Pathways to Top Corporate Management"; Zweigenhaft and Domhoff, *Diversity in the Power Elite.*

19. Frank Aydelotte, *The American Rhodes Scholarships: A Review of the First Forty Years* (Princeton, N.J.: Princeton University Press, 1946); Rhodes Scholarship Trust, *The Rhodes Scholarship Trust* (Claremont, Calif.: Rhodes Scholarship Foundation, 1995); Robert I. Rotberg, *Cecil Rhodes and the Pursuit of Power* (New York: Oxford University Press, 1988).

20. Martin Trow, "The Democratization of Higher Education in America," *European Journal of Sociology* 3 (1962): 231–62; Robert Lerner, Althea K. Nagai, and Stanley Rothman, *American Elites* (New Haven, Conn.: Yale University Press, 1996).

21. See Youn, Arnold, and Salkever, "Baccalaureate Origins and Career Attainments of American Rhodes Scholars."

22. Ibid.

23. Thomas J. Schaeper and Kathleen Schaeper, *Cowboys into Gentlemen: Rhodes Scholars, Oxford, and the Creation of an American Elite* (New York: Berghahn Books, 1998).

24. In 1980 the Carnegie Council on Policy Studies in Higher Education documented the expansion in American higher education following World War II. After increasing more than 50 percent between 1940 and 1950, enrollment more than doubled in each of the next two decades.

25. Cf. E. Digby Baltzell, " 'Who's Who in America' and 'The Social Register': Elite and Upper Class Indexes in Metropolitan America," in Reinhard Bendix and Seymour Martin Lipset, eds., *Class, Status and Power: A Reader in Social Stratification* (Glencoe, Ill.: Free Press, 1953), 172–84; Cookson and Persell, *Preparing for Power;* Useem and Karabel, "Pathways to Top Corporate Management."

26. Baltzell, "Who's Who"; Cookson and Persell, *Preparing for Power;* Useem and Karabel, "Pathways to Top Corporate Management." Elite boarding schools include Choate, Deerfield Academy, Episcopal High School, Groton, Hill, Hotchkiss, Kent, Lawrenceville, Middlesex, Milton, Phillips Academy (Andover), Phillips Exeter, Portsmouth Priory, St. George's, St. Mark's, St. Paul's, Taft, and Woodberry Forest School.

27. Jay Mathews, *Class Struggle: What's Wrong (and Right) with America's Best Public High Schools* (New York: Random House, 1998). Rankings based on index measuring number of advanced placement (AP) courses per graduating senior. Only public schools selecting half or less of the student body by examination or other academic criteria were included.

28. A. B. Hollingshead, *Two Factor Index of Social Position* (New Haven, Conn.: Author, 1957).

29. Baltzell, "Who's Who."

30. All cohorts took the SAT prior to test score recentering in 1993.

31. Neil J. Dorans, *The College Board Technical Handbook for the Scholastic Aptitude Test and Achievement Tests* (New York: College Entrance Examination Board, 1984).

32. *Who's Who in America*, 90th ed. (New Providence, N.J.: Marquis Publishing Company, 1989).

33. Baltzell, "Who's Who," 271.

34. Ibid.

35. David W. Hosmer Jr. and Samuel L. Lemeshow, *Applied Logistic Regression* (New York: John Wiley and Sons, 1989).

36. The logistic model is based on the cumulative logistic probability function and specified as:

$$\text{Probability} \quad [Y_i = 1] = P_i = \frac{1}{1 + e^{-(a + \beta X_i)}} \quad (1)$$

where P_i is the probability that Y, the outcome in question will take place for the inth individual, e represents Euler's constant, α is the intercept parameter, X_i is a vector of explanatory variables, and β is a vector of parameter estimates for each of independent variables in the vector X_i.

Transforming this equation by taking logs, we have:

$$\text{logit } (P_i) = \alpha + \beta_1 X_i + \beta_2 X_j + K \beta_n X_k \qquad (2)$$

The logarithm of the odds that a particular outcome will occur (the log odds ratio) is a linear function of the independent variables.

37. Youn, Arnold, and Salkever, "Baccalaureate Origins and Career Attainments of American Rhodes Scholars."

38. Aydelotte, *American Rhodes Scholarships.*

39. Dorans, *College Board Technical Handbook;* Neil J. Dorans, "Correspondence between ACT and SAT I scores," *College Board Research Report* 99, no. 1 (New York: College Board, 1999).

40. The Rhodes Scholarship Trust does not collect test information as part of the application process. We obtained SAT and ACT scores from their respective testing organizations.

41. William G. Bowen and Derek Bok, *The Shape of the River: Long-Term Consequences of Considering Race in College and University Admissions* (Princeton, N.J.: Princeton University Press, 1998).

42. Michael Young, *The Rise of the Meritocracy, 1870–2033* (New York: Random House, 1959); Pierre Bourdieu, "Cultural Reproduction and Social Reproduction," 43; Pierre Bourdieu, *Outline of a Theory of Practice* (Cambridge: Cambridge University Press, 1977); Randall Collins, "Functional and Conflict Theories of Educational Stratification," *American Sociological Review* 36 (1971): 1002–19; Useem and Karabel, "Pathways to Top Corporate Management."

44. See Arnold, Youn, and Savitz, "Baccalaurcate Origins and Career Attainments of American Rhodes Scholars."

45. Boris Bernstein, *Class, Codes, and Control* (London: Routledge and Kegan Paul, 1975), 1:289.

46. Arnold, Youn, and Savitz, "Baccalaureate Origins and Career Attainments of American Rhodes Scholars."

Appendix 1
Opportunities for Competitive Scholarships

Objectives and Brief Descriptions of Selected Nationally and Internationally Competitive Fellowship Programs

Beinecke Scholarship

(Annually 20, two-year duration)
Each year approximately one hundred colleges and universities are invited to nominate a student for a Beinecke Scholarship, and a maximum of twenty scholarships are awarded. Each school invited to participate in the Beinecke Scholarship Program is permitted to make a single nomination each year.

To be eligible for a Beinecke Scholarship, a student must:

- have demonstrated superior standards of intellectual ability, scholastic achievement, and personal promise during his or her undergraduate career;
- be a college junior who plans to continue full-time undergraduate study and who expects to receive a baccalaureate degree between December and August of the following year;
- be a U.S. citizen or a U.S. national from American Samoa or the Commonwealth of the Northern Mariana Islands;
- have a documented history of receiving need-based financial aid during his or her undergraduate years. The amount of financial need is not a major factor; nevertheless, preference is given to candidates for whom the awarding of a scholarship would increase the likelihood of the student's being able to attend graduate school.

www.beineckescholarship.org

Churchill Scholarships

(Annually 10, one-year duration, participating institutions only)
Churchill Scholarships enable American students of exceptional ability,

enrolled at one of the 80 participating institutions, to study engineering, mathematics, or science at Cambridge, one of the world's great universities. The Churchill Scholarships also provide the opportunity to experience life in Britain, to get to know and forge friendships with British students and those from many other lands who are enrolled at Cambridge, to see something of Europe and lands beyond, to see the United States from a new perspective, and to gain insights about oneself that come from living abroad and adjusting to new challenges.

The criteria for the selection of Churchill Scholars include the following:

- achievement in academic work as indicated by course grades
- scores on the Graduate Record Examination
- capacity for original, creative work as shown by special recognition and letters of reference
- character, adaptability, and a demonstrated concern for the critical problems of society
- good health

www.thechurchillscholarships.com

Commonwealth Scholarships and Fellowships Plan

(Annually 600, up to three-year duration)

The Commonwealth Scholarships and Fellowships Plan was instigated at the first Conference of Commonwealth Education Ministers in 1959. The intention was that awards would be offered by a range of Commonwealth countries, with each country determining the size and nature of its own contribution. At present, awards are available in Australia, Brunei, Cameroon, Canada, India, Jamaica, New Zealand, Nigeria, Malaysia, Mauritius, South Africa, Trinidad, Tobago, and the United Kingdom. In total, almost 22,000 individuals have held awards since the scheme commenced.

The United Kingdom is the largest contributor to the Plan, currently making 350–400 awards each year. The main funding for Britain's contribution comes from the Department of International Development (DFID), which supports awards to developing Commonwealth countries, and the Foreign and Commonwealth Office (FCO), which supports scholarships to Australia, Bahamas, Brunei, Canada, Cyprus, Malta, New Zealand, and Singapore. The two sponsors have different but overlapping objectives. DFID policy is concerned with meeting international poverty reduction targets; FCO, with making long-term friends for the United Kingdom and thus enhancing our role in the world. Both approaches, however, require recruitment of high-quality students who can be expected to return and make a significant impact in their home country following their award. Awards in the United Kingdom now divide into six categories, as follows:

- General Scholarships. The largest category, with about 150 awards per year for conventional doctoral or masters-level study. Open to citizens of all Commonwealth countries other than the United Kingdom.
- Academic Staff Scholarships. Approximately 30 awards per year for postgraduate study. Open to young staff of universities in selected developing countries.
- Academic Fellowships. Support established academic staff in developing country universities to spend six month periods of collaboration or professional updating in the United Kingdom. About 80 awards per year.
- Split Site Doctoral Scholarships. Support scholars already undertaking doctoral research in developing countries to spend up to one year at a U.K. university, under joint supervision, as part of their studies. About 30–35 awards per year.
- Scholarships by Distance Learning. A pilot scheme offering scholarships on four masters-level courses, offered by U.K. universities in partnership with developing country institutions. Typically 60–70 awards annually.
- Professional Fellowships. Awards which support established professionals in areas key to international development to spend three-month periods of updating and career development with a U.K. host institution. Approximately 30 awards.

Selection methods vary between schemes but generally emphasize partnership between home and host country. In the General Scholarships scheme, for example, nominating agencies in each Commonwealth country make nominations after national competition. Of these, about one third are selected for awards in a competitive process in the United Kingdom. www.acu.ac.uk/

Jack Kent Cooke Graduate Scholarship Program

(Annually 35, two-year duration)

This new graduate scholarship competition provides funding for tuition, room and board, required fees, and books for up to six years of graduate study. Scholarship amounts vary for each recipient based on several factors, including costs at the institution he or she attends; awards cannot exceed $50,000 annually. Scholars may use the award to attend any accredited graduate school in the United States or abroad to pursue any graduate degree or any professional degree, including medicine, law, or business. Each award will be renewable annually as long as the student maintains high academic performance, exhibits good conduct, and makes significant progress toward a degree.

A panel of academic professionals will review and evaluate all eligible fellowship applications for recommendation to the Jack Kent Cooke Foundation. The Foundation will make the final selections. Award selection criteria include the following:

- academic achievement and intelligence
- financial need
- will to succeed
- leadership and public service
- critical thinking ability
- potential to make a significant contribution to field of study and/or society
- appreciation for/participation in the arts and humanities

www.jackkentcookefoundation.org/

Deutscher Akademischer Austauschdienst (DAAD)

The purpose of DAAD is to promote relations between institutions of higher education in Germany and abroad, primarily through the exchange of students, academics, and scientists. Goals include: encouraging leading young academics and scientists from abroad to study and do research in Germany; helping young German academics and research scientists to qualify themselves at the very best institutions all around the world; assisting the developing countries in the South and the reforming states of the East to establish efficient higher education structures. These objectives take on structure in more than two hundred DAAD programs, which are open to all disciplines and all countries, and to foreigners and Germans alike.

Criteria for the selection of DAAD scholars are:

- academic excellence, intellectual promise, creativity, and critical thinking
- potential for future leadership in the fields of science and culture, business, and politics in the spirit of international and intercultural experience
- a sense of social and political responsibility

Study Scholarships for Graduates of All Disciplines

OBJECTIVE

Study scholarships are awarded to provide foreign graduates of all disciplines with opportunities to complete a postgraduate or master's degree course at a German higher education institution and to gain a degree in Germany (master's/diploma).

DURATION

Depending on the length of the chosen degree course or study project, the study scholarship will be awarded for between 10 and 24 months. Initially, scholarships are awarded for one academic year and can be extended for students with good study achievements to cover the full length of the chosen degree course.

VALUE

- The DAAD will pay a monthly award of 715 euros or, in exceptional cases for applicants holding advanced qualifications (e.g., a doctorate/Ph.D.), 975 euros plus travel and luggage costs and a health insurance allowance. In addition to these payments, the DAAD will pay a study and research allowance and, where appropriate, a rent subsidy and family allowance.
- Tuition fees cannot be paid by the DAAD.

REQUIREMENTS

- Applications for DAAD study scholarships are open to excellently qualified graduates who, when they commence their scholarship-supported studies, hold a bachelor's, diploma, or comparable academic degree. Doctoral candidates cannot be considered for this program. The DAAD "Research Grant" program is available for such candidates.
- Besides previous academic achievements, the most important selection criterion is a convincing presentation of the applicant's academic and personal reasons for the planned study project in Germany.
- Applications must either include the notification of admission issued by the German host institution for the desired degree course, or the notification of admission must be presented to the DAAD before the scholarship-supported studies begin. The award letter from the DAAD only becomes effective once the holder has been admitted to studies.
- Good German language skills are generally a requirement for studying in Germany. Exceptions are possible when scholarship holders are enrolled in degree courses which are instructed in English. The DAAD may fund attendance of a German language course at a language school in Germany before the scholarship-supported studies begin. This is free of charge to the scholarship holder.
- The age limit at the time of when the scholarship-supported stay begins is 32.
- Applicants who will already have been in Germany for more than two years at the time they begin the scholarship-supported studies cannot be considered.

Research Grants for Doctoral Candidates and Young Academics and Scientists

OBJECTIVE

Research grants provide young foreign academics and scientists with an opportunity to carry out a research project or a course of continuing education and training at a German higher education institution or non-university research institute. Research grants can be used to carry out:

- research projects at a German higher education institution for the purpose of gaining a doctorate in the home country (this includes the doctoral programs offered for developing and transformation countries under the "DAAD Sandwich Model");
- research projects at a German university for the purpose of gaining a doctorate in Germany;
- research projects or continuing education and training, but without aiming for a formal degree/qualification.

DURATION

- The length of the grant is set by the grant committee at the selection session. Depending on the project in question and on the applicant's work schedule, grants can be paid generally for one to ten months; in the case of full doctoral programs in Germany, for up to three years; and in exceptions, for a maximum of four years.
- Support can only be provided for the completion of a full doctoral program in Germany when special support reasons exist, for example, the lack of comparable research or academic supervision opportunities in the home country or a doctoral topic that requires several years of research in Germany.
- Support for full doctoral programs in Germany is based on a program length of three years; if foreign graduates first have to qualify for admission to a doctoral program, then grants can be awarded for a period of four years. Even when support has been awarded for a full doctoral program, that award will initially be limited to a maximum of one year.

VALUE

- Depending on the award holder's academic level, the DAAD will pay a monthly award of 715 euros (graduates holding a first degree), 795 euros (doctoral candidates) or 975 euros (doctoral candidates with at least two years' academic work experience), plus travel and luggage costs and a health insurance allowance.
- Award holders completing a stay of more than six months receive a study and research allowance plus, where appropriate, a rent subsidy and family allowance. Funding for attendance of a language course is decided on a case-by-case basis.
- When award holders take doctoral programs run under the "DAAD Sandwich Model," then the award may include the travel expenses of an academic supervisor—if applied for in the first application.

REQUIREMENTS

- Applications for DAAD research grants are open to excellently qualified university graduates who hold a diploma or master's degree at the time they commence the grant-supported research and, in exceptional cases, graduates holding a bachelor's degree or already holding a doctorate.
- Doctoral candidates wishing to take a Ph.D. in their home country will already have been admitted to an appropriate course at their home university.
- The application papers must generally include written confirmation of academic supervision by a professor in Germany and expressly refer to the applicant's project, thereby confirming that the host institute will provide a workplace. If the applicant is planning to complete a doctorate at the German host university, the letter of confirmation must come from the academic supervisor (Doktorvater/Doktormutter) for the applicant's doctoral program/thesis.
- The most important selection criterion is a convincing and well-planned research or continuing education and training project to be completed during the stay in Germany and which has been coordinated and agreed with an academic supervisor at the chosen German host institute.
- German language skills are generally required, although the level depends on the applicant's project as well as on opportunities for learning German in the home country. In the natural sciences and in engineering, and when English is spoken at the host institute, proof of good English language skills may be accepted. The DAAD decides on a case-by-case basis whether the applicant can attend a German language course before beginning the research grant.
- The award of DAAD research grants for doctoral candidates and young academics is subject to an age limit of 32, although exceptions are possible.

www.daad.de

ERASUMUS/SOCRATES Program (European Commission)

(One semester or one-year duration)

ERASMUS is the higher education section of the European Community action program called SOCRATES. ERASMUS is an EU-funded program which contains a wide range of measures designed to support the European activities of higher education institutions, including mobility and exchange of their students and teaching staff. ERASMUS is an acronym for EuRopean Action Scheme for the Mobility of University Students.

The program is open to the fifteen member states of the European

Union; the three EEA countries (Iceland, Liechtenstein, and Norway); and the twelve associated countries (Bulgaria, the Czech Republic, Cyprus, Estonia, Hungary, Latvia, Lithuania, Malta, Poland, Romania, the Slovak Republic, Slovenia). Turkey is presently negotiating its possible future participation.

Background

The SOCRATES II program supports European cooperation in eight areas, from school to higher education, from new technologies to adult learners. The higher education section of SOCRATES II, ERASMUS, was established in 1987. It is named after the philosopher, theologian, and humanist Erasmus of Rotterdam (1465–1536). An untiring adversary of dogmatic thought in all fields of human endeavor, Erasmus lived and worked in several parts of Europe in quest of the knowledge, experience, and insights which only such contacts with other countries could bring.

Objectives

Higher education plays a crucial role in producing high-quality human resources, disseminating scientific discovery and advanced knowledge through teaching, adapting to the constantly emerging needs for new competencies and qualifications, and educating future generations of citizens in a European context. All such functions are of vital importance to the long-term development of Europe. The increasing speed at which existing knowledge becomes obsolete and the rapid changes in the means by which it is delivered and renewed will require the higher education sector to adopt new methods and commit itself wholeheartedly to the provision of lifelong learning.

Against this background, ERASMUS contains a wide range of measures designed to support the European activities of higher education institutions and to promote the mobility and exchange of their teaching staff and students.

Participating Countries

Adopted on 24 January 2000 and spanning the period until the end of 2006, SOCRATES and its ERASMUS action are now open to the participation of the 30 countries described above.

Key Features

As in the past, ERASMUS is open to all types of higher education institutions (for which the term "universities" is generally used), all academic disciplines, and all levels of higher education study up to and including the doctorate.

While the promotion of "physical mobility," mainly of students, constituted the main thrust of ERASMUS Phase I and II, the higher education section of SOCRATES seeks to integrate such mobility into a wider framework of cooperation activities which aim at developing a "European Dimension" within the entire range of a university's academic programs. "Bringing students to Europe, bringing Europe to all students" is the new spirit of ERASMUS. While student mobility retains a position of central importance within the program, stronger incentives are now available to encourage universities to add a European perspective to the courses followed by students who do not participate directly in mobility.

From 1987/88 to 1999/2000, about 750,000 university students have spent an ERASMUS period abroad, and more than 1,800 universities (or other higher education institutions) are presently participating in the program.

The EU budget of SOCRATES/ERASMUS for 2000–2006 amounts to around 950 Mio (of which approximately 750 Mio is for student grants). Additional funds are provided in each country by public authorities, by the universities themselves, and by other organizations.
http://europa.eu.int

Ford Foundation International Fellowships Program (IFP)

(Duration varies by program, 300–400 annually; 3,500 awardees by 2010)

The Ford Foundation International Fellowships Program (IFP) provides opportunities for advanced study to exceptional individuals who will use this education to become leaders in their respective fields, furthering development in their own countries and greater economic and social justice worldwide. To ensure that Fellows are drawn from diverse backgrounds, IFP actively seeks candidates from social groups and communities that lack systematic access to higher education.

IFP is the largest single program ever supported by the Ford Foundation. By investing $280 million over ten years through 2010, the Foundation intends to build on its half-century of support for higher education. Foundation programs have long promoted the highest educational standards and achievement. Ford fellowship recipients have become leaders in institutions around the world and have helped build global knowledge in fields ranging across the natural and social sciences as well as the humanities and arts. IFP draws on this tradition and underscores the Foundation's belief that education enables people to improve their own lives as well as to assist others in the common pursuit of more equitable and just societies.

Fellows are chosen on the basis of their leadership potential and commitment to community or national service as well as for their academic achievement and potential. Fellows may enroll in master's or doctoral programs and may pursue any academic discipline or field of study that is consistent with the interests and goals of the Ford Foundation. Support is provided for up to three years, and Fellows may choose to study in their home countries or regions or internationally. Placement assistance is provided to Fellows who do not have prior admission to recognized graduate-level programs and may be combined with pre-academic training of up to one year in language, research, computer, and intercultural skills. The program also provides Fellows with opportunities for networking, building leadership skills, professional development, and post-fellowship activities. There is no age limit for applicants.

Applicants must be resident nationals or residents of an eligible IFP country. In addition, successful candidates will:

- demonstrate superior achievement in their undergraduate studies and hold a baccalaureate degree or its equivalent;
- have substantial experience in community service or development-related activities;
- possess leadership potential evidenced by their employment and academic experience;
- propose to pursue a post-baccalaureate degree that will directly enhance their leadership capacity in a practical, policy, academic, or artistic discipline or field corresponding to one or more of the Foundation's areas of endeavor;
- present a plan specifying how they will apply their studies to social problems or issues in their own countries and commit themselves to working on these issues following the fellowship period. IFP selects Fellows on the strength of their clearly stated intention to serve their communities and countries of origin, and expects that they will honor this obligation.

IFP Fields of Study

IFP Fellows may choose to study in any academic discipline or field of study that fosters the Foundation's goals of strengthening democratic values, reducing poverty and injustice, promoting international cooperation, and advancing human achievement. At present, the Foundation achieves these goals by providing grants to individuals and institutions working in three major fields: asset building and community development; peace and social justice; and education, media, arts, and culture.

Applicants must demonstrate a clear connection between their proposed academic discipline and the social issue or problem they wish to address.

How Will the IFP Experience Be Documented and Evaluated?

The International Fellowships Fund (IFF), the organization responsible for the overall management of IFP, works with its various partner organizations around the world to produce articles, reports, and videos on the program. Press clippings and other publicity materials will be posted on the IFP website (www.fordifp.net); and a video of the first Fellows Leadership Institute, held at the School for International Training in Brattleboro, Vermont, is already available. The first IFP Annual Report was published in spring 2003.

The Center for Higher Education Policy Studies (CHEPS) at the University of Twente in the Netherlands will design an evaluation framework for IFP that will be applied in 2004 in order to incorporate the results—to the extent possible—while the program is still in progress. The evaluation will assess the program's decentralized design, implementation, and educational effects, including the Fellows' academic placements and performance, completion rates, and subsequent employment. Particular emphasis will be given to the recruitment and selection processes in thirteen international sites and whether they are reaching the program's target groups. The quality of placement and the impact of leadership training and cohort-building activities will also be evaluated.

Finally, the Ford Foundation will commission several independent studies to document how IFP was designed and implemented and how it compares to other major Foundation programs in the United States and abroad. www.fordifp.net

Fulbright U.S. Student Program

Sponsored and managed by the U.S. Department of State, the Fulbright U.S. Student Program is administered through a cooperative agreement with the Institute of International Education (IIE), and by binational Fulbright Commissions and U.S. Embassies overseas.
(Annually 900, typically one-year duration)

The U.S. Fulbright Student Program is designed to increase mutual understanding between Americans and peoples of other countries by giving recent B.S./B.A. graduates, master's and doctoral candidates, and young professionals and artists opportunities for personal and academic development and international experience. Most grantees plan their own programs but are affiliated with a foreign university or other host institution during their stay. Along with opportunities for intellectual, professional, and artistic growth, the Fulbright Program offers the chance to meet and work with people of the host country, sharing daily life as well as professional and creative insights. The program offers overseas placements in approximately 140 foreign countries.

Selection is made on the basis of the applicant's academic or professional record, leadership qualities and potential, language preparation, proposed study project, personal qualifications, and preference factors as established by the Fulbright Scholarship Board and Fulbright Commission/Foundation or U.S. Embassy ("Post") abroad. Among other factors, selections are affected by:

- the extent to which the candidate and the project will help to advance the program aim of promoting mutual understanding among the people of the United States and other countries;
- the ability of the Post/Commission abroad to arrange supervision of the student;
- program requirements (fields of study, level of participants) in individual countries;
- the ratio between the number of awards offered in a given country and the number of applications received. For example, the competition for some countries is especially keen, and many well-qualified applicants cannot be accommodated. Chances for success in the competition may be enhanced by applying in the less-stringent country competitions.
- the desirability of achieving wide institutional and geographic distribution.
- Other qualifications being equal, U.S. military veterans receive preference.

The selection process is extensive, beginning with university screening for currently enrolled students, followed by a review by national screening committees consisting of specialists in various fields and area studies, which review all applications and recommend a panel of candidates to Commissions/Posts overseas. These in turn select the awardees according to their program priorities. Final approval is made by the Fulbright Foreign Scholarship Board in Washington D.C. Independent candidates and professionals apply directly to IIE rather than through a U.S. university.

In reviewing applications, the national screening committee takes into consideration the nature of the proposed project, its originality, the necessary academic preparation for completing the project described, including language proficiency, and the interest of the student as evidenced by any advance research he/she may have done to determine that the required resources are in fact available in the host country requested.

The curriculum vitae (personal narrative) provides the national screening committee with a picture of the student as a whole person, particularly in the area of leadership potential. Applicants are asked to include information concerning their future career plans and the effect a Fulbright grant might have on those plans.

The Fulbright Commissions/U.S. Embassies overseas receive the panel of candidates from the national screening committee in rank order. Each Commission or Embassy will evaluate candidates according to the feasibility of their project, prior experience in the country, and how well the candidate fits into the program priorities for that particular country.

Fulbright students come from large and small universities, liberal arts institutions, state colleges and universities, schools of music and art, and professional schools. Applicants may also be employed and without formal institutional affiliation. The Fulbright Program seeks to achieve the broadest representation of U.S. academic institutions on all levels and from all geographical areas of the country.

U.S. Department of Education (USED) Fulbright Program

(Annually 130+, duration varies)

This program is designed to develop and improve knowledge in the fields of modern foreign languages and area studies by providing opportunities for doctoral dissertation research abroad by U.S. graduate students. It is expected that these students will contribute to meeting the nation's need for specialists in these fields. Projects deepen research knowledge on, and help the nation develop capability in, areas of the world not generally included in U.S. curricula. Projects focusing on Western Europe are not supported.

Applicants apply through their university departments, are screened by USED-appointed national screening committees, are passed through binational commissions and/or American Embassy/Posts for feasibility and political sensitivity, and finally approved by the Fulbright Board. Grantees are expected to be self-sufficient in the host country, although they are encouraged to contact the binational Commission for assistance with visas, affiliations, and other matters. Unlike State Department Fulbrighters, who are paid in local currency, USED Fulbrighters receive their stipends in U.S. dollars through their home institutions. This can sometimes affect the value of their stipends because of fluctuating exchange rates.

Fulbright Visiting Student Program

Sponsored and managed by the U.S. Department of State, the Fulbright Visiting Student Program is administered through cooperative agreements with Institute of International Education (IIE), American Mideast Educational and Training Services (Amideast), Latin American Scholars Program of American Universities (LASPAU), and by binational Fulbright Commissions and U.S. Embassies overseas.

(Annually 2,200+, typically one-year duration)

The Fulbright Visiting Student Program is designed to increase mutual understanding between Americans and people of other countries by giving B.S./B.A. graduates, master's and doctoral candidates, and young professionals and artists from approximately 140 countries opportunities for personal and academic development and experience in the United States. Most awards are for one or two years. It is fairly common for Fulbright students to receive fellowships or graduate assistantships from a U.S. university to complete work on an advanced degree at the conclusion of their Fulbright grant.

Fulbright Visiting Students usually represent the academic elite of their nations. Frequently, Fulbright may be the only program, or the most prestigious program, to provide scholarships for advanced study in the United States. While each country may have its own specifications, all must follow the basic Fulbright principles of open competition on a national level and selection based on individual merit and binational peer review without regard to race, gender, religion, and political or institutional affiliation. Growing attention is being given to increasing diversity in the applicant pool according to ethnic origin and geographic location (candidates from rural areas, outside capital city, etc.).

Unlike the U.S. student program, grants are not awarded to graduating university seniors. Depending on the country, awards may be for advanced degree or non-degree study, for students or professionals, and for full, partial, or travel-only awards.

In the 51 countries that have binational Fulbright Commissions, they conduct the selection. The U.S. Embassy, in consultation with the partner government, manages the selection process in other countries. In countries with large programs, there may be several discipline-oriented committees; in the smaller programs, one committee usually evaluates all applicants. All nominees are subject to final approval by the Fulbright Foreign Scholarship Board and admission to a U.S. academic program.

Placement at a U.S. university also varies according to country. Normally, IIE, Amideast, or LASPAU coordinates the admissions procedure according to preferences indicated by the candidate, although often placement is determined according to the financial assistance offered by an institution in the form of tuition waivers. In fact, the annual cooperative agreements awarded by the State Department to the three partner organizations stipulate that they will seek the maximum amount of cost-sharing by U.S. host institutions. In some countries with well-established educational advising services about U.S. universities, grantees are responsible for their own admission process. Once Fulbright students are in the United States, the respective cooperating agency is responsible for their supervision, including financial administration of the grant, although some Fulbright programs pay benefits directly to the grantee.

The Department of State, through the cooperating agencies, conducts several midyear enrichment conferences in various parts of the United States to which most students are invited. These conferences feature prominent speakers and focus on broad themes such as the environment, civil society, the role of law, and most recently, the response to terrorism. The conferences are considered by both the grantees and administrators as distinguishing factors of the Fulbright program, contributing to building transnational networks and raising the students' awareness of their Fulbright identity.

The Fulbright Senior Scholar Program

(Annually 800 grants, duration varies)

For over 56 years, the Department of State has sponsored and managed the Fulbright Senior Scholar Program, part of the U.S. government's flagship academic exchange effort. The program is administered by the Council for International Exchange of Scholars (CIES) and by binational Fulbright Commissions and U.S. Embassies abroad. The Fulbright Scholar Program is open to a range of participants. Every academic rank—from instructor to professor emeritus—is represented. Untenured faculty, including adjuncts and professionals outside academe, are also encouraged to apply.

For eligibility requirements and special programs, see the website: www.iie.org

Fulbright Teacher Exchange Program

(Approximately 600 U.S. and foreign educators exchanged annually)

The program is funded by the U.S. Congress, sponsored and managed by the U.S. Department of State, and administered through a cooperative agreement with the Graduate School, U.S. Department of Agriculture (USDA), and by Fulbright Commissions and U.S. Embassies abroad. For eligibility and selection process, see the website: www.iie.org

Gates Cambridge Scholarships

(Annually 100–120; 40–60 in United States, 1–4 years duration)

A benefaction from the Bill and Melinda Gates Foundation of $210 million established in 2001 an independent Gates Cambridge Trust at the University of Cambridge. Gates Cambridge Scholarships allow students from any country of the world other than the United Kingdom to pursue a course of graduate study at Cambridge. Scholarships are awarded to students on the basis of intellectual ability, leadership capacity, and desire to use their knowledge to contribute to society throughout the world by providing service to their communities and applying their talents and knowledge to improve the lives of others.

Over time, Gates Cambridge Scholars will form an integral and dynamic part of Cambridge University's influential international alumni network, bringing vision and commitment to improving the lives of citizens throughout the world. Gates Cambridge Scholars will be expected to be leaders in addressing global problems relating to learning, technology, health, and social equity, which are among the prime purposes of the benefactors of the Trust. The scholars are thus expected to use their education for the benefit of others and to show commitment to improving the common weal.
www.gates.scholarships.cam.ac.uk/

German Chancellor Scholarships (Humboldt Foundation)

(Annually 10, one-year duration)

It is the philosophy of the German Chancellor Scholarship Program that leaders in German-American relations come from a wide variety of fields. Leadership can therefore take many different forms appropriate to the respective field. Applicants should present a record of high achievement, evidence of potential for continued professional accomplishment, and a clearly defined career interest. In addition, the foundation looks for evidence that a candidate will be a leader both within the chosen profession and within the broader community. Initiative, creativity, maturity, strength of character, self-confidence, sensitivity, and a sense of responsibility contribute to the foundation's definition of leadership.

Ten scholarships are awarded annually to prospective U.S. leaders in academia, government, public service, and the private sector. Candidates must be U.S. citizens, possess a bachelor's degree by the start of the award, and be no more than 35 years old. The scholarship is open to all fields of professional endeavor and offers the opportunity to conduct study or research at a German university or research institution. The scholarship period begins September 1 and lasts 12 months; it is preceded in August by language classes taught in Germany. Recipients will receive a monthly stipend; and special allowances are available for accompanying family members, travel expenses, and German language instruction.
www.avh.de/en/programme/stip_aus/

Hertz Fellowship

(Annually 25, five-year duration)

The Fannie and John Hertz Foundation seeks to support the graduate education of America's most promising technical talent, the Ph.D.-directed effort of the young men and women who can be expected to have the greatest impact on the application of the physical sciences to human problems during the next half-century. Candidates should demonstrate evidence of exceptional creativity, broad understanding of physical principles, and outstanding potential for innovative research. Qualities believed to be indicators of future professional accomplishment and success include:

- exceptional intelligence and creativity with particular emphasis on those aspects pertinent to technical endeavors
- excellent technical education, evidenced not only by transcripts and reference reports from senior technical professionals but also by the results of a personal, technical, interview
- orientation and commitment to the *applications* of the physical sciences
- extraordinary accomplishment in technical or professional studies may offset slightly lower academic records, or add luster to outstanding ones
- features of temperament and character conducive to high attainment as a technical professional
- appropriate moral and ethical values
- difference the award of the Hertz Fellowship is likely to make in the kind, quality, and/or personal creativity of the student's graduate research

Any winner of a Graduate Fellowship by the Hertz Foundation must formally accept it before commencing its tenure. This acceptance includes a statement that the Fellow makes a moral commitment to make his or her skills "available to the United States in times of national emergency." What does this mean, and why does the Foundation require it?

John Hertz felt he owed the United States more than he could repay for the opportunities he had been given when he arrived here as a young immigrant, fleeing oppression in Central Europe. Thus, it is not surprising that he wanted any young person supported by his wealth through the course of their graduate education to answer deliberately, on at least one occasion, the question, "What do I owe my country?" Hence, the Foundation asks for the statement on the Foundation's Fellowship acceptance form. This is *not* a legal or contractual obligation, but rather a freely given moral commitment. No one from the Foundation has ever approached a present or former Fellow and told him or her that the United States faces a national emergency and that she or he is obligated to address it. No one ever will.

The Foundation believes that each individual Fellow must decide for him- or herself, at any point in time, whether the country faces a truly serious problem and, if so, whether he or she is capable of employing the technical skills to help address it. The Foundation offers no definition of what constitutes a "national emergency"—these are reasonably well-recognized only in distant hindsight—but one might consider as examples the following historical events in which scientists and engineers have played a major role:

- the development of radar by British scientists and engineers in the late 1930s that enabled the RAF to win the Battle of Britain;
- the Manhattan Project in the United States;
- the Apollo Program that fulfilled President Kennedy's declaration: "I believe this nation should commit itself to achieving the goal, before the decade is out, of landing a man on the Moon and returning him safely to Earth."

In the future, we might reasonably expect our nation to face emergencies in

- fuel shortages and quests for new energy sources, e.g., nuclear fusion
- materials supplies
- transportation and communication system overloads
- deterioration of environmental quality
- malevolent utilization of cyberspace
- misuse of modern molecular biology

In every case, the Foundation believes that it is up to the individual Fellow to determine whether a serious problem exists and whether or not she or he can help. We do not support students pursuing advanced professional degrees other than the Ph.D., although we will support the Ph.D. portion of a joint M.D./Ph.D. study program.
www.hertzfndn.org

Howard Hughes Medical Institute/EMBO Scientists

Administered by the European Molecular Biology Organization (EMBO)
(Annually 6, three-year duration)

The EMBO Young Investigator Program (YIP) was established to support young scientists who are within the first three years of having established their own independent laboratories. The objective of the YIP is to give selected young scientists help in beginning their careers through EMBO funding and recognition. The HHMI/EMBO Scientists Program is part of the review process for the EMBO YIP and focuses on three countries in which the HHMI International Research Scholars Program operates: the Czech Republic, Hungary, and Poland.

Financial Benefits

The stipend is $26,000 per year and the possibility of additional funds from a pool provided by EMBO. But a major benefit is expected to be the possibility to use the selection as leverage for more funds nationally and internationally.
www.hhmi.org/grants/

Howard Hughes Medical Institute Research Training Fellowships for Medical Students

Competition and program is administered by HHMI.
(60 first-year research awards, 3–14 awards for continued support)
The goal of the HHMI Research Training Fellowships for Medical Students is to strengthen and expand the nation's pool of medically trained researchers. The fellowships provide funds to support fellows and meet their research- and education-related expenses. Through annual competitions, HHMI supports three types of medical student fellowships under this program: (1) a year of research training, (2) a second year of research training, and (3) completion of medical studies.

Initial Year Research

Fellowships provide support for one year of full-time research training in fundamental biomedical research. The fellowship includes a stipend ($23,000), a research allowance ($5,500), and a fellow's allowance to be used for health care, tuition, and fees ($5,500). Fellowship research must be conducted at an academic or nonprofit research institution in the United States, excluding the National Institutes of Health (NIH) in Bethesda, Maryland. Sixty awards are made annually.

Continued Research Support

At the end of the initial year of research training, fellows may compete for continued support for a second year of full-time research. Only a small number of these fellowships are awarded.

Support for Completion of Medical Studies

In order to mitigate some of the debt burden that has been implicated as a factor steering promising students away from careers in academic medicine and research, fellows may apply for continued fellowship support for up to two years of full-time study toward the completion of the M.D. or D.O. degree. The fellowship includes a stipend ($21,000) and an education

allowance on behalf of the fellow to defray tuition and any other education-related expenses ($16,000). Only a small number of these fellowships are awarded.
www.hhmi.org/grants/

Howard Hughes Medical Institute/National Institutes of Health Research Scholars Program

Competition and program are administered jointly by HHMI and NIH. (42 first-year research awards; 14 first-year continued support for medical studies awards)

The HHMI-NIH Research Scholars Program, also known as the Cloister Program, was established to give outstanding students at U.S. medical schools the opportunity to receive research training at the National Institutes of Health in Bethesda, Maryland.

Students in good standing at U.S. medical and dental schools are eligible to apply to the program. Research Scholars spend nine months to a year on the NIH campus, conducting basic translational or applied biomedical research under the direct mentorship of senior NIH research scientists.

The Howard Hughes Medical Institute provides the administration and funding for the program, including the salaries and benefits for the Research Scholars. The NIH provides advisors, mentors, laboratory space, equipment, and supplies for laboratory work. NIH also supports a limited number of fellowships for a second year of research.

Research awards provide an annual salary of $17,800; medical insurance; moving expenses; housing; conference travel, books, and courses. Research areas include cell biology, epidemiology and biostatistics, genetics, immunology, neuroscience, and structural biology.

Continued Support for Completion of Medical Studies

In order to mitigate some of the debt burden for promising students, research fellows may apply for continued fellowship support for up to two years of full-time study toward the completion of the M.D. or D.O. degree. The fellowship includes a stipend ($21,000) and an allowance to defray tuition ($16,000). Only a small number of these fellowships are awarded each year.
www.hhmi.org/grants/

Jacob K. Javits Fellowships

(Annually 75, four-year duration)

The program provides financial assistance to students who have demonstrated (1) superior academic ability and achievement; (2) exceptional promise; and (3) financial need to undertake graduate study leading to a doctoral degree or a master's degree in which the master's degree is the terminal highest degree in the selected field of study. The U.S. Department of Education awards fellowships in selected fields of study of the arts, humanities, and social sciences.

Panels of experts, appointed by the Javits Fellowship Board, select fellows according to criteria established by the board. Students must demonstrate financial need by filing the Free Application for Federal Student Aid.

Eligibility

Fellowships can be offered to individuals who at the time of application have not yet completed their first full year of doctoral program or a master's degree program (terminal degree for the field of study) or are entering graduate school for the first time in the next academic year. Students who have already received a Javits fellowship in previous years are not eligible.

Twenty percent of the fellowships are awarded in the social sciences, 20 percent in the arts, and 60 percent in the humanities. A minimum of 60 percent of the awards are made to students who have no graduate credits. Eligibility is limited to U.S. citizens or nationals, permanent residents of the United States, or citizens of any one of the Freely Associated States.

Applicants must be eligible to be accepted to or currently attending a graduate program leading to a doctorate or a terminal master's degree in an eligible field of study at an institution of higher education approved by an accrediting agency recognized by the Secretary of the Department of Education. Applicants attending a foreign institution are ineligible.

Services

Subject to the availability of funds, a Fellow receives the Javits Fellowship annually for up to the lesser of 48 months or the completion of their degree. The fellowship consists of an institutional payment (accepted by the institution of higher education in lieu of all tuition and fees for the fellow) and a stipend (based on the fellow's financial need as determined by the measurements of the Federal Student Assistance Processing System). In Fiscal Year 2002, the institutional payment was $11,031 and the maximum stipend was $21,500.
www.ed.gov

Kennedy Memorial Scholarships

(Annually 12, normally one-year duration)
The Kennedy Scholarships, along with a landscaped site at Runnymede, form the British National Memorial to President John F. Kennedy. An appeal was launched in the United Kingdom in 1964 to enable British people

to contribute to a fund to commemorate the assassinated president. The Memorial at Runnymede was opened by the Queen in 1965, and the first Kennedy Scholars went to the USA in 1966.

Kennedy Memorial Scholarships are tenable at Harvard University and the Massachusetts Institute of Technology (MIT). They can be used to fund any graduate course of study offered by Harvard and MIT, including Special Student (non-degree) and Visiting Fellow status. They cannot be used by post-doctoral candidates for further research in their own field. They provide tuition fees, health charges, travel, and a stipend adequate to cover living expenses. They are normally tenable for one year, but in certain circumstances extra funding may be considered to help support a second year. Students wishing to apply for the Scholarships must also apply separately to Harvard or MIT for a place in the graduate program of their choice.

Applicants must be British citizens who normally live in the United Kingdom and who have attended secondary school in Britain. They must *either* be recent graduates of a U.K. university (those who graduated more than three years before the year in which the scholarship is to begin will not be eligible) *or* be studying for a first or higher degree and have spent two of the last five years at a U.K. university.

In awarding Scholarships the Trustees take into consideration:

- intellectual ability
- personal and communication skills
- wider interests and attainments
- the focus and value of the candidate's proposed study at Harvard or MIT
- capacity for future influence and leadership

www.kentrust.demon.co.uk/

Luce Foundation Scholars Program

(Annually 18, one-year duration)

The Luce Scholars Program provides stipends and internships for young Americans to live and work in Asia each year. Dating from 1974, the program's purpose is to increase awareness of Asia among future leaders in American society.

Those who already have significant experience in Asia or Asian studies are *not* eligible for the Luce Scholars Program. Candidates must be American citizens who have received at least a bachelor's degree and are no more than 29 years old on September 1 at the beginning of the program. Nominees should have a record of high achievement, outstanding leadership ability, and a clearly defined career interest with evidence of potential for professional accomplishment.

Luce Scholar candidates are nominated by sixty-five colleges and universities. Applications are submitted by eligible institutions in early December. The Luce Foundation cannot accept applications submitted directly to the foundation. After interviews with the foundation's staff, finalists meet with one of three selection panels who choose the eighteen Luce Scholars. Placements and support services for the Luce Scholars are provided by the Asia Foundation, an organization with field offices throughout Asia. The program begins in late August and concludes the following July.

Luce Scholars have backgrounds in virtually any field—other than Asian studies—including medicine, the arts, business, law, science, environmental studies, and journalism. Placements can be made in the following countries in East and Southeast Asia: Brunei, Cambodia, China and Hong Kong, Indonesia, Japan, Malaysia, Mongolia, Philippines, Singapore, South Korea, Taiwan, Thailand, and Vietnam.

How does a candidate demonstrate a capacity for leadership? Given the level of this competition, if there is any doubt about a candidate's leadership potential, that candidate is unlikely to be successful. It is worth noting that evidence is looked for that a candidate will be a leader both within his or her profession and within the broader community. Initiative, creativity, the respect of one's peers, maturity, strength of character, self-confidence tempered by self-awareness, a sense of responsibility, sensitivity, a positive personality; all these are aspects of what we refer to broadly as leadership. www.hluce.org/3scholfm.html

MacArthur Fellows Program

(Annually 20–30, five-year duration)

The MacArthur Fellows Program awards unrestricted fellowships to talented individuals who have shown extraordinary originality and dedication in their creative pursuits and a marked capacity for self-direction. There are three criteria for selection of Fellows: exceptional creativity, promise for important future advances based on a track record of significant accomplishment, and potential for the fellowship to facilitate subsequent creative work.

The MacArthur Fellows Program is intended to encourage people of outstanding talent to pursue their own creative, intellectual, and professional inclinations. In keeping with this purpose, the Foundation awards fellowships directly to individuals rather than through institutions. Recipients may be writers, scientists, artists, social scientists, humanists, teachers, activists, or workers in other fields, with or without institutional affiliations. They may use their fellowship to advance their expertise, engage in interdisciplinary work, or, if they wish, to change fields or alter the direction of their careers.

Although nominees are reviewed for their achievements, the fellowship is not a reward for past accomplishment but rather an investment in a person's originality, insight, and potential. Indeed, the purpose of the MacArthur Fellows Program is to enable recipients to exercise their own creative instincts for the benefit of human society. The Foundation does not require or expect specific products or reports from MacArthur Fellows and does not evaluate recipients' creativity during the term of the fellowship. The MacArthur Fellowship is a "no strings attached" award in support of people, not projects. Each fellowship comes with a stipend of $500,000 to the recipient, paid out in equal quarterly installments over five years.

How Fellows Are Chosen

Each year the MacArthur Fellows Program invites new nominators on the basis of their expertise, accomplishments, and breadth of experience. They are encouraged to nominate the most creative people they know within their field and beyond. Nominators are chosen from as broad a range of fields and areas of interest as possible. At any given time, there are usually more than one hundred active nominators. While there are no quotas or limits, typically 20 to 30 Fellows are selected each year. Between 1981 and 2003, 659 Fellows were named.

Nominators, evaluators, and selectors all serve anonymously, and their correspondence is kept confidential. This policy enables participants to provide their honest impressions, independent of outside influence. The Fellows Program does not accept applications or unsolicited nominations. www.macfound.org

Marshall Scholarship

(Annually 40, for up to two years with a third year considered)

Marshall Scholarships finance young Americans of high ability to study for a degree in the United Kingdom. Up to forty Scholars are selected each year to study either at graduate or occasionally at undergraduate level at a U.K. institution in any field of study. The scheme allows the Scholars, who are the potential leaders, opinion formers, and decision makers in their own country, to gain an understanding and appreciation of British values and the British way of life. It also establishes long-lasting ties between the peoples of Britain and the United States. Each scholarship is held for two years.

Description

The Marshall is tenable at any British university and covers two years of study in any discipline, at either undergraduate or graduate level, leading to the award of a British university degree. Selection is based on outstanding academic achievement (minimum GPA of A–), remarkable participation in cocurricular activities, and evidence of individual initiative and public leadership ability. "A British Marshall Scholar should possess keen intellect and a broad outlook." Application is made through the region where the candidate resides or attends college.

In appointing Scholars, the selectors will look for distinction of intellect and character as evidenced both by scholastic attainments and by other activities and achievements. Preference will be given to candidates who combine high academic ability with the capacity to play an active part in the life of the university in the United Kingdom to which they go and to those who display a potential to make a significant contribution to their own society. Selectors will also look for strong motivation and seriousness of purpose, including the presentation of a specific and realistic academic program. www.marshallscholarship.org

Andrew Mellon Fellowships in Humanistic Studies

(Administered by the Woodrow Wilson Foundation)
(Annually 85, one-year duration)
The Andrew W. Mellon Fellowships in Humanistic Studies are designed to help exceptionally promising students prepare for careers of teaching and scholarship in humanistic disciplines. The Mellon Fellowship is a competitive award for first-year doctoral students. Fellows may take their awards to any accredited graduate program in the United States or Canada.

A high grade point average and high scores on the Graduate Record Examination (GRE) are important but are not the only measures of excellence. Selection committees will want to see evidence of outstanding future promise as well as any academic honors or awards earned.

Other Programs Administered by the Woodrow Wilson Foundation

Graduate and Undergraduate Fellowships

THE MMUF DISSERTATION AND TRAVEL/RESEARCH GRANTS

In years past, the Woodrow Wilson Foundation administered the Mellon Minority Undergraduate Fellows (MMUF) program. While no new undergraduate fellowships are now being offered through MMUF, Woodrow Wilson and the Mellon Foundation continue to support past MMUF recipients through the MMUF Dissertation and Travel/Research Grants. The Dissertation Grants offer up to $20,000 for twelve months of dissertation work, while the Travel/Research Grants provide $5,000 for one summer or one semester in support of dissertation development. Only previous MMUF recipients are eligible. The program provides the finest minority students with some continuity of assistance through the dissertation years.

THE THOMAS R. PICKERING UNDERGRADUATE AND
GRADUATE FOREIGN AFFAIRS FELLOWSHIPS

Since 1992, the Woodrow Wilson Foundation has partnered with the U.S. Department of State to recruit to the Foreign Service talented students in academic programs relevant to international affairs, political and economic analysis, administration, management, and science policy. The goal is to attract outstanding students from all ethnic, racial, and social backgrounds, helping the State Department ensure that America's face to the world represents today's America. Undergraduate Pickering Fellows receive tuition and fees, plus room and board, for their junior and senior years; they commit to pursue a humanities-rich, internationally focused core curriculum, attend a seven-week summer institute, and complete a master's program in international studies at one of several accredited schools, plus two State Department summer internships. Graduate Pickering Fellows begin their commitment as they enter their master's programs.

CHARLOTTE W. NEWCOMBE DOCTORAL
DISSERTATION FELLOWSHIPS

Funded by the Charlotte W. Newcombe Foundation and administered by the Woodrow Wilson Foundation, the Newcombe Fellowships encourage original and significant dissertation work on ethical or religious topics in all fields of the humanities and social sciences. Since 1981, more than 800 Newcombe Fellows have been named, many of them now on the faculty at colleges and universities throughout the United States and abroad. In 2003, Newcombe Fellowships went to 29 doctoral candidates selected from among more than 400 applicants; each received $16,500 to support 12 months of full-time dissertation research and writing.

WOODROW WILSON DISSERTATION GRANTS IN WOMEN'S
STUDIES/WW–JOHNSON & JOHNSON DISSERTATION
GRANTS IN WOMEN'S HEALTH

The Woodrow Wilson Women's Studies Dissertation Grants, which date back to 1974, have supported more than 450 dissertations since the program's inception. The program was the nation's first to support doctoral work in women's studies. The awards in Women's and Children's Health, funded by Johnson & Johnson and given annually since 1996, have supported nearly 80 dissertations over the years. Both awards offer a one-time stipend of $3,000 in support of dissertation travel and research. In 2003, 23 Ph.D. candidates at 21 universities received these grants—12 in women's studies, 11 in women's health.

Postdoctoral and Faculty Fellowships

WOODROW WILSON ACADEMIC POSTDOCTORAL FELLOWSHIPS IN THE HUMANITIES

(Approximately 18)

Postdoctoral appointments are common in the sciences but rare in the humanities. Woodrow Wilson's Academic Postdocs, the first of their kind in the nation, provide recent Ph.D. graduates in the humanities with two-year, full-time appointments at prestigious colleges and universities. During their appointments, the Postdoctoral Fellows combine scholarly research with mentored teaching, strengthening their credentials and jumpstarting their scholarly work before they formally enter the highly competitive humanities job market. Host institutions identify opportunities for Woodrow Wilson Postdocs and commit to supplement their Fellowships with additional salary, space, and resources. From among some 600 applicants in 2002, Woodrow Wilson selected 18 Academic Postdocs from 12 different institutions nationwide. Altogether, 50 Woodrow Wilson Postdocs have been named since the program's inception in 2000.

THE MILLICENT C. MCINTOSH FLEXIBLE FELLOWSHIPS

Introduced as a pilot program in 2002, the McIntosh Fellowships support especially promising, recently tenured faculty in the humanities at liberal arts colleges. While many faculty, soon after they receive tenure, take sabbatical leave to travel and conduct research for their next scholarly projects, some young academics have family and other obligations that make it difficult for them to be away. The McIntosh Fellowships offer such faculty year-long stipends of $15,000. Each recipient's home institution continues to pay full salary and faculty benefits during the fellowship year and augments the stipend with an additional $5,000. The 2002 competition was open to faculty members at nine premier liberal arts colleges. Three McIntosh Fellows were selected in this first year of the program. www.woodrow.org/students_graduate.html

George J. Mitchell Scholarships

(Annually 12, one-year duration)

The US-Ireland Alliance has established the George J. Mitchell Scholarships to educate future American leaders about the island of Ireland and to provide tomorrow's leaders with an understanding about, an interest in, and an affinity with, the island from which 44 million Americans claim descent. Scholars are eligible to attend institutions of higher learning in Ireland, including the seven universities in the Republic of Ireland and the two universities in Northern Ireland, for one academic year of graduate study.

Prospective Mitchell Scholars must have a demonstrated record of intellectual distinction, leadership, and extracurricular activity, as well as personal characteristics of honesty, integrity, fairness, and unselfish service to others which indicate a potential for future leadership and contribution to society. There are no restrictions as to academic field of study, although the proposed course of study must be available at the university elected by the applicant, and the applicant's undergraduate program must provide sufficient basis for study in the proposed field. Previous educational or personal experience in Ireland or Northern Ireland is usually not a factor in selection. Because the objective is to introduce Ireland to outstanding young Americans, however, among otherwise equally qualified candidates, those without prior experience there are favored.

The universities participating in the Mitchell Scholarships contribute tuition and room for the Scholar. In addition, each Scholar will receive a stipend of $11,000 to cover other necessary expenses for the term of study. The US-Ireland Alliance will assist successful applicants with their traveling expenses to and from Ireland and Northern Ireland.

Usit Now, Ireland's leading travel service for students, will contribute a IR£750 travel stipend to each Mitchell Scholar. It is envisaged that the Mitchell Scholars will use the stipend not only to explore the island of Ireland but also to develop an understanding of the relationship between Ireland and Britain as well as Ireland's relationship with Europe.
www.us-irelandalliance.org/scholarships.html

National Science Foundation (NSF)
Graduate Research Fellowships

(Annually 1,000, three-year duration)
The National Science Foundation (NSF) seeks to ensure the vitality of the human resource base of science, mathematics, and engineering in the United States and to reinforce its diversity. A competition is conducted for Graduate Research Fellowships, with additional awards offered for women in engineering and computer and information science. NSF Graduate Fellowships offer recognition and three years of support for advanced study to approximately 900 outstanding graduate students in the mathematical, physical, biological, engineering, and behavioral and social sciences, including the history of science and the philosophy of science, and to research-

based Ph.D. degrees in science education. Approximately 90 awards will be in the Women in Engineering (WENG) and Women in Computer and Information Science (WICS) components. It is a highly competitive program that is merit-based rather than need-based.

The two basic merit review criteria are: intellectual merit, and broader impacts of support. In the case of the first criteria, the question is: Does the applicant demonstrate highly meritorious scholarly characteristics and credentials? In the second, the question is: Does the applicant demonstrate through past experience, scholarship, and other activities the values of diversity, contributions to community, and commitment to the integration of research and education that are of significant importance to the NSF?

In responding to the second criteria, the applicant should consider past experiences in volunteer activities, mentoring or teaching other students or young people, leadership activities, and other examples the applicant deems appropriate. Each individual will have different experiences that relate to these criteria, and the above are provided as examples only.
www.ehr.nsf.gov/dge/programs/grf/

Open Society Institute—Network Scholarship Programs

(Annually 1,000, typically one-year, some multi-year duration)

The goal of the Network Scholarship Programs (NSP) is to train future generations of academic and public leaders by supporting fellowships in the humanities and social sciences.

Network Scholarship Programs provide fellowships, scholarships, and related activities that empower students, professors, and professionals to improve the social, political, and intellectual environments of their home communities. Network Scholarship Programs currently target the Caucasus and Central Asia, with an emphasis on the humanities in general, and social science disciplines such as human rights, social work, law, public health, and education in particular. Support for advanced study in the humanities favors individuals positioned to improve the quality of higher education instruction in their home country. Professional degree programs emphasize applied expertise, with a focus on policy analysis and systemic reform. Internships, pre-departure orientations, mid-year conferences, and an alumni grants program all serve to reinforce the grantees' connections to each other as well as to their international peers.

Network Scholarship Programs are supported by generous grants from the U.S. Department of State and the Agency for International Development (USAID), matching funds from the British Foreign and Commonwealth Office, the German DAAD, and the French government as well as substantive contributions from universities around the world. The Network Scholar-

ship Program's international network includes administrative and regional expertise provided by Soros-supported Educational Advising Centers and Soros national foundation staff.
www.osi.hu/

Rhodes Scholarship

(Annually 92; 32 for U.S.; two- to three-year duration)

The Rhodes Scholarships were established in 1903 by Cecil Rhodes, who dreamed of improving the world through the diffusion of leaders motivated to serve their contemporaries, trained in the contemplative life of the mind, and broadened by their acquaintance with one another and by their exposure to cultures different from their own. Mr. Rhodes hoped that his plan of bringing able students from throughout the English-speaking world and beyond to study at Oxford University would aid in the promotion of international understanding and peace. Each year, 32 U.S. citizens are among the 92 Rhodes Scholars worldwide who take up degree courses at Oxford University.

Intellectual distinction is a necessary but not a sufficient condition for election to a Rhodes Scholarship. Selection committees are charged to seek excellence in qualities of mind and of person which, in combination, offer the promise of effective service to the world in the decades ahead. The Rhodes Scholarships, in short, are investments in individuals rather than in project proposals. Accordingly, applications are sought from talented students without restriction as to their field of academic specialization or career plans, although the proposed course of study must be available at Oxford, and the applicant's undergraduate program must provide a sufficient basis for further study in the proposed field.

Mr. Rhodes' will contains four criteria by which prospective Rhodes Scholars are to be selected:

- literary and scholastic attainments
- energy to use one's talents to the full, as exemplified by fondness for and success in sports
- truth, courage, devotion to duty, sympathy for and protection of the weak, kindliness, unselfishness and fellowship
- moral force of character and instincts to lead and to take an interest in one's fellow beings

Proven intellectual and academic ability of a high standard is the first quality required of applicants, but in considering applications, Committees of Selection will have regard to those qualities which Mr. Rhodes expressly listed in order to define the type of Scholar he desired.

Mr. Rhodes believed that the energy to use talents to the full was best tested through participation and success in sports. Sporting prowess, however, is not essential if applicants demonstrate in other ways the physical vigor which will enable a Rhodes Scholar to make the effective contribution to the world, which Mr. Rhodes clearly expected in expressing the hopes that a Rhodes Scholar would come to "esteem the performance of public duties as his (her) highest aim."

Financial need gives no special claim to a Rhodes Scholarship. Cecil Rhodes' will lays down that "no students shall be qualified or disqualified for election to a Scholarship" because of "race or religious opinions." www.rhodesscholar.org (US)

Rotary International Ambassadorial Scholarships

(Annually 1,000, one-year duration)

The Rotary Foundation's oldest and best-known program is Ambassadorial Scholarships. Since 1947 more than 30,000 men and women from 100 nations have studied abroad under its auspices. Today it is the world's largest privately funded international scholarship program. More than 1,200 scholarships were awarded for study in 2000–2001. Through grants totaling approximately $26 million, recipients from some 69 countries studied in more than 64 nations.

The purpose of the Ambassadorial Scholarships program is to further international understanding and friendly relations among people of different countries. The program sponsors several types of scholarships for undergraduate and graduate students as well as for qualified professionals pursuing vocational studies. While abroad, scholars serve as ambassadors of goodwill to the people of the host country and give presentations about their homelands to Rotary clubs and other groups. Upon returning home, scholars share with Rotarians and others the experiences that led to greater understanding of their host countries.

Generous contributions from Rotarians worldwide represent continued faith that the students who are Ambassadorial Scholars today will be tomorrow's community and world leaders. www.rotary.org/foundation/educational/amb_scho

Rotary World Peace Scholars

(Annually 70, two-year duration)

Each year, Rotary selects 70 scholars to study at one of the seven Rotary Centers worldwide. These Rotary World Peace Scholars undertake two-year master's-level degree programs in conflict resolution, peace studies, and international relations at one of the seven Rotary Centers. Each Rotary district may nominate one candidate for a world-competitive selection process. The inaugural Rotary Center program took place during the 2002–03 academic year.

Rotary World Peace Scholars must meet all requirements for admission into their chosen university for a master's-level program. They must possess excellent leadership skills and relevant work or volunteer experience, demonstrating a commitment to a career devoted to peace, conflict resolution, and international understanding. Rotary World Peace Scholars also must be proficient in a second language, including that of the host university.

Candidates may have diverse life experiences and a wide range of professional backgrounds. What unites them is personal experience dealing with conflict situations and a common dedication to promoting world peace.

Rotary Centers

> Duke University and University of North Carolina at Chapel Hill, USA
> Sciences Po, Paris, France
> University of Bradford, West Yorkshire, England
> University of Queensland, Brisbane, Australia
> International Christian University, Tokyo, Japan
> Universidad del Salvador, Buenos Aires, Argentina
> University of California, Berkeley, USA

www.rotary.org/foundation/educational/amb_scho/centers/scholars/index.html

The Paul and Daisy Soros Fellowships for New Americans

(Annually 30, two-year duration)

The purpose of the Paul and Daisy Soros Fellowships for New Americans is to provide opportunities for continuing generations of able and accomplished New Americans to achieve leadership in their chosen fields. The Fellowship is established in recognition of the contributions New Americans have made to American life.

Selection Criteria

Candidates must demonstrate the relevance of graduate education to their long-term career goals and potential for enhancing their contributions to society. Fellowships are not awarded solely on the basis of academic record. The academic record is relevant as evidence of the candidate's ability to successfully complete a graduate degree program.

A successful candidate will give evidence of at least two of the following three attributes or criteria for selection: (1) creativity, originality, and initia-

tive, demonstrated in any area of her/his life; (2) a commitment to, and capacity for, accomplishment, demonstrated through activity that has required drive and sustained effort; and (3) a commitment to the values expressed in the U.S. Constitution and the Bill of Rights. The third criterion includes activity in support of human rights and the rule of law, in opposition to unwarranted encroachment on personal liberty, and in advancing the responsibilities of citizenship in a free society.
www.pdsoros.org

The Spencer Foundation Dissertation Fellowship Program

(Annually 30)
The Dissertation Fellowship Program seeks to encourage a new generation of scholars from a wide range of disciplines and professional fields to undertake research relevant to the improvement of education. These fellowships support individuals whose dissertations show potential for bringing fresh and constructive perspectives to the history, theory, or practice anywhere in the world.

Eligibility

Applicants must be candidates for the doctoral degree at a graduate school in the United States. The fellowships are intended to support the final analysis of the research topic and the writing of the dissertation. Award is $20,000.
www.spencer.org/

The Studienstiftung des deutschen Volkes (German National Merit Foundation)

(Annually 1500 scholarships, EU citizens and foreign students, up to five years)
The Studienstiftung sponsors outstanding students at German universities and other tertiary institutions. The selection of students is based on their academic abilities (Leistung), initiative (Initiative) and sense of responsibility (Verantwortung). The Studienstiftung currently supports around 6,000 students, that is, less than 0.5 percent of all students studying in Germany.

The Studienstiftung is funded by the Federal Government of Germany, the German States, and local authorities; by a variety of other foundations and enterprises; and by more than 6,000 private contributors.

In its unique role as Germany's largest sponsor of the most talented students, the Studienstiftung puts strong emphasis on equal opportunity in the selection process. It operates independently from political views and religious beliefs. The award programs of the Studienstiftung assist and complement the academic-scientific education of students by developing cosmopolitan and interdisciplinary abilities and key qualifications for their forthcoming professional activity. Students cannot directly apply for a scholarship of the Studienstiftung; they must be recommended by university lecturers, academic supervisors (for *doctoral students*), headmasters, or high school principals (exception: *open scholarships*). Only the most qualified students will be considered for a scholarship.

Candidates for a scholarship of the Studienstiftung must demonstrate excellence within their peer group in their chosen field of study. They must also show that they have used their abilities fully while being aware of their responsibility to science, society, their profession, and themselves.

The Studienstiftung can sponsor any EU citizen who is currently enrolled at a German university. Other foreign students of German universities can be considered if they passed the German Abitur (high school certificate) and their parents are taxable under German taxation laws. www.studienstiftung.de/

Truman Scholarship

(Annually 75–80, up to four-year duration)

The Harry S. Truman Scholarship—America's federal memorial to its thirty-third president—awards merit-based $26,000 scholarships to college students who plan to pursue careers in government or elsewhere in public service and wish to attend graduate or professional school to help prepare for their careers. Truman Scholars participate in leadership development programs and have special opportunities for internships and employment with the federal government.

The mission of the Truman Scholarship Foundation is to find and recognize college juniors with exceptional leadership potential who are committed to careers in government, the nonprofit or advocacy sectors, education or elsewhere in the public service; and to provide them with financial support for graduate study, leadership training, and fellowship with other students who are committed to making a difference through public service. The Foundation seeks candidates who:

- have extensive records of public and community service;
- are committed to careers in government or elsewhere in public service;
- have outstanding leadership potential and communication skills.

Financial need is not a consideration.

Selection of Truman Scholarship Finalists

A committee examines all nominations and selects about 200 finalists to be interviewed for Truman Scholarships. Finalists are selected on the basis of

- extent and quality of community service and government involvement
- leadership record
- academic performance and writing and analytical skills
- suitability of the nominee's proposed program of study for a career in public service

Regional selection panels interview finalists in late February and March and select Truman Scholars largely on the basis of leadership potential and communication skills, intellectual strength and analytical ability, and likelihood of "making a difference" in public service.
www.truman.gov

The Thomas J. Watson Fellowship Program

(Annually 50, one-year duration, 50 invited liberal arts colleges only)

The Thomas J. Watson Fellowship offers college graduates of unusual promise a year of independent, purposeful exploration and travel abroad in order that Watson Fellows in their future lives will bring resourcefulness, originality, vision, and leadership to their chosen fields and be humane and effective participants in the world community. Inaugurated in 1968 by the Thomas J. Watson Foundation, the Fellowship gives talented college graduates the freedom to pursue a project of their own devising for a year overseas following their graduation. During their year abroad, Fellows have an unusual and demanding opportunity to take stock of themselves, to test their aspirations and abilities, to view their lives and American society in greater perspective, and to develop a more informed sense of international concern.

In selecting Watson Fellows, the foundation seeks individuals of high ability and energy who are resourceful, imaginative, courageous, and independent. They look for leadership and integrity. A candidate's academic record, while not of primary importance, is considered together with those extracurricular activities that reflect both initiative and serious dedication.

The proposed project should reflect a candidate's genuine interest in, and longstanding commitment to, a specific concern; one that can be pursued with great independence and adaptability. The project cannot involve formal study at a foreign institution and should be personally significant, imaginative, and feasible.

Administered in cooperation with fifty outstanding private colleges and universities throughout the United States, the Watson Fellowship provides a grant of $22,000 to each recipient. In addition, the Fellowship Program will supply, as a supplement to the stipend, 12-months' payment of outstanding federally guaranteed student loans. The purpose of the loan program is to ease the financial burden during their Fellowship year and to encourage all students, regardless of student loan debt, to apply for Watson Fellowships. The Fellowship is taxable. The Thomas J. Watson Fellowship Program welcomes applicants from a diverse range of backgrounds and academic disciplines.

www.watsonfellowship.org

Appendix 2
Bellagio Conference Participants
Rockefeller Study and Conference Center Villa Serbelloni

Participants

Irid Agoes, Director
The Indonesian International Education Foundation (IIEF)
Indonesia

Peter J. Bruns
Vice President Grants and Programs
Howard Hughes Medical Institute
USA

Marianne Craven
Managing Director of Academic Programs
U.S. Department of State
USA

Joan Dassin
Director
Ford Foundation International Fellowships Fund
USA

Dorothea Fitterling
Director for Europe, North America, and the Former Soviet Union
Deutscher Akademischer Austauschdienst
Germany

Elena Grigorenko
PACE Center (Center for the Psychology of Abilities, Competencies, and Expertise)
Yale University
USA

Stanley Heginbotham
Selection Consultant
USA

Alice Stone Ilchman
Director
Jeannette K. Watson Fellowships
Thomas J. Watson Foundation
USA

A. Sarah Ilchman
African Fulbright Program
Institute for International Education
USA

Warren F. Ilchman
Director
Paul & Daisy Soros Foundation
USA

Gordon Johnson
Provost, Gates Cambridge Trust
UK

John Kirkland
Director
Association of Commonwealth Universities
UK

Michele Lamont
Harvard University
USA

Martha Loerke
Director of Network Scholarship
Programs
Open Society Institute
USA

Brian O'Connell
Vice Chancellor and Rector
University of the Western Cape
South Africa

Jairam Reddy
Independent Consultant in Higher
Education
South Africa

Francis X. Rocca
The Chronicle of Higher Education
USA

John S. Rowett
Warden of Rhodes House
The Rhodes Trust
UK

Robert J. Sternberg
PACE Center (Center for the Psychology of Abilities, Competencies,
and Expertise)
Yale University
USA

Catharine Stimpson
Dean of the Graduate School
New York University
USA

Mary Hale Tolar
Deputy Executive Secretary
Harry S. Truman Scholarship Foundation
USA

Bernd Wächter
Director
Academic Cooperation Association
Belgium

Robert Weisbuch
President
Woodrow Wilson National Fellowship Foundation
USA

Martin West
Deputy Vice Chancellor (International Relations)
University of Capetown
South Africa

Julian Wolpert
Woodrow Wilson School
Princeton University
USA

Ms. Caroline Matano Yang
Chair, Board of Foreign Scholarships
USA

Contributors

ALICE STONE ILCHMAN is director of the Jeannette K. Watson Fellowship of the Thomas Watson Foundation. She served as the dean of Wellesley College and as Assistant Secretary for Educational Affairs in the U.S. State Department before becoming president of Sarah Lawrence College. She was formerly chair of the Rockefeller Foundation.

WARREN F. ILCHMAN is director of the Paul and Daisy Soros Fellowships for New Americans. He has held appointments at the University of California, Berkeley; at State University of New York, Albany; at the Pratt Institute; and as director of the Indiana University Center on Philanthropy. He has received Fulbright and Marshall scholarships.

MARY HALE TOLAR is the director of the Kansas Campus Compact. She has over a decade of experience with national scholarships, serving most recently as the deputy executive secretary of the Truman Scholarship Foundation. She was a co-founder of the National Association of Fellowship Advisers. She was a recipient of both a Truman and Rhodes scholarship.

KAREN D. ARNOLD is Associate Professor of Educational Administration and Higher Education at Boston College. She is author of *Lives of Promise: What Becomes of High School Valedictorians?* and *Remarkable Women: Perspectives on Female Talent Development*.

ELENA L. GRIGORENKO is deputy director of the Pace Center for the Psychology of Abilities, Competencies, and Expertise at Yale. She holds a joint appointment at the Department of Psychology and in Yale's Child Study Center. She is winner of a number of early career awards in educational psychology.

STANLEY J. HEGINBOTHAM has served as a faculty member of Columbia University, with the Congressional Reference Service of the Library of Congress, as program officer of the Ford Foundation, and as vice president of the Social Science Research Council (USA). He is senior selection advisor to the Paul and Daisy Soros Foundation and to numerous other scholarship programs.

MICHELE LAMONT is Professor of Sociology at Harvard University. She taught at the University of Texas at Austin before joining the faculty at Princeton University. She is the author of *Money, Morals, and Manners: The Culture of the French and American Upper-Middle Class* and *The Dignity of Working Men: Morality and the Boundaries of Race, Class, and Immigration*. Professor Lamont has been a Guggenheim Fellow and a visiting scholar at the Institute for Advanced Study and at the Center for Advanced Study in the Behavioral Sciences.

SUSAN LEGERE is a graduate student at the Lynch School of Education at Boston College.

MANDY SAVITZ is a graduate student at the Lynch School of Education at Boston College.

ROBERT J. STERNBERG is IBM Professor of Psychology and Education at Yale University and director of the Center for the Psychology of Abilities, Competencies, and Expertise at Yale. He has authored numerous books and articles and is known for his theory of successful intelligence. His work has been recognized by a host of awards, fellowships, and honorary degrees. Robert J. Sternberg is currently president of the American Psychological Association.

TED I. K. YOUN is Professor of Education at Boston College and focuses on qualitative methods of sociological research. He has written numerous articles and books and is currently working with Professor Karen D. Arnold on a major longitudinal study of American Rhodes Scholars.

Index

Philanthropic and Nonprofit Studies